The Politics of East –West Migration

Edited by

Solon Ardittis
Senior Research Manager at ECOTEC
Research and Consulting Ltd, Brussels
Co-Director of the European Bureau for
Research on Immigration (BRISE)

Foreword by Jacques Attali

St. Martin's Press

Selection, editorial and introductory matter, and Chapter 1
© Solon Ardittis 1994
Foreword © Jacques Attali 1994
Chapters 2–13 © The Macmillan Press Ltd 1994

First published in Great Britain 1994 by
THE MACMILLAN PRESS LTD
Houndmills, Basingstoke, Hampshire RG21 2XS
and London
Companies and representatives
throughout the world

A catalogue record for this book is available
from the British Library.

ISBN 0–333–59237–9

Printed in Great Britain by
Antony Rowe Ltd
Chippenham, Wiltshire

First published in the United States of America 1994 by
Scholarly and Reference Division,
ST. MARTIN'S PRESS, INC.,
175 Fifth Avenue,
New York, N.Y. 10010

ISBN 0–312–12140–7

Library of Congress Cataloging-in-Publication Data
The politics of east–west migration / edited by Solon Ardittis :
foreword by Jacques Attali.
p. cm.
Includes index.
ISBN 0–312–12140–7
1. Europe, Eastern—Emigration and immigration. 2. Central
Europe—Emigration and immigration. 3. Europe—Emigration and
immigration. I. Ardittis, Solon.
JV7590.P65 1994
304.8' 0947—dc20
93–48290
CIP

THE POLITICS OF EAST–WEST MIGRATION

Contents

List of Tables

vii

Foreword

Today the people of western Europe are much more conscious of what is wrong than what is right. The prevalent feeling in this post Cold War period is not one of victory, but rather of uncertainty; not of achievement but rather of deepening crisis. The factors behind this mood change are well known. On the economic front, persistent high levels of unemployment throughout Europe, monetary instability and growing fiscal imbalances; and on the political front, domestic turbulence in many countries and an apparent growing popular disenchantment with the European whole. Disenchantment not only with the economic ills of these countries, but also of the governments concerned. This feeling is compounded by an impression of inaction before the flagrant disregard of human rights in the former Yugoslavia.

Behind everything, there seems to lie a deeper crisis of identity – one which is linked to the ending of the Cold War itself. For the first time in many years the question can be asked: 'What is Europe?' The treaties, projects and plans which so far have contributed to the development of the European idea were in a sense nurtured in a closed system: a familiar world which stopped at the Iron Curtain – a world bound by the horizons of the Treaty of Rome.

The removal of the eastern boundary to this world has changed the nature of Europe's perception of itself. Just as the European explorers of America discovered that to the west lay the vast new ocean of the Pacific, Europeans today are finding that the world they inhabit is much larger and less predictable than they had thought. The prevailing sentiment is not exactly Euro-pessimism or Euro-sclerosis – rather Euro-disorientation. Europe is no longer the Community of Twelve – it stands for something much larger, more daunting and more unknown.

Central to Euro-disorientation has been the issue of East–West migration. Since the end of the Cold War this has risen rapidly up the political agenda in western Europe. Relaxed emigration controls in these countries and severe economic hardship in the face of unprecedented economic reform set the stage for mass migration towards the western half of the continent.

Population movements are of course nothing new. Europeans have been at the forefront of this phenomenon for centuries. In 1492 it was Europeans who discovered the new world of America and thereby engendered the greatest population movement of all time – a movement still going on today as the United States accepts 750,000 new permanent residents a year. However, for western Europeans, today's population movement poses a severe threat. First, this potential mass migration comes at a time western Europe is in recession; the Community is stricken by high levels of unemployment; jobs are scarce and growth limited. Second, within this environment, these countries are coming to terms with the openness engendered by the Single Market. Many people are not prepared to open themselves up any further.

The situation is worsened by the threat of mass migration from Africa. Sometimes referred to as the lost continent of the world, Africa faces ever diminishing growth rates, widespread famine and a vast population explosion – the current population of 450 million is predicted to double in the next twenty years. With this tragic future in store one can see that the prospect of mass migration northwards is a very real one.

Unsurprisingly, this situation engenders a reaction of exclusion in western Europe. Germany's recent constitutional changes are indicative of this. As the Financial Times recently wrote, 'Exclusion is an understandable emergency reaction [but] it needs to be followed by constructive policies, on a Europe-wide basis, for dealing with the reality of large numbers of people who will not disappear because they are denied refugees status' (*Financial Times*, 27 May 1993).

The time has come for politicians from both east and west to move beyond the short termism dictating current policy decisions, and to address the longer term response to migration – a pan-European response. Some co-ordinated efforts are to be seen on the political stage but, as Bimal Ghosh points out in this book, 'the harmonisation efforts are focused more on methods and procedure of inter-state cooperation than on the principles or substance of migration policies'. Countries must move beyond the bounds of the nation-state if they are to coherently address this issue. The concept of European integration is meaningless unless this occurs.

Partnership, tolerance and creativity are the necessary tools, together with the realisation that migration is not a curse, but is in fact the way of the future.

The global market of the next millennium will be characterised by the dominant role of international capital and international companies; by the growth of global markets in goods and services; by fast communications; and by the mobility of ideas and labour. The players in the global market will be compared with the ancient nomads: wandering free, moving easily from one territory to the next, carrying their livelihood with them. Migration is part of this nomadism – unfortunately, however, it is one of nomadism's negative features. In the global economy of the next century, more inhabitants of the poorer countries of the world will wish to migrate to the prosperous regions of Europe and the Pacific Basin.

We cannot avoid this aspect of the next millenium, but we can strive to minimise these foreseen increases in migratory flows by reducing the pressure urging these people to migrate. In short, we should strive to make people want to live in their own country. We must be clear however as to how we can help. Resources do not exist in the west to subsidise consumption in all of eastern Europe on the scale of west German transfers to east Germany since the reunification of that country. The bulk of investment must come from these countries themselves.

The west, and western Europe in particular, can assist however in the integration of eastern Europe into both the global and the regional economic systems. In this respect, one area of crucial importance is that of trade. It will be through trading with the rest of the world, and in the first instance with western Europe, that Eastern Europe will stimulate growth, earn the foreign exchange to service debts and build up reserves.

We must strive to diminish the circulation of people by increasing the circulation of goods. I have called on numerous occasions for the creation of a pan-European free trade agreement, encompassing all the countries of eastern and western Europe. I repeat that call again here. Unless these countries are allowed to trade their goods on the western market, a new Berlin wall will emerge – a wall separating the rich half of Europe from the poorer half. This must not be allowed to happen. If this happens, the migratory flows we have witnessed since 1989 will only serve as a precursor for what is to follow.

JACQUES ATTALI

Acknowledgements

Despite the still severe limitations on information regarding the levels and structure of new migration from the East, this book aims to provide an original exercise in balanced analysis, conducted by both Eastern and Western European experts, of the main issues associated with this phenomenon. During the preparation of this book, a number of policy events have taken place: war in former Yugoslavia; the breakup of Czechoslovakia; Switzerland's rejection, by public referendum, of European integration; new legislation on immigration in Austria; a growing number of xenophobic demonstrations in Germany. Notwithstanding their often dramatic human effects, these events have increased both our enthusiasm in exploring further such a topical subject and the editor's stress in keeping up with new terminology and legal delimitations resulting from such fertile policy developments.

I would thus like to commend all contributors for their rigorous efforts aimed at submitting the most accurate and up-to-date material on migration trends in their respective countries. This has also entailed, in the case of the Estonian contributor, travelling to all three Baltic States to collect primary information on recent Baltic migration.

Professor Ghosh's advice at various stages of the book has been extremely valuable. Our sincere thanks also go to Jacques Attali, who expressed interest in this project since its very beginning and who promptly agreed to support our book by contributing a foreword.

Finally, and above all, I would like to thank Margaret Haffenden, without the invaluable assistance and patience of whom this book would never have been written.

SOLON ARDITTIS

xiii

Notes on the Contributors

Solon Ardittis is Senior Research Manager at ECOTEC Research and Consulting Ltd (Brussels) and joint Director of the European Bureau for Research on Immigration (BRISE), a newly-created policy research network based in Brussels. Specialising in international migration issues, he has been a researcher at the European Centre for Work and Society (Maastricht) and a consultant to the International Labour Office, the Commission of the European Communities, and the International Organization for Migration.

Jacques Attali is former President of the European Bank for Reconstruction and Development (EBRD) in London. Prior to establishing the Bank, he was President François Mitterrand's special advisor and Professor at the University of Paris IX-Dauphine. He is the author of seventeen books, including *Millennium – Winners and Losers in the Coming World Order* (1991).

Rainer Baubock is Assistant Professor at the Department of Political Science of the Institute for Advanced Studies in Vienna. He specialises in migration, ethnicity and nationalism, and is the author of *Immigration and the Boundaries of Citizenship* (1992), *Wertlose Arbeit. Zur Kritik der Hauslichen Ausbeutung* (1991) and *Wohnungspolitik im Sozialdemokratischen Wien 1919 bis 1934* (1979).

Valentina Bodrova is Senior Advisor on population, women and family programmes at the Russian Centre for Public Opinion and Market Research (Moscow). Before joining the Centre, she was teaching at the Centre of Population of Moscow State University. She has also been a consultant to ILO and UNFPA.

Carla Collicelli is Head of the Department for Social Policies of CENSIS (Rome), where she specialises in health, social security, family, the elderly and migration issues. She is a consultant to the Italian government and parliament, and to the Council of Europe, the EC and ILO. She is also the Italian correspondent to the OECD-SOPEMI migration observatory.

Bimal Ghosh is Senior Consultant to the International Organization for Migration and to the United Nations, on migration and development issues.

He is also the Director of the Migration and Refugee Programme at the Centre for Political and Economic Analysis in Geneva and an external consultant to the Council of Europe in Strasbourg. He was formely a Senior ·Director in the United Nations system, consultant to the UNDP Administrator, Director of Technical Cooperation and Development in the ILO and Special Advisor to the ILO Director-General. Previous academic positions include assignments at Johns Hopkins University (SAIS), Institute of Development Studies (Sussex) and the Harvard Institute for International Development.

Patricia Goldey is a lecturer in the Agricultural Extension and Rural Department of Reading University. She has research interests in migration, social movements, rural organisations and gender and development. She has had extensive overseas experience in Latin America, Africa and S.E. Asia.

Vladimir Grecic is Deputy-Director of the Institute of International Politics and Economics in Belgrade. He earned his PhD from the School of Economics of Belgrade University in 1972, where he currently teaches sociology. He has published extensively on international migration issues, including three books (in Serbo-Croat): *Contemporary Migration in Europe* (1975); *Migration and Integration of the Foreign Population in the Countries of Northern, Western and Central Europe* (1989); *Migration of Serbs in the Past and Present* (1990).

Elmar Honekopp is Senior Research Fellow at the Institute of Employment Research in Nuremberg. His main areas of involvement include employment and migration issues in the European Community and in Eastern Europe.

Jarmila Maresova is Research Associate at the Research Institute of Labour and Social Affairs in Prague. She is the author of *New Migration Situation in Czechoslovakia* (1991).

Marek Okólski is Professor of demography and Director of the Polish Policy Research Group at the Department of Economics of Warsaw University. He is also the Polish correspondent to the OECD-SOPEMI migration observatory. He is the co-author of *Stabilisation and Structural Adjustment in Poland* (1993).

Zdenek Pavlik is Professor of demography at the Faculty of Science of Charles University (Prague). His main books include: *Outline of the World*

Population Development (1964), *Demography of Africa* (1967), *Demographic Revolution as a General Regularity of Population Development* (1982), and *Principles of Demography* (1986).

Mary Redei is Advisor to the Hungarian State Secretary for Migration, Ministry of Home Affairs and Researcher at the Institute of Political Science (Budapest). She is the Hungarian correspondent to the OECD-SOPEMI migration observatory and a member of the technical committee of the European Commission's COST-social science programme. She has published extensively on the regional development aspects of both internal and internal migration.

Tatjana Regent is since 1991 Head of the Federal Migration Service of the Russian Federation (Moscow). She was previously Professor at the faculty of geography of Moscow Pedagogical University, and head of laboratory at the Institute of Employment Studies of the Russian Academy of Sciences.

Luule Sakkeus is Research Fellow at the Estonian Interuniversity Population Research Centre in Tallin, where she specialises on the dynamics of migration processes in Estonia. She is also involved in the Fertility and Family Survey (FFS) project implemented by the UN Economic Commission for Europe and the United Nations Fund for Population Activities. She is a former consultant to the Department of Population Statistics of the Estonian Statistical Office.

Franco Salvatori is responsible for social policies at the national board of Italy's CGIL trade union (Rome). He has been Director of the Institute for Migrant Policies and Vocational Training (ECAP) in Frankfurt and a trade union delegate to EEC and ILO committees.

Thomas Straubhaar is Director of the Institute for Economic Policy of the University of the Federal Armed Forces in Hamburg. He has taught at the Universities of Freiburg, Bern, Basel and Konstanz, and has published extensively on European and international migration.

General Introduction
Solon Ardittis

Due to economic and political liberalisation in Central and Eastern Europe and the resulting increase in East–West population movements, the subject of migration in Europe is increasingly attracting attention from a growing, heterogeneous, audience. This, in turn, is leading to an ever-growing need for information on and analysis of the economic and political implications of this new phenomenon.

To date, information on new migration from the former Eastern Bloc has been scarce and poorly disseminated. Relevant studies by Eastern European scholars have only been in print since 1990, usually in their original language and they have more often than not only been accessible to restricted, mostly Eastern European, circles. Similarly, studies undertaken by Western European experts since the 1989 revolutions have been circulated, primarily, in scientific journals or at specialised workshops.

Before the recent political upheavals and liberalisation of population movements in the former Eastern bloc, no systematic research and analysis of the causes and structure of East–West migration had been undertaken. If we except *ad hoc* and exceptional forms of migration to the West, such as the family reunion of Germans, the emigration of Romanian and Soviet jews, the exodus of Bulgarian muslims to Turkey, and the refugee movements from Hungary (1956), Czechoslovakia (1968) and Poland (1956, 1968 and 1981), the insignificant levels of East–West migration until 1989 (approximately 100,000 annually during the last two decades) largely justify the current state of research in the field of Eastern European migration.

The growing concern of major Western European receiving countries over increased migration from Central and Eastern Europe is clearly marked by the current lack of systematic information on the factors, structure and sectoral effects of new movements from the East. At the same time, information gaps in crucial subject areas are increasingly fuelling speculative and uncontrolled assertions on the size and implications of new East–West migration, often to the detriment of a reasoned evaluation of current trends and of the shaping of unbiased policy responses. The lack of any information allowing distinction between permanent immigration and temporary movements, such as those composed of genuine tourist, shopping and leisure visits to the West, shuttle migration in the context of the 'Polish markets' (commuting street vendors), and frontier or seasonal migration, clearly constitutes an insuperable obstacle to assessing the reality and structure of permanent immigration from Eastern Europe. Similarly, official statistics in major receiving countries such as Germany and Austria do not yet provide any information on the skill profile of immigrants, or on the subsequent outflows of Eastern Europeans initially established in Germany and Austria. Such information would help measure the exact geographic extension, within Western Europe, of new population movements from Eastern Europe, since Germany and Austria can in many cases be considered as transit countries.

Speculation about the size and effects of migration from Eastern Europe has thus grown, leading to unjustified anxieties or to ill-founded assertions over the need for new restrictive immigration control measures. Although such speculation has often been conveyed by undiscerning media, it has also, at specific points in time, been articulated by political figures, whether from sending or from receiving countries. A rather spectacular illustration of politically-targeted speculation was proffered in 1991 by the then-Soviet Minister of Labour, who predicted, during an international conference organised by the Council of Europe, a forthcoming outflow of six million Soviets, mainly directed towards Western Europe. As reality soon evidenced, not only had such a prediction to be interpreted in the right political context (i.e. the G7 negotiations over the amount of aid to be granted to the Soviet Union), but its materialisation also proved to be technically unrealistic (the capacity of the former Soviet Union to issue new passports within the predicted period of time being well below the estimated number of potential migrants).

In the face of the widening discrepancy between the recent historical emergence of the migration variable into European economic and social affairs and the absence of comprehensive and reliable information on the structure of these new flows, institutional actors in Europe are increasingly voicing their need for new instruments allowing production of systematic data in the field of European migration, particularly in terms of its labour market implications.

Among the conclusions of the Conference of Ministers on Population Movements from Central and Eastern Europe (Council of Europe, 24–25 January 1991), which shed some light on the contours of future policy attitudes in the field of East–West migration, the following priority actions were identified:

– exchange and dissemination of information on labour market conditions and employment opportunities in the countries of origin.

- economic cooperation with a view to promoting measures to prevent disorganised emigration from Central and Eastern Europe.
- training and employment schemes of short duration, including youth exchanges.
- monitoring and evaluation of factors causing uncontrolled migration from the East, and rapid and mutual information on this subject area.

Similarly, a report of experts commissioned by the EEC on the Immigration Policies and the Social Integration of Immigrants in the European Community (*Immigration Policies and Social Integration of Immigrants in the European Community*, 28 September 1990), put forward as its first recommendation the need 'to improve the collection of information on immigration in Europe, and to centralise and disseminate, among European countries, national data on the migratory situation within each country'. This information effort, according to the same report, must be aimed at both feeding and pacifying the on-going debate on migration in Europe.

The current scarcity of appropriate information and the trend towards biased speculation, therefore call for an independent and scientifically based assessment of migratory trends in Central and Eastern Europe. The aims of such an assessment should be to provide a balanced analysis of well-selected issues, in order to allow for a reasoned evaluation of the new migration phenomenon and the subsequent adoption of unbiased policy responses. Such an analysis should aim, in particular, to:

1. Distinguish the specific characteristics and extent of migratory pressures in each country of origin in order to identify the type of policy measures and international cooperation needed in each sending country, and to measure the potential for future out-migration from each Central and Eastern European country.
2. Identify the current labour market and sociopolitical effects in Western European receiving countries, particularly in the light of specific pull factors stemming from Western European demographic trends, labour market mismatches and skill shortages. This should also allow for measurement of the current and future 'immigration capacity' of each major receiving country.
3. Inform policy-makers in Eastern and Western Europe about the way in which migration is being approached and regulated in other countries, and identify, when applicable, elements of 'good practice' and related normative targets for future policy measures to be implemented on the sending and the receiving sides.

The careful selection of specific issues to be addressed and of the perspectives from which these will be analysed, was therefore critical to the coherent delimitation of the scope of this book. Clearly, migration from Central and Eastern Europe is not evolving in a vacuum. Since the 1989 revolutions, it is governed by five major types of determinant related to traditional factors (i.e. historical, geocultural), political factors (i.e. ethnic antagonism and, to a lesser extent, political persecution), transition-related factors (unemployment and poverty resulting from economic restructuring), family-related factors (i.e. reunion of families in Eastern or Western Europe, a category which applies more specifically to East and West Germany), and 'spontaneous' factors (i.e. unorganised migration often driven by the desire to 'test' the West after a long-lasting ban on emigration). In addition, distinctions between (i) labour migrants and asylum-seekers (let alone, at this stage, the issue of 'genuine' and 'economic refugees'), (ii) permanent, temporary and shuttle migration, and (iii) legal (i.e. contractual) and illegal migration, also need to be taken into account.

East–West population movements, what is more, do not evolve independently of the legislative/policy framework set by both sending and receiving countries. The way in which migration is regulated from the sending or the receiving end is critical to the analysis of current and future migratory trends.

Finally, East–West migration cannot be analysed independently of ongoing migratory trends in developing countries of the South. New migration from the East, clearly, should be approached in the context of the 'immigration capacity' of each Western European state (i.e. labour market requirements, demographic trends, political/humanitarian will), hence in the context of the full range of incoming flows from various migratory fronts.

Against this background, the objectives of this book are threefold:

1. To describe and measure, in the most accurate possible manner, the nature and structure of East–West migration since the 1989 revolutions.
2. To analyse the causes and effects of the phenomenon, and the way in which it is being approached and regulated, in different sending and receiving countries.
3. To relate East–West migration to other migratory fronts and to the overall immigration capacity of Western Europe, and to draw up a prospective analysis of the way in which migration from Eastern Europe is likely to develop and to be regulated according to development targets set by both Eastern and Western European states.

The book is organised in four parts.

Part I introduces the overall subject of migration from Central and Eastern Europe. It analyses the political and economic context in which East–West migration has developed since the 1989 revolutions, and discusses the major causes which determine current East–West migration (i.e. push and pull factors in sending and receiving countries). Part I also introduces major issues raised by East–West migration in both Eastern and Western European countries. These issues, which are analysed in more detail in Parts II, III and IV, focus on the labour market, economic, sociopolitical, demographic and educational trends in both sending and receiving countries.

Part II develops and illustrates the above issues through a detailed analysis of the new migratory fronts in Poland, the Baltic States, Hungary, Russia and the CIS, former Yugoslavia, and former Czechoslovakia. The objective of this section is to differentiate, according to the nature and volume of current flows from each sending country, the relevance and effects of each national migratory front in Central and Eastern Europe. The underlying assumption is that migration from the East is not a homogeneous and uniform phenomenon. Migratory pressures are extremely divergent according to geographic area: some countries, such as Poland, have traditionally acted as labour suppliers to Western European countries. Others, such as the former Soviet Union, have not. What is more, recent flows from the CIS have mainly consisted of highly qualified professionals (scientists, engineers) emigrating on a temporary basis, contrary to other countries which have been exporting lesser skilled manpower, usually for longer stays and often illegally.

From the perspective of the countries of origin, economic and political issues associated with the emigration of nationals can also vary considerably according to country. Migration can be encouraged in order to reduce unemployment or underemployment, or with a view to (i) improving the skill profile of nationals through education, training or work experience in West European countries, or (ii) increasing the flow of remittances sent by expatriate nationals to their countries of origin; or it can be discouraged, e.g. in the case of highly skilled migration, which can lead to dramatic brain drain effects hindering the new development targets set by the countries of origin. The characterisation of flows from each country, including both labour and refugee movements, thus helps to define and measure the economic and political implications of current and future East–West migration.

Within the limits of available statistics and information, each chapter reviews the volume, structure and destinations of recent migration, its major effects and the policy reactions it has generated at the national level. Country-specific issues are addressed by each chapter, thus allowing for a reasonable distinction between the specific migratory pressures in each country. For instance, the chapter on Hungary highlights the specific status of the country as both a sending and a receiving country (Hungary is experiencing substantial immigration of Romanians, a fact which is determining the current revision of national immigration policy towards more restrictive regulations). Interstate migration within the CIS is analysed in the chapter on Russia and the CIS. The increasing problems raised by substantial illegal migration of former Soviets to Poland, and the new policy measures brought about by this phenomenon, are addressed in the chapter on Poland.

Part III focuses on the policy implications of new East–West migration from the perspective of Western European receiving countries. Whatever the range and effects of push factors in the sending countries, migration from Central and Eastern Europe has been, and to a great extent will continue to be, governed by policy attitudes adopted on the receiving end (i.e. legislation and labour market policies). Therefore, in addition to measuring the effects of recent Eastern European migration on the labour market and on the social scene of the receiving countries, the objectives of Part III are to analyse the current immigration capacity of major Western European states.

Part III is divided into five chapters related to Austria, Germany, Italy, Switzerland and the EFTA countries, and the United Kingdom.

Since the 1989 revolutions, Austria, Germany and Italy have been the main countries of destination of Central and Eastern European migration. Detailed analysis, for each one of these countries, of the labour market effects and the social impact of substantial immigration from Central and Eastern Europe, and of the policy measures adopted in each country, should help to define common policy patterns and individual 'good practice' measures of relevance to other receiving countries and of relevance to the definition of a coordinated European immigration policy. This also entails the identification of specific areas (e.g. job offers, housing) where competition between recent immigrants and nationals, or old-time immigrants, is already perceivable. In the case of Germany, the chapter naturally concentrates on the integration problems related to immigration of East and ethnic Germans. These issues are related to the increasing problems of economic competitiveness faced by Germany since reunification and to the resulting xenophobic sentiments voiced by an increasing proportion of the native population. The chapter on Austria stresses issues related to immigration from Yugoslavia, which immigration composes the bulk of in-flows from Eastern Europe. Finally, all three chapters address the evolving policy reactions, including the revision of existing legislation, to growing immigration pressures from the East.

The chapter on the United Kingdom, a country not yet affected by substantial immigration from Central and Eastern Europe, but one which experiences increasing immigration pressures from developing countries of the South, illustrates the main rationale and features of an immigration policy quite distinctive from other national policies in Western Europe. The way in which the United Kingdom is currently preventing susbtantial immigration from Central and Eastern Europe, and the role it plays in EC negotiations related to the shaping of the future European immigration policy, are carefully analysed.

Finally, the study of the EFTA countries, with special emphasis on Switzerland, is justified by, and is related to, the current negotiations on the European Economic Area, involving the EC and EFTA member states. The way in which a country such as Switzerland, which has traditionally implemented a highly restrictive immigration policy, is currently approaching the prospect of increased immigration from both Western and Eastern Europe (despite its recent rejection, by public referendum, of the European Economic Area), should help to identify the contours of the future coordinated immigration policy at the EURO-19 level (i.e. EC and EFTA member states).

Part IV expands upon the scope of the preceding chapters by addressing, in a forward-looking and comparative perspective, the overall issue of migration in Europe. Part IV aims, in particular, to:

1. relate the issue of East–West migration to traditional, on-going, immigration from developing countries of the South;
2. analyse the combined impact of East–West and South-North migration on Western European policies and the prospects of a common European immigration policy;
3. highlight the main elements of a policy package to deal effectively with East–West migration in the 1990s and beyond.

SOLON ARDITTIS

Part I
Overview

1 East–West Migration: An Overview of Trends and Issues
Solon Ardittis

INTRODUCTION

Migration from Central and Eastern Europe is far from being a uniform and homogeneous phenomenon. The causes of such migration, its destinations and levels, have depended heavily upon the state of economic restructuring and development in the countries of origin, as well as upon levels of unemployment and ethnic antagonism.

Despite widespread expectations or calculations, massive emigration towards Western Europe has not yet occurred. Migration has often been confined to Eastern Europe, on an East–East front (i.e. between Eastern European neighbouring countries), or has remained an internal movement structured around the specific ethnic divides of regions or former subnational republics.

Since 1989 migration from the East, broadly categorised, has thus developed in the following five, very different ways:

- labour migration (whether of a temporary or permanent nature, of a legal or illegal character), resulting from economic restructuring and rising unemployment;
- refugee migration, generated by ethnic tension or overt civil war;
- family reunification, a category which applies most notably to East and West Germany;
- return migration to countries of origin;
- 'non-compulsory' migration, driven by the desire to test the West after a long-lasting ban on emigration.

Subaltern forms of migration, which have also been observed, consist of student/trainee migration to Western Europe and various forms of shuttle

3

migration, i.e. street vendors or smugglers commuting across East–East or East–West border regions.

Owing to the heterogeneous forms of current Eastern European migration, sending countries have been increasingly categorised, in terms of cooperation agreements and the policy attitudes of Western institutional actors, as 'safe' or 'unsafe' countries. Safe countries are those where economic transition and political stability have taken a positive course, and where substantial migratory pressures are less likely to arise.[1] As a result, safe countries (e.g. Hungary, and to a lesser extent Bulgaria, Poland and Czechoslovakia) are also those to which Western investments and political cooperation have been more naturally targeted. By contrast, unsafe countries are those where political instability (reflected for instance in overt civil war or ethnic conflicts) or economic transition together have put these countries onto a problematic or conflictual course. These countries (e.g. former Yugoslavia, Russia and other republics of the CIS) are naturally characterised by the limited confidence which they generate among Western investors, and by the discriminatory political treatment to which they are subjected by Western policy-makers.

The nature of Western policy responses to new migration from the East is in effect heavily dependent upon such a divide between safe and unsafe Eastern European countries. Clearly, policy responses are not only directed at economic and political cooperation, but also aim to prevent substantial levels of uncontrolled migration, or, even better, to displace the burdens of such migration to safe Eastern European countries. Thus by helping, for instance, first-asylum countries such as Hungary (which is the destination of substantial numbers of immigrants from other Eastern European countries) and Poland, the West is able to protect its Eastern borders from significant illegal migration or asylum-seeking flows. The role of some Eastern European countries as buffer zones to East–West migration, as illustrated in some of the chapters of this book, is clearly an important aspect of current East–West political cooperation.

Today it can be said that migration from the East still constitutes a nebular phenomenon in the eyes of Western European policy-makers: Owing to its often illegal character, East–West migration can be measured only partially; its effects on receiving countries can be grasped only sectorally, if not anecdotally; models allowing the forecast of the development of East–West migration over the next few years are necessarily incomplete, as they cannot integrate the entire range of such fluctuating variables as ethnic conflict, nationalistic/communist thrust, or secession.

These limitations in part help to explain the lack of any coordinated West European immigration policy *vis-à-vis* Central and Eastern Europe, and the multiplication of *ad hoc* measures aimed at extinguishing localised fires, albeit temporarily, as they break out (e.g. Albanians disembarking on the Italian coast, Bosnians fleeing civil war, etc.). They also explain the almost iterative organisation of international conferences by intergovernmental organisations, such as the Council of Europe and the OECD, or by academia, on the policy aspects of East–West migration. They explain, finally, the increasing role of the media in reporting and interpreting the development of migration from the East, and the surprisingly strong reliance of policy-makers on such day-to-day information.

The frequent presentation of Eastern migration as a powerful threat to political and economic stability in Western Europe, although attributable to a great extent to media influence, can also be explained by the fundamentally unpredictable character of the 1989 revolutions. Not only were the 1989 revolutions difficult to anticipate, they also occurred at a time of accelerated historical course in Western Europe, which in particular consisted of greater political and economic integration in Western Europe and an expanding process of economic and technological competition between Western Europe, the United States, Japan and the NICs. Clearly, the events which occurred in Eastern Europe in 1989, despite having been called for by Western European leaders for over four decades after World War II, were far from having been incorporated into the historical process of Western European political and economic integration engaged upon in the mid-1980s. Not only had they not been integrated into such a process, they also appeared as elements likely to disrupt the continuity of Western European integration and competitiveness. Much has therefore been written on the anomaly of present historical developments which are witness to the concomitant political/economic integration of Western Europe and political/economic dislocation of Eastern Europe and the concomitant opening up of Eastern Europe and closing up of Western Europe.

When addressing the issue of new migration from the East, it is also important to look at the recent history of other forms of migration from or to Western Europe. To a great extent, new migration from the East can be compared to the migration from Southern Europe which occurred throughout the 1960s and 1970s. Similitudes indeed abound: the breakup of dictatorial regimes (Portugal, Greece and Spain only regained democracy in the 1970s), disparities in the levels of economic development, poorly developed infrastructure, relatively low enrolments in post-compulsory education, restricted access to modern consumer or cultural products, to name but a few. The relationship between the dynamics of new Eastern European and recent Southern European migration must thus be kept in mind when devising new policy instruments to regulate migratory pressures in Eastern Europe. This is all the more true since, as this chapter will attempt to demonstrate, comparisons between Eastern and Southern Europe not only apply to the so-called push factors in the countries of origin (i.e. the economic, political or social determinants giving rise to emigration), but can also be related to the pull factors in the Western European receiving countries (i.e. the economic or demographic factors leading a given country to call upon foreign labour to achieve its development goals). It is thus evident that the opening up of Eastern Europe and the resulting process of new migration from that region does not constitute an all-negative phenomenon for the Western world. Although labour shortages in Western Europe are today much less pronounced than during the years of high levels of Southern European migration in the 1960s and 1970s, labour market mismatches today persist, together with skill shortages in particular economic sectors and, in some countries, negative demographic trends.

Comparisons with Southern Europe also bring us to the issue of return migration to countries of origin. In the case of Central and Eastern Europe, return migration comprises two rather distinctive connotations. There is the potential return, on the one hand, of members of expatriate communities established in Western Europe. These communities are composed of refugees or labour migrants who moved to Western Europe from the early 1950s onwards, and of those nationals (i.e. illegal migrants, temporary contract workers, trainees and students) who migrated to the West after the 1989 revolutions. As some of the country chapters in this book indicate, the process of return migration from within these communities has already begun. The lessons drawn from the various forms of return migration to Southern Europe throughout the 1980s would be extremely valuable in the context of Central and Eastern Europe. Evaluative findings on the success of return migration policies implemented by the countries of immigration, and on the success of the policies developed by the Southern European countries of origin to assist the socioeconomic reintegration of their returning nationals, can certainly be transposed to, and form the components of, future return migration policies to be devised for Central and Eastern Europe. These include specific measures to assist the return of potential investors and highly qualified expatriate nationals.

The second form of return migration in Central and Eastern Europe, and one which is also gaining momentum, relates to 'internal' return migration within former national territories. The return to the 'homeland' of ethnic communities which were 'deterritorialised' after World War II and again after the 1989 revolutions is certainly an issue of intrinsic, and often dramatic, importance in the overall study of current Eastern European migration. The most spectacular example of such 'forced' return migration is that of Russians established throughout the republics of the former Soviet Union. Contrary to traditional dynamics of return migration within Western Europe or in other regions of the world, internal return migration in Eastern Europe is characterised both by persecution (ranging from administrative difficulties to physical violence) in the countries of residence, and by dramatic integration difficulties in the countries of return (when, as in the case of Russia, these countries are confronted with economic collapse and massive deficiencies in the social infrastructure, most notably a shortage of housing).

Finally, before closing this introduction, a word needs to be said about the relationship between new migration from the East and traditional migration from the Third World. From the point of view of formal political morale, it will obviously be very difficult for the criteria in relation to which East–West migration will be formally regulated (e.g. economic, demographic, humanitarian criteria) to deviate from those applied to Third World migration. Both in terms of labour recruitment and the granting of refugee status, however, new migration from the East is likely to impact severely on the levels of future South–North migration. Due to easily apprehendable geopolitical factors (i.e. the geographic and cultural vicinity of Eastern and Western Europe, historical linkages, future integration of some Eastern European countries into a broad pan-European economic and political federative body), it is clear that Western permeability to external immigration already discriminates between the national origin of migrants. Conflicts such as those afflicting former Yugoslavia, for instance, have clearly focused the attention of the West, to the detriment of more secular conflicts in other regions of the world, most notably in Africa. Similarly, employers' attitudes towards the recruitment of irregular labour are already showing signs of a shift towards East European migrants (recruitment channels are more manageable and cost-effective given their geographic proximity, but race-related factors also help to explain employers' preference for European low-cost labour).

This chapter aims to introduce the overall subject of East–West migration, its main determinants, structure and effects. The chapter is organised in pointers (i.e. short descriptions of issues) rather than as a comprehensive analysis of the various aspects of East–West migration addressed by this book. More detailed illustrations of the pointers provided in this chapter will be proffered in Parts II and III, which are organised into eleven country chapters. A detailed analysis of these pointers, and of their current and future policy relevance, is provided in Part IV.

THE LEVELS AND CAUSES OF EAST–WEST MIGRATION

How many people have migrated since the 1989 revolutions? The answer is still very difficult to provide given the heterogeneous factors of East–West migration, which combine short and long term, regular and irregular movements, and which rule out any strict quantification of migration from that region. Official statistics, which are based on the declarations of those travelling abroad (where such declarations are actually required), are clearly unreliable. Estimates, nevertheless, help to measure the significance of new migration from the East, particularly the levels of change after the 1989 revolutions. Thus in 1989 alone, more than 1.2 million people emigrated from Central and Eastern Europe, including 700,000 German settlers (*Aussiedler* and *Ubersiedler*), 320,000 Bulgarian Turks, 71,000 Soviet Jews and 80,000 spontaneous asylum seekers (Widgren, 1990). Since 1989, over 400,000 people every year have applied for asylum in Germany (438,000 in 1992, compared, for instance, to 80,000 asylum seekers in France during the same year). From 1989 to 1991, the United States received between 50,000 and 100,000 refugees (see Table 1.1). It is estimated that between 1990 and 1991, Germany received 1.5 million legal and illegal migrants from Central and Eastern Europe. Since 1991, conflicts in former Yugoslavia generated over 2.5 million refugees and displaced persons. Finally, according to the *Institut national d'études démographiques* (Paris), from the 13 million potential new immigrants to Europe until the year 2000, 7.5 million will be from Eastern Europe (4 million) and the former Soviet Union (3.5 million).

Although available figures do not yet allow detailed analysis of the skill profile of new East European immigrants, and despite the fact that large numbers of irregular migrants from Central and Eastern Europe are currently employed, whatever their educational qualifications and professional experience, in the lower positions of the receiving countries' secondary market, there is evidence to show that East–West migration also involves significant numbers of qualified personnel. According to one estimate (Honekopp, 1991), among the 400,000 former Soviets who emigrated in 1990 (mostly Soviet Jews, 70 per cent of whom were economically active), a large proportion was composed of highly qualified professionals or skilled workers. Other data (*The Economist*, 1991) indicate that, in 1990, 250 members of the Soviet Academy of Science went abroad on long-term contracts (compared with only 50 in 1989), a figure which represents 20 per cent of the Academy's total membership.

Figures for Poland (Okoslki, 1990) show that among the 398,000 economically active Poles who emigrated between 1983 and 1988, 15 per cent

Table 1.1   Major destinations of Eastern European immigration (various years)

Country	Period	Nature of immigration flows
GERMANY	1950–89	– 3.5 million Germans from the GDR ('Ubersiedler') – 2.0 million ethnic Germans from the former USSR, Poland and other East bloc countries ('Aussiedler') – 3.5 million non-Germans (Turks, Spaniards, Greeks, Italians, Yugoslavs and others)
	1990–1	– since the beginning of 1990, 1.5 million legal and illegal immigrants.
ISRAEL	1950–89	– Several thousands, including 192,000 Soviet jews from 1952 to 1984, and 18,200 between 1985 and 1989.
	1990–	– Nearly 400,000 Soviet Jews
USA	1989–91	– Between 50,000 and 100,000 refugees.
CANADA	1980–89	– More than 200,000 immigrants from Eastern Europe (Poles, Hungarians, etc.).
OTHERS	1980–9	– Less than 10,000 immigrants per year

Source: BIPE Conseil, based on INED data (in ERECO: *Europe in 1996 – Economic Analysis and Forecasts*, May 1992).

had been to university. The number of emigrants in this category (i.e. 59,600) corresponds to the yearly average output of university graduates in Poland. Another estimate (Heyden, 1990) indicates that approximately 70 per cent of East European migrants of German origin who settled in the Federal Republic of Germany possess high-level professional qualifications.

According to a report prepared by a group of experts commissioned by President Eltsine, the number of scientists based in Russia decreased from 1,385,269 in 1989 to 1,227,388 on the 1st of January 1991, which corresponds to an erosion of 11 per cent within a single year (Dufour, 1992). Some data indicate that in 1990 and 1991, approximately 1,500 researchers from Eastern Europe were recruited in France, and 6,000 in Germany. Israel received 31,000 former Soviet researchers between 1989 and 1991, and another 30,000 were recruited in the United States. According to a counsellor of former President Bush, a susbstantial number of US industries recruited former Soviet experts, particularly in the field of software development. Most American universities are employing former Soviet teaching staff and students (*Le Monde*, 24 April 1992).

Not all Eastern European scientists, however, have chosen to migrate. It appears that a number are still present in their countries of origin but are engaged in commercial activities. The effects of such a phenomenon, which has been referred to as an 'internal brain drain', can be even more dramatic than those resulting from skilled emigration, as they can lead to the gradual obsolescence and eventually the extinction of a country's scientific capacity.

Although the full phenomenon of East–West migration cannot yet be quantified without resorting to estimates and approximations, it is evident that population movements generated by the opening up of former COMECON countries cannot remain indifferent to Western Europe's historical, political and economic developments. Although the effects of such population movements can only be of a transitory nature, reflecting the suddenness of new migration from that region and the resulting period of policy adjustments engaged upon by Western governments, new migration from Central and Eastern Europe has signified a series of changes in both sending and receiving countries:

- It has signified, in the first place, a radical change in Europe's immigration trends and configuration. Due to the size of the stock of immigrants from Central and Eastern Europe before 1989, immigration from that region was of minor concern to Western European governments before the 1989 revolutions (see Table 1.2). Post-1989 population movements from that region thus contributed to opening up new migratory fronts in the very heart of Europe, the effects of which are now combining with those generated by traditional immigration from the developing South.
- Maritime borders no longer 'protect' Western Europe from traditional migratory fronts. The opening up of Central and Eastern Europe has created major sources of migration across Western Europe's actual land borders.
- Substantial immigration to the two major receiving countries, Germany and Austria, has started to put into question the economic competitiveness of these countries. It is also undermining social cohesion, particularly in Germany where xenophobic sentiments strengthened throughout 1992.
- New migration from the East also revealed the way in which humanitarian, political and economic criteria clashed in shaping Western Europe's political and security-related responses to unexpected developments such as sudden immigration pressures from the East. Italy's reaction to the massive exodus of Albanians in 1991 (a reaction which successively combined firmness, flexibility, and eventually, by allow-

Table 1.2 Number of East European residents in major West European receiving countries

Nationality	Germany (1989)	Austria (1981)	France (1986)	Sweden (1985)	Switzerland (1988)
Albania	297	124	561	23	
Bulgaria	5,670	432	1,122	322	
Former Czechoslov.	31,695	2,032	2,871	1,136	5,900
Hungary	31,627	2,526	3,750	1,993	4,700
Poland	220,443	5,911	67,189	15,445	4,600
Romania	21,101	1,253	5,058	1,140	
Former USSR	11,533	495	5,576	1,101	
Former Yugoslavia	610,499	125,890	69,251	38,450	100,867

Source: J.C. Chesnais: *Les Migrations d'Europe de l'Est vers l'Europe de l'Ouest: de l'histoire à la prospective* (Strasbourg: Council of Europe, 1991).

ing Albanians to stay in Italy, the open violation of existing national legislation) is certainly a case in point.

– The emergence of new migratory fronts in the Eastern part of Europe also emphasised the need for greater coordination of national immigration policies implemented by Western States. The interdependence, between all member states, of issues and effects stemming from new East–West migration has contributed to speeding up the process of coordination, if not harmonisation, of national asylum policies already foreseen (but never implemented owing to lack of agreement) by the European Single Act of 1986.

– Finally, as already suggested in the introductory part of this chapter, new migration from the East highlighted the distinct migratory status of each Central and Eastern European state. New migration has led some states (i.e. Hungary and Poland) to act as immigration countries, while others have become net migrant exporters as a result of poor economic performance or geopolitical factors.

The levels of current migration, however, and their foreseeable effects on both sending and receiving countries, cannot be analysed independently of the causes, hence of the structure, of new East–West migration. It is also on the basis of a close identification of the range of causes determining current migration that policy responses can be fully developed in both Eastern and Western states.

As in other types of migration, East–West population movements have often been approached in terms of push and pull factors. Although the relative weight and significance of determinants at each end of the migratory process is always difficult to measure, this delimitation nevertheless help to distinguish the geographic origin (hence the directions of any future measures) of the causes and trends which currently determine East European migration.

THE PUSH FACTORS IN CENTRAL AND EASTERN EUROPE

As already suggested in the typology of migration movements presented in the introduction, push factors in Central and Eastern Europe have mainly consisted of economic and ethnic determinants. The next section draws attention to the main economic and ethnic indicators which, combined with the political and economic liberalisation after 1989, have stimulated significant levels of migration within or from Central and Eastern Europe. An illustration and analysis of these indicators is proffered in Parts II, III and IV.

Economic Determinants

The on-going process of economic restructuring and adjustment to a market economy, which is resulting in numerous privatisation measures, a dramatic decrease in subsidies, severe budgetary restrictions, and a gradual decline in industrial production, has led to a dramatic increase in unemployment in Central and Eastern Europe over the next few years.

At the end of 1990, nearly 600,000 East Germans, 360,000 Czechoslovakians, 1.2 million Polish, and 2 million Soviets were considered to be unemployed as a direct or indirect consequence of the reforms (Okolski, 1991). It is estimated that industrial areas will experience sharp rises in unemployment over the coming years. Thus in East Germany, areas dependent on heavy industry are affected to a greater extent by economic restructuring and unemployment reaches its highest levels in Neubrandenburg, Schwerin and east Berlin. Similarly, data from July 1991 show that high levels of unemployment are gradually shifting towards the urban and industrial areas (Commission of the European Communities, 1992). Participation rates of women being higher in Central and Eastern Europe than in Western Europe (cf. Table 1.3), job losses have hit women harder than men

Table 1.3   Labour force participation rates of women in the European Community and in Central/Eastern Europe in 1988 (per cent)

Country	Participation rate of women (%)
Belgium	35.9
Denmark	60.0
Germany	41.7
Greece	35.2
France	45.9
Ireland	33.5
Italy	34.2
Luxembourg	33.9
Netherlands	41.3
Portugal	45.9
Spain	31.0
United Kingdom	49.9
EC	41.2
Bulgaria	50.0
Other Central and Eastern European Countries	46.0

Source: *Eurostat Labour Force Survey, 1988*; Employment Observatory: *Employment Trends in Central and Eastern Europe*, no. 1 (January 1992).

(by the third quarter of 1991, the female unemployment rate was over 2 per cent higher than the rate for men in Poland, and over 1 per cent in former Czechoslovakia and Romania) (Employment Observatory, 1992).

Existing social security systems are still unable to compensate for rising unemployment, a situation which is unlikely to improve in the coming years due to financial constraints inherent in economic restructuring (although between 60 per cent and 70 per cent of the unemployed in most Central and Eastern European countries receive unemployment benefits, the duration of such benefits is shorter than in Western Europe).

While GDP per capita in Eastern Europe at the end of the 1980s was about 1/8th of the average in the rest of Europe, GDP in 1990 fell in real terms by over 7 per cent and in 1991 by 10 per cent (in Bulgaria and in the former USSR, the decrease was even more significant).

Privatisation has mainly translated into the creation of SMEs, cooperatives and joint ventures, rather than into the actual privatisation of state enterprises (the latter, however, is gradually being implemented through distribution of ownership rights to employees, or through joint ventures with foreign capital) (Fischer and Standing, 1991). In addition, due to the

Table 1.4   Comparison between the number of hours of work needed to purchase various consumer goods in Central and Eastern Europe, and in the Federal Republic of Germany in 1988 (Federal Republic of Germany = 1.0)

	FRG	Bulgaria	ex-Czechoslovakia	Hungary	Poland	ex-USSR
Foodstuffs						
Pork (kg)	1.0	4.1	3.4	2.4	2.0	2.7
Beef (kg)	1.0	5.9	3.7	2.6	1.7	3.0
Chicken (kg)	1.0	5.4	4.7	3.5	2.8	5.5
Eggs (1)	1.0	5.5	3.8	2.6	6.6	4.2
Butter (kg)	1.0	6.0	3.6	8.5	3.5	4.0
Sugar (kg)	1.0	7.1	3.3	3.2	3.6	4.5
Wine (litre)	1.0	2.9	5.8	2.9	10.6	13.4
Coffee (kg)	1.0	18.2	10.4	7.2	17.8	11.3
Tea (kg)	1.0		3.2	0.7	0.7	2.4
Cigarettes (20)	1.0	1.7	1.0	0.7	0.6	1.4
Non-food products						
Car	1.0	4.0	2.5	2.3	9.2	3.6
Petrol (litre)	1.0	8.1	7.0	5.7	5.0	4.0
Television	1.0	5.3	6.6	4.0	13.4	4.6
Washing powder (kg)	1.0	1.5		4.1	5.1	4.2
Men's shoes (pair)	1.0	1.2	1.2	1.8	2.0	1.7

Source: UNECE: *Economic Survey of Europe* (New York: UN, 1989).

drastic decline in trade between former Council for Mutual Economic Assistance (CMEA) partners,[2] and due to new arrangements stipulating that intra-CMEA trade should be conducted in hard currency, the securing by former COMECON countries of new markets in Western Europe has become critical to the success of the new economic reforms. This is all the more true since Western firms are increasingly becoming tough competitors for new markets in the former CMEA region.

Finally, in this review of major economic determinants of potential out-migration, it is worth referring to the wage differentials with most Western European countries, differentials which have continued to widen after 1989. In the case of East Germany, and according to an estimate by the IMF, it will take at least 10–15 years until labour productivity in East Germany reaches the level prevailing in West Germany. The difference in the number of working hours necessary to acquire food products and durable goods varies from +100 per cent and +1,300 per cent between most Central and Eastern European countries and West Germany (see Table 1.4). In the 1980s, the savings from one average salary in the EEC was equivalent to 6–10 average salaries in Central and Eastern European countries. Moreover, with the exception of Hungary and Czecoslovakia, the power of purchase in Central and Eastern European countries has decreased throughout the 1980s.

Ethnic Determinants

Migration within or from Central and Eastern Europe, which, with the displacement of Goths, Huns, and the Altaic and Slavic Populations, can be traced back to the early stages of the first millenium before Christianity, should clearly be seen as a recurrent factor in the continuous shaping and reshaping of Eastern Europe's history, cultural identities and legal boundaries. Not even after emancipation, in the 19th and 20th centuries, from the occupying Austrian and Prussian powers, and from the Ottoman and Russian Empires, did migration cease to symbolise the salient and often dramatic effects of Eastern Europe's historical convulsions. The territorial and other claims by national minorities which erupted after the 1989 revolutions should thus be related to the aftermath of World War II and to the resolutions of the Yalta Conference, through which Central and East European legal boundaries were determined until 1991.

Quite distinctively, then, pre-1989 East–East and East–West migration should be characterised first of all by its political determinants. For a period of more than four decades, military conflicts, followed by political/ideological/religious antagonism, have acted as major push factors in East European migration. Population movements from or within that region have constituted, more often than not, what must be referred to as involuntary migration. On the whole, migrants from Central and Eastern Europe have been expellees or political refugees.

A typology of East European migration since World War II would thus broadly distinguish four major stages or types of movement:

1. Population displacements and return migration in the aftermath of World War II and following the Yalta resolutions.
2. East–West migration from the German Democratic Republic and other East European countries until the erection of the Berlin Wall in 1961. German population movements constituted the largest stream of migrants in the aftermath of World War II. To date, they still represent

the most important forced displacement of population in modern European history (see Table 1.5).
3. Incidental refugee movements closely linked to political and military upheavals in specific Central and East European countries.

Table 1.5   East and ethnic German population before and after World War II

	Reich Germans, Oder–Neisse Territories (a)	Sudeten Germans, Czechoslovakia (b)	Ethnic Germans, East Europe	Total
German population in May 1939	9,575,200	3,477,000	3,946,300	16,998,500
German population at the end of World War II	9,289,700	3,453,000	3,802,700	16,545,400
German accounted for, 1945–1950				
Number removed	6,817,000	2,921,400	1,865,000	11,603,400 (c)
Number retained (d)	1,134,000	258,700	1,324,300	2,717,000
Total Germans accounted for	7,951,000	3,180,100	3,189,300	14,320,400
Germans not accounted for, 1945–1950	1,338,700	272,900	613,400	2,225,000

Notes:
(a) East Prussia, East Pomerania, East Brandenburg, Silesia
(b) Baltic area including Memel, Danzig, Poland, Hungary, Romania, and Yugoslavia.
(c) To the Federal Republic and West Berlin: 7,900,000 (68 per cent); to the Soviet occupied zone: 3,200,000 (27 per cent); to Austria and other Western countries: 500,000 (5 per cent).
(d) Including POWs and other detained Germans.

Source: *Statistisches Bundesamt, in Die Deutschen Vertreibungsverluste* (Mainz: Kohlhammer, 1968).

4. Labour migration under specific bilateral agreements between Eastern European countries; between Eastern European countries and developing countries; and between Eastern and Western European countries.

Within this typology, ethnic determinants have acted, and continue to act, as major factors of Eastern European migration, at least – for the time being – in terms of 'internal' population movements.

The ethnic divisions in Central and Eastern Europe were largely unknown to Western observers before the 1989 revolutions. As has been emphasised by Rhode (1991: 42–3): 'only institutes of East European studies or expelled people or refugees in the diaspora themselves collected and generated some knowledge on East European ethnic groups, but ethnicity in Europe, as a topic as such, did not raise a lot of interest during the 1960s and 1970s. The strong ethnic segregation and nationalistic movements of the population from the former countries of 'social brotherhood' was thus unpredicted and unexpected from Western studies'.

To a certain extent, this can be explained by the fact that after World War II, massive deportations and redrawing of borders meant that ethnic heterogeneity among Central and Eastern European countries was significantly reduced. Thus Romania retook possession of Transylvania, which was home to over 1.5 million Hungarians, while Bessarabia became a Soviet republic of Moldavia. Bulgaria lost Macedonia which became a Yugoslav republic. With the redrawing of Polish borders, Poland lost its Ukrainen, Bielorussian and Lithuanian minorities. Over ten million Germans were expelled from Poland and Czechoslovakia. As Rupnik (1993: 75) noted, quoting Ernest Gellner: 'Central and Eastern Europe before World War II resembled a painting by Kokoschta, full of subtle nuances of different tones; after the war, it became closer to a painting by Modigliani, dominated by monochromatic scenery.'

The ethnic puzzle, however, is far from having been torn apart after World War II. Table 1.6 gives an overview of the ethnic divisions of the East European population, while Table 1.7 highlights the languages, religions and alphabets in Central Europe. If we except relatively ethnically homogeneous countries such as Hungary and Poland, Table 1.6 aptly reflects the significance of ethnicity in this part of Europe.

Former USSR, which has a population composed of 52 per cent of Russians, 16 per cent of Ukrainens and 32 per cent of over 100 ethnic groups, is a certainly a case in point. Tables 1.8 to 1.11 provide some insight into the current and future significance of each ethnic and linguistic group within the former USSR. Table 1.9, for instance, shows the significant growth of the Central Asian population until 2010 (+61.5 per cent, compared to a growth rate of only 4.5 per cent for the Slavic population), while

Table 1.6   Ethnic Divisions of the East European population (1989)

	Population (thousands)	Growth rate	Ethnic divisions
Albania	3,208.0	1.9	96% Albanian 4% Greek, Vlachs, Gypsy, Serb and Bulgarian
Bulgaria	8,972.7	0.1	85.5% Bulgarian 8.5% Turk 2.6% Gypsy 2.5% Macedonian 0.3% Armenian 0.2% Russian 0.6% Other
Former Czechoslovakia	15,658.1	0.2	64.3% Czech 30.5% Slovak 3.8% Hungarian 0.4% German 0.4% Polish 0.3% Ukrainen 0.1% Russian 0.2% other
Hungary	10,566.9	0.2	96.6% Hungarian 1.6% German 1.1% Slovak 0.3% Southern Slav 0.2% Romanian
Poland	38,169.8	0.5	98.7% Polish 0.6% Ukrainen 0.5% Belorussian 0.5% Jewish
Romania	23,153.5	0.5	89.1% Romanian 7.8% Hungarian 1.5% German 1.6% Ukrainen, Serb, Croat, Russian, Turk and Gypsy
Former USSR	288,742.3	0.8	52% Russian 16% Ukrainen 32% from over 100 ethnic groups

Source: Central Intelligence Agency: *The World Factbook 1989* (Washington: US Government Printing Office).

Table 1.7   Languages, religions and alphabets in Central Europe

People	Language	Religion	Alphabet
Belorussian	ES	O	C
Ukrainen	ES	O	C
Polish	WS	C	L
Czech	WS	C	L
Slovakian	WS	C	L
Slavonian	SS	C	L
Croatian	SS	C	L
Bosnian	SS	M	
		O	C
		C	L
Serbian	SS	O	C
Montenegrian	SS	O	C
Macedonian	SS	O	C
Bulgarian	SS	O	C
Latvian	B	L	L
		C	
Lithuanian	B	C	L
Romanian	L	O	L
Moldavian	L	O	C
			L
Greek	G	O	G
Albanian	A	M	L
Finn	FU	L	L
Estonian	FU	L	L
Hungarian	FU	C	L

Languages	Religions	Alphabets
A = Albanian	C = Catholic	C = Cyrillic
B = Baltic	L = Lutheran	G = Greek
FU = Finno-Ugric	M = Muslim	L = Latin
G = Greek		O = Orthodox
L = Latin		
ES = Eastern Slavic		
WS = Western Slavic		
SS = Southern Slavic		

Source: A. and J. Sellier: *Atlas des peuples d'Europe centrale* (Paris: Editions La Découverte, 1991).

Table 1.8   Population of the former USSR republics (including the Baltic States) in 1988 (in thousands)

Armenia	3,280
Azerbaijan	7,020
Belorussia	10,200
Estonia	1,570
Georgia	5,540
Kazakhstan	16,530
Kirguizia	4,290
Latvia	2,680
Lithuania	3,690
Moldavia	4,340
Russia	147,380
Tajikistan	5,110
Turkmenistan	3,530
Uzbekistan	19,900
Ukraine	5,160
Total	286,710

Source: *Le Courrier des Pays de l'Est* (Paris, April 1990).

Table 1.9   Current and future population in the former USSR, by major nationality (in thousands)

	1990	2000	2010	2010/1990
Slavic	201,880	207,269	211,076	+4.5%
Other European	12,711	13,152	13,536	+6.5%
Central Asian	37,802	49,071	61,050	+61.5%
Caucasian	25,161	27,958	30,449	+21.0%
Others	15,220	16,254	17,326	+13.8%
Total former USSR	292,775	313,705	333,438	+13.9%

Source: W.W. Kingkade: *USSR, Estimates and Projections of the Population by Major Nationality, 1979 to 2050* (Washington: Center for International Research, US Bureau of the Census, 1988).

Table 1.10   Population in the former-USSR by major linguistic group in 1979 (in thousands)

Armenian:	4,151	Iranian:	3,629
Baltic:	4,290	Mongolic:	497
Caucasian:	6,062	Romanian:	3,097
Finno-Ugric:	4,520	Samoyed:	34
Germanic:	1,936	Slavic:	180,746
Greek:	344	Turkish:	32,777
Indian:	209	Tungusic:	33

Source: Calculations based upon R. Caratini: *Dictionnaire des Nationalités et des minorités en URSS* (Paris: Larousse, 1991).

Table 1.11   Proportion of Russians in the republics of the former USSR in 1979 (%)

Armenia:	2.3	Azerbaijan:	7.9
Belorussia:	11.9	Estonia:	27.9
Georgia:	7.4	Kazakhstan:	40.8
Kirghizia:	25.9	Latvia:	32.8
Lithuania:	8.9	Moldavia:	12.8
Russia:	82.6	Tajikistan:	10.4
Turkmenistan:	12.6	Uzbekistan:	10.8
Ukraine:	21.1		

Source: R. Caratini: *Dictionnaire des nationalités et des minorités en URSS* (Paris: Larousse, 1991).

Table 1.11 allows the problems currently faced by Russians established outside of Russia to be understood. With the exception of Armenia, Azerbaijan and Lithuania, where the Russian population does not exceed 10 per cent of the total population (2.3 per cent, 7.9 per cent and 8.9 per cent respectively in 1979), all other former republics of the USSR are composed of substantial levels of Russians (e.g. 40.8 per cent of the total population in Kazakhstan, 32.8 per cent in Latvia and 27.9 per cent in Latvia). Not surprisingly, then, in 1990 alone, over 36,000 Russians arrived in the Russian Federation from other former Soviet republics. A survey carried out in 1991 indicated that 50 per cent of those who arrived in Russia were of Russian nationality (cf. Chapter 5). The case of former Yugoslavia is perhaps even more dramatic, with figures showing that in September 1992 over 1,900,000 Yugoslav refugees were present on the territory of former Yugoslavia (cf. Chapter 7). The ethnic unrest in Central and Eastern Europe has thus emerged as the principal variable in relation to which any predictions of both the levels and nature of future migration from Eastern Europe, and the directions and nature of future West–East cooperation, can be made.

THE PULL FACTORS IN WESTERN EUROPE

The breakup of the Soviet Union, which was followed by the relative decentralisation of the supervision of nuclear arms and by spending cuts in the former Soviet defence industry, have raised widespread concern in the West over the export of brains to the 'unsafe' developing countries of the South.

In fact, beyond the specific domain of the defence industry, the 1989 revolutions in Central and Eastern Europe, and the resulting freedom to migrate from that region, have contributed to revealing the way in which the opening up of Eastern Europe could also be exploited, in terms of human resources and in a highly selective manner, by Western societies.

As referred to in the introduction, East–West migration cannot be approached as an all-negative phenomenon for Western receiving countries. Pull factors exist; if they did not, new migration from the East would have reached significantly lower levels. The way in which receiving countries actually regulate and/or tolerate (legally, socially or politically) subtantial inflows of foreign labour or population is obviously a major causal factor of such migration.

Pull factors in Western Europe can be related to demographic evolution, educational and training output, quantitative/qualitative mismatches on the labour market, and the R&D activity of Western countries (Ardittis, 1991 and 1992).

Demographic decline in most Western European countries, as increasing numbers of reports are evidencing, is due to generate a constant decrease in the indigenous labour force as from the end of the present decade. Active labour force in the age group 20–30 is currently decreasing by -1.7 per cent annually (compared with -1.3 per cent in the USA, $+0.75$ per cent in Japan, and with a slight increase in most Eastern European countries), while retirements are expected to exceed new entries into the labour market by the year 2000 (IRDAC, 1990). If the European Community's overall labour force will experience a growth of nearly 2 million by the end of the present decade, it is expected to drop by 15 million within the first 25 years of the next century. Both the anticipated growth of 2 million within the next

Table 1.12   EC population until 2020 (thousands)

	1989	1995	2000	2020	2020/ 1989 (%)
Denmark	5,131.6	5,186.6	5,312.2	4,967.9	–3.2
Germany*	62,104.1	63,958.9	64,300.5	58,817.3	–5.3
Greece	10,033.0	10,300.0	10,400.0	10,500.0	4.7
Spain	38,888.3	39,244.1	39,440.8	37,409.3	–3.8
France	56,160.3	57,060.9	57,882.9	58,664.1	4.5
Ireland	3,515.0	3,500.4	3,472.6	3,347.5	–4.8
Italy	57,540.6	57,585.4	57,610.9	53,484.3	–7.0
Luxembourg	376.7	378.4	383.4	385.1	2.2
Netherlands	14,848.8	15,420.9	15,859.8	16,516.8	11.2
Portugal	10,320.8	10,518.6	10,632.0	10,629.0	3.0
UK	57,236.4	58,280.0	59,079.0	60,740.0	6.1
Benelux	9,937.7	9,913.8	9,893.3	9,422.8	–5.2
EC 12	326,093.1	331,197.9	333,962.5	324,525.1	–0.5

Source: 'Eurostat and ERECO', *Europe in 1996, Economic Analysis and Forecasts* (May 1992).

decade (the slowest ever since World War II), and the subsequent contraction of 15 million have no parallels in European history (Rajan, 1990). The total EC population itself is due to experience a decline of 9 million people during the first two decades of next century (see Table 1.12).

Total fertility in Eastern Europe is currently higher than in North-Western Europe, the Mediterranean, Japan and the USA (see Tables 1.13 and 1.14). In 1989, Eastern Europe was also the region with the lowest proportion of foreign population (9 foreigners per 1,000 nationals, compared with 83/1000 in North-Western Europe, and 211/1000 in Japan and the NICs).[3] On the other hand, in 1989 Eastern Europe also had the lowest participation rate of females in secondary education (72.7 per cent, compared with a rate of 95.6 per cent in North-Western Europe).

In order to alleviate effects of the ageing of native Western populations such as the reduction in labour supply and contributions to social security systems, specific policies have been mainly confined to measures to stimulate the female labour supply, to raise the age of retirement, to restructure professional qualifications among the adult workforce, and to promote technological change to reduce overall needs for human resources (OECD, 1991).

If the migration variable is not yet overtly taken into account by most Western European governments, recent simulations of the demographic

Table 1.13   Demographic characteristics of major regions around 1989

	NW Europe	Mediterranean	East Europe	ACUN	Japan and NICs
Total fertility	1.67	1.77	2.07	1.87	1.71
Mean age at first birth	26.2	24.5		26.0	26.8
Age at first marriage (M)	27.3	27.0	25.1	26.0	28.8
Age at first marriage (F)	24.9	24.0	22.0	24.1	26.0
Married women in workforce (%)	59.5	52			60.5
Females in secondary education (%)	95.6	81.3	72.7	97.0	83.0
Proportion of foreign population (per 1000)	83	13	9	137	211

ACUN = Australia, Canada, USA, New Zealand

Source: Compiled from different sources by D.A. Coleman: 'European Demographic Systems in the Future', *Conference on Human Resources in Europe at the Dawn of the 21st Century* (Eurostat, Luxembourg, 27–29 November 1991).

evolution of four countries with a different migratory history (Austria, Canada, Belgium and Spain) help nevertheless to measure the future demographic implications of new migration to Europe. Suffice it to say that, in the absence of any additional immigration, and with a fertility rate of 2.1 (i.e. a rate higher than the one currently experienced by these four countries), population would start to decrease, and the number of deaths to exceed the number of births, in 2020 in Belgium, 2025 in Austria and Canada, and 2040 in Spain (Wattelat and Roumans, 1991).

Table 1.14   Total fertility rates in the EC member states, 1970–88

	1970/74	1975/79	1980/84	1985	1988
B	1.94	1.71	1.59	1.51	1.57
D	1.62	1.44	1.36	1.28	1.42
DK	1.96	1.70	1.42	1.45	1.56
E	2.89	2.63	1.83	1.61	1.52(a)
F	2.31	1.86	1.87	1.82	1.82
GR	2.32	2.32	1.97	1.68	1.52(b)
IR	3.80	3.46	2.87	2.49	2.17
I	2.27	1.92	1.55	1.41	1.30(b)
L	1.96	1.54	1.48	1.39	1.41(b)
NL	1.97	1.58	1.51	1.51	1.54
P	2.76	2.42	1.99	1.70	1.56(b)
UK	2.04	1.72	1.80	1.79	1.84

(a)   1986
(b)   1987

Source: Central Bureau of Statistics of the Netherlands, 1990.

In order to prevent such a decline, and bearing in mind current fertility rates, immigration would need to be promoted as from 1990 in Austria and Belgium, in 2000 in Spain and 2010 in Canada. In the case of Belgium and Canada, new immigration would need to double the net rates experienced by these countries in the recent past.

The evolution of the educational attainment of national students, and of labour market requirements, which, to a great extent, stems from Western European current demographic trends, offers further illustration of future implications of immigration to Europe.

Although between 1960 and 1970 the number of higher education enrolments in West European countries almost doubled, this evolution is currently being reversed at a time when all European governments are encouraging higher participation rates in tertiary education in order to fill rising skill gaps in the labour market. Moreover, available information clearly points to the fact that the above-mentioned increase in participation rates in higher education until the late 1970s involved, to a great extent, areas with less economic and industrial relevance, thus contributing to growing hidden unemployment (i.e. under-employment and under-utilisation of aquired skills) among graduates. In turn, a constant decrease in participation in scientific and technological areas has also been experienced, the share of engineering among higher education courses dropping by half over the last twenty years (IRDAC, 1990).

In the same vein, it is worthy of reminder that the share of *foreign students* within the total population enrolling in graduate studies in science and engineering has been increasing constantly over the last decade. Hence, among other examples, over 52 per cent of all graduate enrolments in science and engineering in the United Kingdom are presently composed of foreign students. In France, foreign students participate in graduate studies at double the rate of French nationals (Chandler, 1989).

Thus, in addition to growing *qualitative mismatches* between skilled labour demand and output of graduates, Western Europe is clearly confronted with a *rising shortage* of adequately trained manpower to fill

Table 1.15   Major educational and employment indicators in Eastern and Western Europe around 1989

	Bulgaria	Czechoslovakia	Hungary	Poland	Russia	Germany	UK
% of population under 15 (in 1990)	20	23.3	19.9	25.2	n.a.	15	18.9
Rates of enrolment in Secondary education	75	85	100	80	n.a.	99	83
Rates of enrolment in tertiary education	25	18	25	18	n.a.	32	23
% of adult literacy	93	99	99	98	99	99	99
Employment by sector (%)							
Primary	19	12	20	n.a.	17	3	2
Manufacturing	38	37	(38)*	36	29	41	(30)*
Construction	8	9	(38)*	9	9.3	7	(30)*
Tertiary	35	42	42	n.a.	44.6	49	68

*Total figure for construction and manufacturing.

Source: Compiled from *The Economist Atlas of the New Europe* (1992).

domestic labour market requirements. In this context, it is interesting to note that the current growth of labour demand is much higher for technical professions than for all other areas of the labour market. At the same time, the supply of new entrants in technical professions is lower than average.

The above trends cannot but be compared to major education and employment indicators in Eastern Europe. As Table 1.15 indicates, rates of enrolment in tertiary education and adult literacy in Eastern and Western Europe are of a comparable level, while the proportion of the population under 15 is more significant in Eastern Europe.

As the Industrial R&D Advisory Committee of the Commission of the European communities recently observed:

'all evidence points to a greater need for engineers, scientists and technicians in the future, and the current fear is that the education and training systems will not be in a position to deliver the number and range of school-leavers and graduates required. Moreover, without appropriate measures, the situation will worsen in the first decades of the 21st century. Worse even, skill shortages could become so severe that they significantly decrease Europe's competitive position' (IRDAC, 1990: 20).

Another area related to the current evolution of structural needs for foreign skilled manpower in Western Europe concerns R&D investments and activity within the European Community (see Table 1.16). In this respect, two main developments are indicative of current and future needs for an increase in skilled personnel. Firstly, available figures (OECD 1988 and 1990) show that most West European R&D activity is currently taking place in three countries, i.e. France, the United Kingdom and the Federal Republic of Germany (the latter employing 35 per cent of the European Community's R&D personnel). This trend clearly implies a future increase in investment in human resources, both in the above-mentioned countries (in order to deliver the appropriate number of scientists and engineers needed to implement growing R&D activity), and in the rest of Europe (in order to close development gaps with Western partners).

Against this background, existing figures also indicate that, per head of population, the number of researchers in Western Europe is less than half that of Japan and the United States, while other countries such as South Korea and Singapore have reached the European average figures and are continually progressing. On the other hand, although public expenditure in the field of education in Eastern Europe is still lower than in Western Europe, the percentage of GDP spent on R&D is of a comparable level (see Table 1.17).

Table 1.16   Indicators of R&D skill needs in the European Community

Member state	R&D as a percentage of GDP (1987)	Researchers (per 1,000 employed)	R&D index (EC = 100)*
B	1.5	2.6	76
D	2.8	4.8	131
DK	1.3	2.7	68
E	0.7	1.0	18
F	2.3	3.9	108
GR	0.3	0.6	—
I	1.5	2.7	61
IR	0.8	2.8	53
NL	2.3	3.7	103
P	0.4	0.7	—
UK	2.3	3.1	106

*This is a composite R&D index, based on a consideration of different factors, used as an indicator of the current variations between EC member states.

Source: The Industrial R&D Advisory Committee of the Commission of the European Communities: *Opinion on Skill Shortages in Europe* (Brussels: IRDAC, 1990).

Table 1.17   Basic indicators in education and R&D in selected East and West European countries 1986

	Czechoslovakia	France	Germany	Hungary	Poland	UK
% of total expenditure in education	5.2	7.8		2.3	3.8	2.2
% of age group enrolled in education						
Secondary	37	95	72	70	80	85
Tertiary	15	30	30	15	17	22
% of GDP in R&D	3.9	2.3	2.7	2.5	1.2	2.4

Source: World Bank: *World Development Report 1989* (Washington, DC); *L'Etat du Monde, 1989–1990* (Paris: Editions la Découverte).

Finally, due to the uneven progression of R&D investments, and, more widely, to uneven economic development within Western Europe, internal migration within the European Community of highly qualified personnel from less developed regions can indeed be expected in the coming years, which in turn will create notable sectoral shortages of skilled labour in Southern European areas (Ardittis, 1990).

As a summary of the developments in the field of West European demography, education and labour market trends identified above, and as a synthetic typology of the current imbalances in labour force developments, which could generate increasing needs for skilled migration to Europe, it is worth referring to Rajan's typology of know-how and training challenges in the European Community (Rajan, 1990). In order to examine the prospective skilled labour demand and imbalances in West European labour markets, Rajan identified six major categories of *gaps*, which he defines as possible future 'time bombs':

- the numbers gap (quantitative imbalances between skilled labour demand and supply);
- the skills gap (qualitative mismatches between skilled labour demand and supply);
- the gender gap (effects of the current evolution of female labour participation, which is due to become a dominant component of growth in the labour force);
- the racial gap (effects of increasing labour participation of ethnic minorities, a group which has not yet experienced a decrease in fertility rates, but whose participation in higher education is comparatively lower);
- the revenue gap (decreasing contributions to social security systems due to the ageing of native populations);
- the productivity gap (effects of the ageing of the labour force on productivity improvement).

THE POLICY ISSUES

As already mentioned in previous paragraphs, the politics of East–West migration to date have to a great extent consisted of emergency measures rather than sustainable, long-term policies. This can be explained by the fact that the full potential of East–West migration is still difficult to assess: for some countries, for which future membership of the EC is a realistic prospect, economic transition has not yet resulted in significant out-migration, and market economy benefits experienced so far support the belief that significant migratory pressures will decline rather than increase over the coming months; for other countries, the process towards a market economy has been engaged upon rather timidly and political pressure and uncertainties have the potential to reverse this process anytime in the near future; in countries like former Yugoslavia, ethnic conflict and over civil war is ongoing, and Western policy attitudes can only fluctuate according to the day-to-day development of conflicts.

Although the bulk of new policy which has been, or will be, devised by Western European governments can only be of a transitory nature, major areas where policy efforts made today can be of benefit, both in terms of the transitory and the post-transition periods of East–West migration, can be identified. One such area relates to information. As was mentioned in the introduction to this book, institutional actors in Europe are increasingly voicing their need for new instruments to allow the production of systematic data in the field of European migration, with particular focus on labour market implications.

The labour market analysis of East–West migration is indeed of intrinsic importance for devising future policies. In the countries of origin, such analysis should concentrate on the current domestic labour supply/demand (skill shortages, training needs) and on the skill profile of emigrants. This analysis should aim at surveying both the economic consequences of current East–West migration and the conditions for the possible return of East European nationals who emigrated throughout the 1970s and 1980s.

The comparative analysis of domestic skill shortages in the countries of origin and the skill profile of new emigrants should allow for a better definition of the future implications of increased East–West migration. The question must be asked whether these movements are merely an 'overflow' (excess or ill-trained labour which cannot, at the present time, be absorbed into domestic labour markets) or whether they are actually feeding a brain drain phenomenon. Similarly, and available figures permitting, a detailed analysis must be conducted of the skill profile of Eastern European immigrants established in the West since the 1970s. As this chapter will show on page 33, it is believed that some of these immigrants, should they return to their countries of origin, could play a significant role in the process of economic restructuring in Central and Eastern Europe.

Another major component in the labour market analysis to be undertaken in the countries of origin relates to measures able to prevent future massive emigration. To a great extent, the identification of appropriate preventive measures should focus on the detailed analysis of skill shortages and training needs in the countries of origin, and on realistic schemes to develop East–West economic cooperation. In addition to surveying/ compiling existing data on unfilled job offers on domestic labour markets in Eastern Europe, there is a need for empirical research on the impact of Western investments and the establishment of Western companies in Eastern countries, as a preventive factor for future migration. The need to analyse the staff composition of Western companies and the training schemes for local professionals promoted by these companies (or by cooperative ventures with local enterprises) in the East, and the need to study the possible relationship between Western investments in Eastern Europe and the absorption of local skilled and semi-skilled manpower, should be taken into account.

From the perspective of the receiving countries, the study of the labour market implications of increased East–West migration can only be a demand-oriented analysis, as it would aim at identifying the range of pull factors currently stemming from Western economic and demographic trends. As indicated in the previous sections, the gradual decrease in the domestic labour supply experienced by most Western European countries as a result of demographic decline, and the existence of large numbers of unfilled job opportunities in the labour market, suggest that the input of current and future labour migration must be approached primarily from a labour market point of view.

Thus, since the outbreak of the reform process in 1989, West Germany and Austria have been negotiating a number of economic migration agreements with Eastern countries to allow for a temporary 'exchange' of workers. Similarly, West Germany has been revising certain regulations relating to frontier migration, and has suspended, in a number of economic sectors, the general ban on new labour immigration. The latter measure has also been adopted by Italy, and is under consideration in other major receiving countries such as France.

Available channels permitting, a detailed analysis of the occupational distribution of new Eastern immigrants who, more often than not (ethnic Germans and contract migrants excepted), are in an irregular situation in Western European receiving countries, would help to measure the rate of absorption of new labour immigration from Central and Eastern Europe, and would shed some light on the mechanics of massive irregular migration (e.g. analysis of recruitment networks in Western and Eastern Europe, of the increasing transfers of capital from the official to the clandestine sector in the receiving countries, of the marginalisation process and discriminatory working environment of new Eastern immigrants, etc.).

The study of the long-term implications of East–West labour migration would also require a detailed analysis of the future demand for foreign labour in Western Europe. Although such a demand is hard to predict since, whatever the requirements of the labour market, the social consequences of increased inflows of foreigners will continue to govern the contours of Western immigration policies, available forecasts nevertheless allow the identification of certain general trends.

Thus in West Germany, a labour-scenario up to the year 2000, devised by the Institute for Labour Market and Occupational Research of the Federal Employment Agency at Nurnberg, indicates the possibility of 2.5 million *additional* employment opportunities in West Germany up to the end of the present millennium (Heyden, 1990). A breakdown of this figure, however, shows an important decline in production-related jobs (i.e. those requiring unskilled labour) and an important rise in skilled and highly skilled positions in the tertiary sector. According to the same Institute, a considerable increase will also occur in the stock of available manpower up to the end of the current decade (i.e. +1.4 million by the year 2000), due to the inflow of ethnic and Eastern Germans and to the increased female labour participation (which still amounts to 56 per cent in West Germany, compared to a rate of 81 per cent in East German landers).

Although they tend to overlook the future demographic deficit in many Western receiving countries, available figures thus point to the increased *selectivity* of future labour immigration to Western Europe. The anticipated needs for brain migration over the next few years are also confirmed by the increased estrangement of *national* students in Western European countries from postgraduate studies in key disciplines (science, technology, management). Hence, as already mentioned, between 50 per cent and 75 per cent of PhDs in most Western countries are now awarded to foreign students.

Finally, the consequences of increasing migratory pressures in Central and Eastern Europe, and the filling, by regular or irregular Eastern labour, of available positions in Western European countries, would have to be looked at from the perspective of other existing migratory fronts (Bohning and Werquin, 1990). The way in which East–West population movements are affecting South–North migration, in terms of new recruitments and the release of new work permits, is clearly an issue the implications of which, of growing concern to major Southern emigration countries, would need to be addressed in the context of a future European immigration policy.

The second major area in relation to which policy action today could benefit both the transitory and post-transition era in Central/Eastern

Europe, relates to return migration. Currently, a number of indicators point to the possible contribution of selected return migration to the development of the countries of origin:

- Most Central and Eastern European countries are increasingly affected by a shortage of managers and technology implementers/innovators able to conduct the process of economic restructuring and integration into a market economy to its full potential.
- At the same time, foreign investors with new technology and managerial techniques, and international technical cooperation aimed at the development of former COMECON countries, are equally confronted with the limited reservoir of appropriately trained manpower; in turn, the restricted availability of adequate local skills is contributing to restraining the full development of investments in former COMECON countries, due in particular to a similar shortage of West Europeans appropriately trained (culturally and linguistically) for taking up new key positions in Central and Eastern Europe.
- Former COMECON countries are still faced with considerable difficulties in importing Western technology and systems, due to considerable external debt and scarcity of hard currency.
- Since the reform era was begun, growing numbers of expatriates (independent of their professional qualifications) have been voicing their interest in exploring suitable means for a return to, and a successful economic reintegration into, their countries of origin. Due to the nature of emigration from Central and Eastern Europe throughout the 1970s and 1980s, remittances to the countries of origin have been scarce, and it can easily be assumed that significant numbers of expatriates, given appropriate opportunities, would be in a position to reintegrate with a substantial investment capability.

Returnees could thus consist of both expatriates with capital (i.e. potential investors) and expatriate nationals with specific skills in great demand in the countries of origin. With regard to the first category, a number of former COMECON countries today offer suitable conditions for a selective return, with capital, of expatriate nationals:

- Due to the accelerated process of economic liberalization and restructuring, the drastic decline in trade and economic relations among former COMECON members, and the multivocal needs for external capital, foreign investments are increasingly being supported and facilitated by Eastern European governments.

- While all restrictions and barriers, including taxes, are gradually being removed, a common feature of all joint ventures in Eastern Europe is their low initial capitalisation. For example, about 80 per cent of joint ventures established in Poland in 1990 were small firms which invested the minimal capital required, i.e. about US$50,000.
- The range of economic sectors offering opportunities for foreign investment, as economic and industrial restructuring evolves, is widening. The bulk of investments in Eastern Europe in 1990 was allocated to a variety of sectors covering the food-processing industry, construction, the hotel and catering business, the chemical and machine industry, and the electronics industry.
- Due to the increasing momentum gained by Western investments in former COMECON countries and to the growing interest of Western corporations and credit institutions in potential markets and opportunities in Eastern Europe, partnerships and joint ventures are being facilitated.
- The potential for foreign investment in Eastern Europe and the former Soviet Union was estimated in 1990 at over US$33 billion (assuming foreign investments equalling 1.5 per cent of GDP) (AMEX Bank Review, 1990), while the flow of direct investment to former COMECON countries by mid-1990 barely exceeded the equivalent of US$2 billion.

Despite *prima facie* suitable conditions, and drawing upon the experience of return migration to Southern Europe throughout the 1970s and 1980s (Ardittis, 1988), the promotion of *ad hoc* plans for reintegration with capital of expatriate nationals will clearly need to integrate a number of prerequisites and specific measures, among which:

- The supply of information on existing (or forthcoming) regulations and fiscal policies for returnees and/or expatriate investors.
- The promotion of contacts between expatriate nationals and public and private investment institutions in the countries of origin.
- The promotion of contacts between expatriate nationals and Western firms investing or intending to invest in former COMECON countries.
- Assistance in the development of network activities or in the setting up of associations by expatriate nationals intending to reintegrate and/or to invest in their countries of origin (i.e. creation of joint ventures, cooperatives, common investment funds, etc.).

– Creation of information and assistance centres for returnees, both in the countries of origin and, through consular sections, in the countries of immigration.

In this respect, multilateral financial and development institutions currently in charge of new assistance programmes for Eastern Europe (e.g. the European Bank for Reconstruction and Development, the Group of 24 and PHARE, the EC and the World Bank), would certainly be instrumental in supporting, in cooperation with recipient countries, *ad hoc* surveys to identify suitable opportunities for returnee investors and entrepreneurs, and to promote appropriate information campaigns in Western European immigration countries.

With regard to the second category of returnees, the attraction of desperately needed expatriate professionals in salaried positions in priority economic areas is also of crucial importance for the sustainable economic development of Central and Eastern Europe. For at least three major reasons, however, the design, at unilateral, bilateral or multilateral level, of measures to stimulate a selective return of expatriate professionals, is an exercise of particular complexity in the case of former COMECON countries:

– Migration of highly qualified professionals is not always the result of mismatches between educational output and labour market requirements, but can equally derive from a lack or inadequacy of infrastructure, equipment, subsidiary technology or intermediary technical staff to implement otherwise needed skills. In the case of former COMECON countries, the latter cause should indeed be retained as a major determinant of past and present skilled migration from Eastern Europe. Due to several decades of relative isolationism, poor economic and technological relations with the Western world, and scarcity of foreign exchange (or economic embargos) which restrained appropriate imports of foreign technology and equipment, infrastructural and technological gaps between Eastern and Western Europe today are very wide.

– Qualified professionals who emigrated to the West over the past two decades, and for that matter expatriate nationals who completed their scientific and engineering graduate studies in Western Europe and who subsequently found employment in the country of immigration, must be seen today as rather improbable candidates for permanent return to the countries of origin. Assimilation of Western technological advances, adequate infrastructure and research means, high standards of living, are but few of the current obstacles to substantial return migration of highly qualified expatriate nationals.

–   Recent expatriates, and resident professionals who intend to migrate in the coming months, will clearly be aiming at experiencing for a number of years the employment conditions prevailing in Western Europe and at exploring career developments outside their countries of origin.

In contrast with brain drain dynamics in most other developing regions, the effects of the long-lasting ban on emigration on current East–West outflows should thus be fully taken into account when considering the impact of, and the remedies for, rising skilled migration from Eastern Europe. More than in other developing areas, the current brain drain from Central and Eastern Europe is therefore evolving in a vicious circle. On the one hand, significant return of highly qualified expatriates can only occur upon completion of the current reform era and the closing of technological gaps with the Western world; on the other hand, expatriate professionals are clearly the best-fitted agents to promote and implement the necessary technological change and innovation to reduce development disparitieis.

Against this background, two multilateral programmes which were devised in the mid-1970s are able to respond to the characteristics of potential return migration to Central and Eastern Europe. The first, the so-called TOKTEN programme ('Transfer of Knowledge Through Expatriate Nationals'), which is administered by UNDP and already operates in some Eastern European countries, promotes the temporary return of highly skilled expatriates through short-term consultancy periods in their countries of origin. The programme does not infringe on the career motivations of the recruited professionals, and it is targeted to well-selected sectors of development in the countries of origin.

The second programme, which operates in Latin America and a number of African and Asian countries, is administered by the International Organization for Migration (IOM). The programme assists the permanent return of expatriate professionals through such integrated services as the search for suitable job openings in the countries of origin, the recruitment of appropriate expatriate professionals, free transportation to the countries of origin, salary adjustments and the provision of professional equipment to support the priority needs of the returnees within their new employing en- tities. The cost-effectiveness and the development benefits (particularly through their substantial multiplier effects) deriving from the above programmes in a number of regions have often been evidenced (Ardittis, 1985 and 1991), and these are clearly the types of programme which could be easily adapted to the particular development situation prevailing in Central and Eastern Europe.

The third major area which calls for policy action relates to education and training in Central and Eastern Europe.

In order to allow for sustainable economic and technological development in former COMECON countries, the design of *ad hoc* training schemes and appropriate long-term educational policies, constitutes a top priority in the context of the present reform era.

Whatever the potential risks of non-subsequent return to the countries of origin, short-term training programmes for Eastern Europeans, currently promoted in a number of Western European countries, clearly offer an *ad hoc* and highly targeted contribution, in terms of specific know-how transfer, to the reform process in former COMECON countries.

An example of newly created training schemes is the COPERNIC programme, jointly organized by major engineering graduate schools in France, and sponsored by major French corporations. The programme aims at training students from Czechoslovakia, Hungary, Poland and Romania, in France, in a number of business and engineering disciplines, for a period of one year (including three months of internship). While there is a clause that stipulates that students must return to their countries of origin upon completion of the programme, the programme is also highly interactive and integrated in nature, as it is primarily designed to train suitable skilled manpower to work in French firms recently established in Central and Eastern Europe.

Similar short-term programmes are also being managed under specific agreements between Poland and the Federal Republic of Germany, France and the Netherlands, and between former Czechoslovakia and the Federal Republic of Germany.

A more sizable programme which also needs to be mentioned is the European Community TEMPUS progamme, which was initiated in mid-1990 with a view to organising East–West joint education programmes, exchanges of faculty members and students, and cooperation between enterprises and higher education institutions. For the period 1990–1, 300 projects were selected, mainly in the fields of engineering, scientific and business administration (i.e. priority education areas selected by recipient countries) (see Table 1.18).

Although the above schemes would need to be thoroughly evaluated in terms of their real output and their major effects (i.e. rate and duration of returns to the countries of origin, effective use of newly acquired skills, subsequent training of local personnel and other multiplier effects, etc.), the development of *ad hoc* training mechanisms able to respond to selected and immediate shortages of qualified manpower can certainly be seen as a *sine qua non* for the effective implementation of the current transition towards a market economy.

Table 1.18   TEMPUS Joint European Projects (JEP) in priority areas in former Czechoslovakia, Hungary and Poland in 1990–1 (in %)

	1	2	3	4	5	6	7	8	9
Czechoslovakia	30	13	5	10	5	5	5	0	27
Hungary	25	8	6	11	6	0	5	8	31
Poland	34	19	7	6	6	6	3	2	17

1. = Applied sciences, technologies and engineering.
2. = Management and business administration.
3. = Environmental protection.
4. = Social and economic sciences related to the process of economic and social change.
5. = Modern European languages.
6. = Applied economics.
7. = Medical sciences.
8. = Agriculture and agro-business.
9. = Other.

Source: Tempus Office (Brussels), 1992.

Similarly, the relationship between the transfer of modern technology by Western enterprises established in former COMECON countries and the training and absorption of local skilled manpower, should be taken into account fully. Internal training schemes within newly created enterprises can help to reduce skill shortages deriving from the process of economic restructuring, at least until Eastern European educational systems can adapt to new labour market requirements. Major firms, by the internal training of rising numbers of managers and technicians, can thus contribute not only to reducing structural outmigration caused by economic reform, but also to diffusing (through the multiplier effect of initial training) and distributing (according to real employment opportunities and industrial locations), the training capacity in Central and Eastern European countries. This type of scheme seems particularly adapted to the skill structure of most Central and Eastern European countries: the labour force in that region is generally well trained and the process of economic restructuring mainly calls for the initiation of programmes for retraining rather than for initial training. Thus in the former Soviet Union, the labour force in 1991 included some 35 million skilled workers and employees with higher education and 82 million skilled blue-collar workers. Each year, 2.6 million people graduate from vocational training schools and over 33 million workers and 10.5 million managers and specialists are trained on an on-going basis (Samorodov, 1992). Due to the mismatch between new labour demand and the existing occupational structure brought about by economic restructuring, retraining is critical to the reduction of structural unemployment. In 1991, a number of retraining centres were thus established in the former Soviet Union and surveys indicate that the majority of workers made redundant were prepared to enroll in these programmes (Samorodov, 1992).

In the longer term, the design of viable educational policies closely related to newly set development targets would also need to be promoted. A viable policy would imply matching educational output with new labour market requirements, but also with adequate infrastructure. As a scientist from the Soviet Institute for Molecular Biology recently declared: 'If we do not take the next step, which is to allow us to organise our laboratories on the level accepted in the West, our science will come to a stop. We will turn into a supplier of scientific minds' (*The Economist*, 1991).

Futhermore, the design of viable educational policies should also contribute to rising participation rates in higher education. As already mentioned, the percentage of age group enrolled in higher education in many Eastern European countries is still half that of the Federal Republic of Germany, France and Japan, and four times lower than in the United States.

Increased enrolments in tertiary education should be eased, in particular, by the current movement to gradually reduce the defence industry in Eastern Europe, a move which will allow for the higher participation rates of male students in education. In 1986, the number of females per 100 males in secondary education was equal to 187 in Hungary and 265 in Poland, against a proportion of slightly under 100 in the Federal Republic of Germany, Japan and the United States, and slightly above 100 in France (World Bank, 1990).

CONCLUSION

History will almost certainly cast the 1990s as the decade of substantial population movements towards Europe, be these movements governed by economic or political determinants. Contrary to other periods in recent European history, which also witnessed high levels of migration (e.g. overseas emigration of Europeans in the 1940s and 1950s, immigration from former colonies and from Southern Europe during the 1960s and early 1970s, return migration to Southern Europe in the late 1970s and the 1980s), European migration in the 1990s is exhibiting a number of unique characteristics.

The first and foremost of these characteristics is that contrary to earlier periods when labour shortages in Western European markets impelled energetic policies of labour recruitment in peripheral countries, migration to Europe has now become a mostly unwanted phenomenon. As a result, Western European immigration policies have had to move from pro-active to reactive. While this process of political mutation can be traced back to the mid-1970s, with the official halt of new immigration to Western Europe, the range of policy adjustments which this process has required are far from having reached completion. While economic criteria act as a key regulative element of pro-active immigration policies, restrictive or reactive immigration policies cannot but draw upon a range of additional geopolitical, historical, social or humanitarian variables. In democracies which father the actual principles of, and conventions on, political asylum and the free movement of people and ideas, restrictive immigration policies form a temporary, albeit necessary anomaly: as such, they are difficult to ground, to implement and to sustain; restrictions can only be modulated according to geopolitical developments, economic/trade interests or political/humanitarian cooperation. A once-and-for-all *modus operandi* for Western Europe's restrictive immigration policies has not yet been, and will probably never be, established.

The second, interrelated, characteristic of European migration in the 1990s consists of the recent juxtaposition of two major migratory fronts, Eastern Europe and the South, with quite distinct determinants, structure and growth potential. Due to its geographic proximity, its unpredictability and its current levels, post-1989 migration from Central and Eastern Europe has focused the attention and centralised the alarmed policy reactions of Western leaders. The alarm has reverberated even louder since substantial migratory pressures in the actual heart of Europe generate a deeper sense of urgency than traditional, cross-maritime immigration from developing countries of the South. This is despite the fact that the levels of migration from developing countries continue to outstrip the levels of new migration from the East. It is despite the fact, also, that the anticipated growth potential of South–North migration over the next few years has no common measure with the growth potential of East–West movements. Development gaps between Eastern European transition economies and the Western world, what is more, will be considerably reduced by the close of the decade, just as Southern European countries gradually succeeded, throughout the 1980s, in aligning their economies with their Northern European neighbours and in reducing migratory pressures. This process will be clearly enhanced by some Eastern European countries' current association agreements with, and future membership of, the European

Community. By contrast, the developing South is increasingly affected by its strongly rooted trio of evils: demographic explosion, poverty, and external debt; not to mention its secular ethnic unrest and environmental degradation which will generate growing numbers of asylum seekers chiefly directed to the more affluent North. The resemblance between East–West and South–North migration therefore can only consist of the confluence of both streams towards Western Europe at a given point in time. It is quite obvious that migration-related policy measures currently devised by Western leaders by no means reflect the relative weight and future implications of both streams.

The third characteristic of European migration in the 1990s relates to the state of the receiving countries' economies. With recession hitting most of Western Europe's national economies, and long-term and youth unemployment reaching unprecedented levels, little flexibility can be expected from Western societies with respect to future immigration from non-member states. Even considering Western Europe's negative demographic trends (which, according to some experts, will be largely compensated for by future female labour supply), short and medium-term immigration pressures will largely outstrip the 'immigration capacity' of the West.

It can thus be anticipated that Western Europe's policy responses to the migration challenge will continue to be chiefly modulative, building upon the current hierarchy of urgencies. In such a hierarchy, it is obvious that Eastern Europe, due to ethnic unrest and overt civil war, will continue to overshadow the less immediate and – as yet unarmed challenges posed by South–North migration. From signs visible today, much points to the fact that Western Europe's new policy apparatus will lean more towards protection than cooperation.

Explicit signs, such as the categorisation of Central and Eastern Europe into safe and unsafe countries, are eloquent indeed. Cooperation with Central and Eastern European countries is increasingly conditional: aid in exchange for displacement of the burdens of migration to safe Central European countries. Thus the negotiations of March 1993 between Hungary, Poland, Austria, Slovenia, the Czech Republic and Slovakia aimed at harmonising immigration rules and setting up special police units to curb illegal immigration. These negotiations also foresee the establishment of common visa regulations and a common intelligence network.

In his enlightening book, Dahrendorf (1990) identified three conditions for successful transition to democracy in Central and Eastern Europe: the establishment of new political institutions, a market economy and a civil society. As Rupnik (1993) correctly remarked, however, the major obstacle which Eastern European countries have encountered in implementing the above transition relates to the lack of synchronisation between these three conditions. So far the transition process has been characterised by the acceleration of political reforms and delays in economic reforms. Thus, as Rupnik observed, free elections were organised within six months of the 1989 revolutions; within an optimistic scenario, six more years will be required to establish a market economy and another sixty years to establish a civil society.

In Part IV of this book, the pros and cons of trade, aid and foreign direct investment as a means of reducing emigration pressures are addressed. As Ghosh notes, aid has traditionally been used for general development purposes with little attention being paid to its effect on migration. Only recently has the European Community, through its newly funded programmes for cooperation with Mediterranean countries in the field of migration, started to analyse the impact on migration of development cooperation policies implemented in recent years (Ardittis, 1993).

Although observers increasingly express their concern over the relatively low level of aid and cooperation granted to the new Eastern European democracies after the 1989 revolutions, it is obvious that the level of such aid is also, to a great extent, dependent upon the pace and success of reforms implemented by the Eastern European countries themselves. Institutional reforms, new legislation and the development of sound managerial capabilities to absorb and optimise foreign aid and investment should indeed precede any substantial transfer of resources from West to East. During this process, however, the importance of technical assistance for the new Eastern European democracies cannot be stressed enough.

The European Community has conceived a range of instruments and structural funds to help the development of its own lagging regions and to contribute to greater economic convergence between its member states. These instruments include, in particular, the European Social Fund and the European Regional Development Fund. In conformity with development targets set by six-year Community Support Frameworks (CSFs), which are jointly negotiated by the beneficiary member states and the European Commission, these two funds contribute to substantial development projects (e.g. in education and training, creation of SMEs, industrial restructuring, research and development, etc.) in the lagging regions of the Community. The Community not only finances a significant proportion of the cost of these projects but also provides the technical assistance necessary to their successful implementation. In addition, within the European Community, a growing number of networks aimed at the exchange of experience among member states or regions are being set up in a number of fields. The integration of some or most Central and Eastern European countries into these networks should gradually be promoted. Lagging regions of the European Community (i.e. the so-called Objective 1 regions, which currently consist of the entire territory of Greece, Ireland and Portugal, in addition to the new German Lander and specific regions in Belgium, France, Italy, Spain and the UK) share a number of deficiencies in common with Central and Eastern European countries. Integration of Eastern European countries into EC networks would thus constitute an exemplary way of promoting East–West cooperative development based on the mutual transfer of experience and know-how. EC networks such as INTERREG, which aims to promote transnational cooperation between border regions, would be particularly relevant to the newly liberalised Eastern European states. Integration of these states into EC networks would, however, require better coordination and synergy between such instruments as PHARE (i.e. the G24 coordinated aid to Central and Eastern Europe managed by the European Commission), TACIS (i.e. the EC's technical assistance fund for the CIS), and the EC's 'internal' structural funds (i.e. the European Social Fund, the European Regional Fund, and the European Agricultural Fund). It would also require aid and technical assistance to Central and Eastern Europe to be viewed not as 'one-off' external assistance initiatives, but as internal, long-term integrative actions aimed at promoting the economic and social cohesion of Europe at large. The EC and wider European regional entities should thus be seen as formally responsible for the evolution of reforms undertaken in Central and Eastern Europe. Such responsibility is not only justified by historical, geopolitical factors, but also by the realistic prospect of some Eastern European states' future membership of the EC. EFTA countries themselves are increasingly invited to participate in a number of EC networking activities.

Cooperative development between Central/Eastern Europe and the EC's regions and member states could prove to be a relatively efficient means of overcoming the 'unpreparedness' of former COMECON countries to absorb and optimise substantial financial aid from the West. As the report of the 'Task Force on Western Assistance to Transition in the Czech and Slovak Federal Republic, Hungary and Poland' concluded: 'the greatest impediments to optimal use of the pledged assistance are the lack of adequate infrastructure in the recipient countries and the lack of overarching coordination of the actual needs, resources and aims involved' (Institute for East–West Studies, 1992). By participating in sectorally targeted EC networks on the exchange of experience, and by benefiting from *ad hoc* technical assistance to implement the much-needed reforms, the 'unpreparedness' of Central and Eastern European countries could gradually be alleviated on a sector by sector basis, and Western aid increased accordingly. As the above Task Force aptly recommended, the monitoring of the operational efficiency of Western aid could be entrusted to several committees which would be responsible for macro-economic assistance (under the chairmanship of the IMF), structural transformation and adjustment (under the chairmanship of the World Bank), technical assistance (under the chairmanship of the EC), micro-economic policies and privatisation (under the chairmanship of the EBRD), and non-economic assistance (under the chairmanship of the Council of Europe).

The gradualness of Western assistance for Eastern European economic reforms should not, however, imply any gradualness in Western Europe's humanitarian assistance and cooperation. In 1992, 15 per cent of PHARE's resources were allocated to humanitaran and emergency aid. Ethnic unrest, and in some countries, political turmoil, will continue to generate high levels of asylum-seeking migration towards the West. Unemployment and low levels of social protection will themselves give rise to occasional increases in migratory pressures in some Central and Eastern European countries. Although Western Europe cannot openly influence the evolution of ethnic antagonism in those regions and can only contribute to reducing economic deficiencies in the long-term, it should however assume full responsibility for providing whatever level of humanitarian assistance is needed today to alleviate the adverse effects of transition in Central and Eastern Europe.

Notes

1. Originally, the term 'safe countries' was applied to those countries which signed the international conventions on refugees.
2. The expected drop, for instance, in Hungarian/Soviet trade in 1991 from the 1990 level was as high as 40–50 per cent (Okolocsanyi, 1991)
3. Until the late 1980s, Eastern Europe promoted selective guest worker immigration designed to close certain manpower gaps and to attract cheap labour from less developed communist countries. In 1990, guest workers in Eastern Europe (including East Germany and excluding the Soviet Union) amounted to approximately 280,000 people, mainly Vietnamese and Cubans (Reed, 1990). Since the 1989 revolutions and the rising unemployment and social antagonism, the foreign worker population of Eastern Europe has gradually been declining either through voluntary return migration or through non-renewal of labour-exchange agreements.

References

AMEX Bank Review, no. 4, 1990, p. 5

Ardittis, S. *The Assisted Return of Qualified Migrants to their Countries of origin: The UNDP and ICM Multilateral Programme*, Geneva: International Labour Office, 1985.

Ardittis, S. *Migration de retour en Europe du Sud*, Geneva: International Labour Office, 1988.

Ardittis, S: 'Labour Migration and the Single European Market: A Synthetic and Prospective Note', *International Sociology*, vol. V, no. 4 (December 1990).

Ardittis, S. 'Prospects and Issues in Skilled Migration from Eastern to Western Europe', *Fifth International Workshop on the Transfer of Knowledge through Expatriate Nationals*, organised jointly by the United Nations Development Programme and the Department of Foreign Affairs of the Philippines, Manilla, 8–12 October 1991.

Ardittis, S. *Evaluation of the EEC-IOM Project for the Reintegration of Qualified Latin American Nationals in Five central American Countries*, Brussels and Geneva: European Commission and International Organisation for Migration, 1991.

Ardittis, S. 'The New Brain Drain from Eastern to Western Europe', *International Spectator*, vol. XXVII, no. 1 (January 1992).

Ardittis, S. *Rapport de synthèse sur les besoins en matière d'information et de recherche dans le domaine des migrations de la Méditerranée vers la Communauté européenne*, Brussels: Commission of the European Communities (DGI), June 1993.

Bohning, W.R. and Werquin, J. *Some Economic, Social and Human Rights Considerations concerning the Future Status of Third-Country Nationals in the Single European Market*, Geneva: International Labour Office, April 1990.

Chandler, A. *Obligation or Opportunity: Foreign Student Policies in Six Major Receiving Countries*, New York: Institute of International Education, Research Report no. 18, 1989.

Commission of the European Communities: *Immigration Policies and Social Integration of Immigrants in the European Community*, Brussels: CEC, 28 September 1990.

Commission of the European Communities: *Regional Development Studies, no. 2 – The socio-Economic Situation and Development of the Regions in the Neighbouring Countries of the Community in Central and Eastern Europe*, Brussels: CEC, 1992.

Dahrendorf, R. *Reflections on the Revolution in Europe*, London: Chatto & Windus, 1990.

Dufour, J.P. 'Le naufrage de la science russe', *Le Monde*, 24 April 1992, p. 11.

The Economist, 1 June 1990, p. 80.

Employment Observatory (European Commission): *Central and Eastern Europe Employment Trends and Developments*, no. 1 (January 1992).

Fischer, G. and Standing, G. Restructuring in Eastern and Central Europe: Labour Market and Social Issues, *ILO/OECD/CCEETT Conference on the Labour Market and Social Policy Implications of Structural Change in Central and Eastern Europe*, Paris, OECD, 11–13 September 1991.

Ghosh, B. 'Money Can't Buy Reform in East Europe', *European Affairs*, no. 3 (Autumn 1990).

Gwiazda, A. 'Eastern Europe is Ripe for Joint Ventures', *European Affairs*, no. 4 (Winter 1990).

Heyden, H. 'South–North Migration', Ninth IOM Seminar on Migration, organised by the International organisation on Migration in Geneva (4–6 December 1990).

Honekopp, E. 'East–West Migration: Recent Developments', International Conference on Migration, organised by the OECD and the Italian Government in Rome (13–15 March 1991).

Institute for East–West Studies. *Moving Beyond Assistance: Final Report of the IEWS Task Force on Western Assistance to Transition in the Czech and Slovak Republic, Hungary and Poland*, Boulder: Westview Press, 1992.

IRDAC. *Opinion on Skill Shortages in Europe*, Brussels: IRDAC, November 1990.

Lipschitz, L. and McDonald, D. *German Unification: Economic Issues*, Washington: International Monetary Fund, Dec.1990.

OECD. *New Technologies in the 1990s*, Paris: OECD, 1988.

OECD. *Employment Outlook*, Paris: OECD, 1990.

OECD. 'Contraintes démographiques et politiques migratoires', *Migrations – Les Aspects Démographiques*, Paris: OECD, 1991.

Okolicsanyi, F. 'Hungary: Drastic Decline in Trade with the USSR', *Report on Eastern Europe*, vol. 2, no. 14 (April 1991).

Okolski, M. 'Mouvements migratoires en provenance des pays d'Europe centrale et orientale', *Conference of Ministers on the Movement of People from Central and Eastern Europe*, organised by the Council of Europe in Vienna (24–25 January 1991).

Rajan, A. *1992, a Zero Sum Game – Business, Know-How and Training Challenges in an Integrated Europe*, London: The Industrial Society Press, 1990.

Reed, H. 'Foreign Workers in Eastern Europe', *Report on Eastern Europe*, vol. I, no. 27 (July 1990).

Rhode, B. *East–West Migration/Brain Drain*, Brussels: Cost Social Sciences, Commission of the European Communities, October 1991.

Rupnik, J. *L'autre Europe – Crise et fin du communisme*, Paris: Points, Odile Jacob, 1993.

Samorodov, A. *The Labour Market, Social Policy and Industrial Relations in the Soviet Union under Transition*, Geneva: ILO, March 1992.

Samorodov, A. 'Labour Mobility in Europe as a Result of Changes in Central and Eastern Europe', *Labour*, vol. VI, no. 3 (Winter 1992).

Standing, G. (ed.). *In Search of Flexibility: The New Soviet Labour Market*, Geneva: ILO, 1991.

Wattelat, C. and Roumans, G. 'Objectifs démographiques et migrations: quelques simulations', *Migrations – Les Aspects Démographiques*, Paris: OECD, 1991.

Widgren, J. 'International Migration and Regional Stability', *International Affairs*, vol. 66, no. 4 (October 1990).

World Bank. *World Development Report* (various years).

Part II
Central and Eastern Europe

Introduction
Solon Ardittis

Part II, which is divided into six chapters devoted respectively to Poland, the Baltic States, Hungary, Russia and the CIS, former Yugoslavia and former Czechoslovakia, aims to illustrate the range of socio-economic, legal and political contexts in which migration from Central and Eastern Europe has developed after the 1989 revolutions.

These six countries (or group of countries), which have constituted major sources of labour and refugee migration since 1989, exhibit a number of common and distinctive migration-related patterns. Common patterns include:

- The restrictive emigration policies which all Central and Eastern European countries experienced until 1989.
- The disruptive of the CMEA employment network after the 1989 revolutions, which determined a redirection of labour migration towards Western European labour markets.
- Return migration of ethnic minorities or political refugees from Eastern or Western European asylum or immigration countries.
- The abolition of special trade arrangements between former COMECON members, which signified the development of trade on a competitive basis.
- The more or less ambitious programmes of reform, particularly in terms of economic restructuring (e.g. privatisations) and introduction of new legislation, which these countries have been implementing since
· 1990.

Major distinctive patterns in turn include:

- The fact that some of these countries (i.e. Poland and former Yugoslavia) acted as traditional countries of labour emigration before the 1989 revolutions, while others (e.g. the former Soviet Union) mainly exported political refugees.
- The fact that some of these countries (i.e. Hungary, Poland, Slovenia, the Czech Republic and Slovakia) became, after 1989, both countries of emigration and of immigration.

- The dislocation of the national territory of some of these countries (i.e. the Soviet Union, Czechoslovakia and Yugoslavia), which signified a range of additional migratory pressures determined by ethnic and political antagonism.

Part II thus aims to address, within each national context, three major series of indicators which allow the assessment of the relative significance of each migratory front:

- The levels and structure of migration after 1989.
- Its main determinants.
- The state of development of new migration-related legislation and policy.

By presenting the above sets of indicators in a concise and mostly factual manner, country chapters in Part II provide a basis for better interpreting the range of policy reactions adopted by Western European countries after 1989 (Part III) and the analysis of policy issues associated with this phenomenon (Part IV).

2 Poland

Marek Okólski

If Central and Eastern Europe were to be considered as a traditional region of emigration, Poland would certainly be ranked as a leading country of emigration. For at least 150 years, Poland has acted as a vast reservoir of labour for many countries, most notably for Germany and for overseas countries of European settlement. The outflow of population from Poland continued even during the years of harshest repression by the communist authorities. With out-migration reaching its peak in the 1980s, Poland undisputably became the major sending country in Europe.

According to scrupulously maintained police records, 222,000 people emigrated officially between 1981 and 1988, in addition to another 533,000 who, by extending their stay abroad after expiry of their visas, became illegal emigrants. On the basis of estimates which draw upon statistics from the central population register of Poland and from the German government, approximately 1,050,000 Polish nationals emigrated between 1980 and 1989 (60,000 in 1980, 220,000 in 1989).

Despite the fact that some 200,000 Polish nationals returned to their country of origin during the 1980s, the total population loss through foreign migration has been quite substantial. In 1988 and in 1989, net migration figures exceeded the respective natural increase figures. Since 1985, when the difference between the net migration of people of working age and the 'natural increase' of that group became negative for the first time, the tendency has been towards an increasing decline in the total resident population of working age. Between 1985 and 1989, the total migration loss among the labour force amounted to 620,000 (nearly 70 per cent above the total 'natural increase'), and the size of the population of working age decreased by some 500,000 (2 per cent).

The structural consequences of the wave of emigration which occurred during the 1980s were by no means less significant; the major effect consisted of a gradual depletion of 'better quality' human resources. For instance, in 1988 (a census year), 44 per cent of emigrants had completed at least secondary school, compared to a proportion of 31 per cent among the total population (Okólski, 1991a). Indeed, throughout the 1980s, the share of highly skilled or educated among the emigrant population increased constantly. Another important consequence of Polish migration

51

during the 1980s resulted from the highly uneven spatial distribution of outflows: since 50 per cent of migrants left from the four main administrative units (i.e. Warsaw, Gdansk, Katowice and Opole), which in 1981 were home to 23.5 per cent of the total Polish population, certain regions underwent virtual depopulation. For example, more than 90,000 people emigrated from the Opole region between 1981 and 1988, a figure which amounted to 18 per cent of the region's total population. Finally, a large number of families have been disunited. According to the population census of 1988, approximately 250,000 household members were left behind by Polish emigrants (including 140,000 spouses or children below the age 25) (Okólski, 1991b).

NEW POLITICAL AND INSTITUTIONAL INFRASTRUCTURES AFTER 1989

Between 1945 and 1989 the legal acts related to foreign migration strictly followed the cardinal principles of the isolationist migration policy of that time: they were simple and predominantly repressive. The relevant institutions, and the transport and service infrastructures, were vastly underdeveloped relative to Western countries. This clearly reflected the low priority which omnipotent governments gave to international movements of people.

Following the adoption, in September 1989, of a liberal migration policy by the first non-communist government, all citizens were granted free passage through the state boundaries,[1] while negotiations on reciprocal visa-free travelling were initiated with many governments. At the same time, Poland started to welcome refugees from abroad. New government and legal entities specifically in charge of migration affairs were established, while a number of international agreements for the exchange of trainees, students and scholars, and programmes in the area of international economic co-operation and assistance were ratified. Various incentives to attract foreign business were gradually implemented. At the same time, the Polish government initiated an active policy aimed at securing wider access to foreign labour markets for Polish workers. All in all, within a period of one to two years, Poland turned into a relatively open country.

MIGRATORY FLOWS IN THE LIGHT OF AVAILABLE STATISTICS

During the first two years following the collapse of the communist regime, the number of emigrants declined considerably. In 1990 and 1991, 49,500 people were registered as emigrants, compared to a figure of 62,900 people in 1988 and 1989. Among them, the large majority (66 per cent) emigrated to Germany, with the United States representing the second major destination (8 per cent of all emigrants in 1990 and 1991).

With regard to immigration to Poland, the number of arrivals rose drastically after 1990. Although available data does not allow a distinction to be made between returning emigrants and other categories of immigrants, it would appear that Polish nationals who left Poland in the period 1975–88 have made a major contribution to the recent increase in immigration. This is also supported by the fact that recent immigration was predominantly composed of males and people aged between 30 and 49.

In 1990 and 1991, the majority of immigrants (51 per cent) came from non-European countries and from the former USSR (22 per cent). On average, the educational attainment of the immigrants who arrived in Poland has been significantly higher than that of emigrants, and this contributed, at least temporarily, to reversing the earlier brain drain which had affected Poland.

Contrary to widely voiced predictions, the radical liberalisation of the government's migration policy in 1989 and 1990, which coincided with a dramatic increase in unemployment and with the deterioration of real incomes, alleviated rather than reinforced emigration pressure in Poland. At the same time, former emigrants found some motivation to return to Poland. By and large, favourable political developments have thus offset the unfavourable effects of the economic slump.

EMIGRATION FOR WORK

In 1990, significant changes occurred regarding foreign employment of Polish labour. On the one hand, the revolutions in Central and Eastern Europe resulted in a radical transformation of the internal labour markets of that region (with the emergence, in particular, of unemployment) and contributed to the disruption of the CMEA employment network. The liberalisation of the movement of people across state boundaries also facilitated spontaneous migration for work. On the other hand, the Gulf War produced an abrupt suspension of nearly all employment contracts held by Polish citizens in Iraq and Kuwait (and to a lesser degree in some other Middle East countries). The traditional migration of Polish employees to the Muslim countries of Africa and the Middle East (more than 15,000 Poles were employed in that region in 1985), which had been substantially weakened during the second half of the 1980s, has thus ceased to play an important role in the export of Polish labour.

Between 1989 and 1990 the total foreign employment of Polish workers (registered in Poland) dropped by 28 per cent (to reach a level of 107,000). A sharp decline in the role of the CMEA member-countries (except Czechoslovakia), particularly the former GDR and the former USSR and the majority of African and Middle East countries, as countries of destination, was in part compensated for by a significant increase in migration to Germany, Greece, Austria, the United Kingdom, Denmark, the Netherlands and Norway. In 1991 and 1992, emigration of Polish workers, in particular for short-term contracts and seasonal work, began to increase due to rising demand from German employers.

THE ROLE OF TOURIST FLOWS: INVISIBLE SHORT-TERM MIGRATION

Due to the considerable disparities between Western European market economies and Eastern European centrally planned economies, in terms of the level of economic development, price levels, real incomes, quality of life, and due also to the difference in prices and availability of consumer goods in various countries of Eastern Europe, foreign travel has developed into a means for improving the standards of living of individuals residing permanently in the countries of Eastern Europe. In the 1980s, the Poles were among those who made the best use of such differentials.

Some of the travellers, mostly the so-called 'false' tourists, became engaged in a particular commercial activity, the essence of which was to sell in the West the relatively cheap goods (i.e. usually the highly subsidised, or lightly taxed, basic commodities of relatively poor quality) purchased in the East, and to bring back home the relatively sophisticated mass-produced Western goods which, if at all available, were non-subsidised and therefore relatively expensive in the East. Another group of travellers consisted of professionals, sportsmen and artists travelling on official business who were able to save a small amount of their *per diem* allowances. The last group was composed of people employed (legally or illegally, on a seasonal or long-term basis) in any of the market economies. According to the exchange rates effective at that time, the average monthly earnings in Eastern Europe in the early 1980s ranged between 20 and 30 US dollars. Even small margins from re-sale activities, *per diem* savings or foreign employment, when expressed in any western currency, therefore signified considerable amounts in a local Eastern European currency and an increase in the individuals' power of purchase. A pendulum movement between the home country and the West thus became a way of making a living for a large part of the Eastern European population, most notably in Poland. It is believed that this phenomenon has turned into growing irregular employment and, by extension, into sizeable emigration.

Whereas after 1989 differences between income and price levels in the West and in a number of Eastern European countries narrowed, differences between various Eastern European countries themselves widened. The pattern of pendular short-term migration started to spread within Eastern Europe, and part of the 'false' tourist movement switched from West to East. Poland, along with a few other countries of the region, thus became a host country for the large numbers of people coming from the neighbouring states officially as tourists, and effectively as petty traders or seasonal labour migrants.

The number of foreigners entering Poland amounted to 6.2 million in 1988 and to 8.2 million in 1989. In 1990, a record 18.6 million foreigners visited Poland. In 1991 and 1992, the number of visitors may even have exceeded the 1990 figure.

The increase in foreign tourist migration in Poland could to a significant extent be attributed to the citizens of the former GDR who, in large numbers (i.e. over 9 million people in 1990), turned into commuting shoppers in the Polish western frontier zone. These movements, which can be related to the effects of the German reunification and to the sharp deterioration of living standards in the former GDR, are of a rather conjenctural, and most likely a transitory, nature.

The increase in the number of people coming from the former USSR, Bulgaria and Romania could be attributed to quite different circumstances. These were the countries most reluctant to go ahead with economic reforms and which experienced, during the transition process towards economic liberalisation, a mix of adverse effects, such as high inflation and unemployment rates, declining real incomes and market disequilibria. The number of visitors from the former Soviet Union rose from 2.9 million in 1989 to 4.3 million in 1990. In 1991 this number went up to more than 5.8 million. As one observer aptly noted, 'the migration of former Soviet citizens to Poland is similar to the one Poles undertook during the 1970s and 1980s when they entered Germany, Sweden and Britain for black market jobs as waiters, plumbers and strawberry pickers' (Battiata, 1992). For the former Soviets who visited Poland, work, however, was not the main objective. According to reliable estimates, in the middle of 1992 only around 10,000 former Soviet citizens worked legally, and some 50,000–70,000 workers from the former USSR were in an irregular situation in Poland (Okólski, 1992). Reports from the customs authorities suggest that 80 per cent of 'tourists' from the former Soviet Union usually come for visits not exceeding three days: their sole intention is to sell the merchandise as quickly as possible (usually in flea markets), and to export the revenues (exchanged into US dollars) back home.

Between 1989 and 1990 the number of Romanians and Bulgarians increased by 650 per cent to reach 470,000 people. As a general rule, visitors from these two countries become involved in various fly-by-night commercial activities, although some take up irregular employment or become, in the case of Romanian gypsies, street beggars. For many of these visitors, Poland is viewed as a transit country allowing future migration to Germany. During the first eight months of 1992, more than 25,000 foreigners (mostly Romanians) were prevented from unauthorised crossing of the Polish-German border.

During the first two years of non-communist rule in Poland, the other activity pursued by false tourists from other Eastern European countries consisted of organised crime. The former Soviets, taking advantage of the still operational Soviet military bases, were particularly active in such activities, which consisted of selling stolen weapons, gasoline and other goods, and of smuggling radioactive substances to the West and stolen luxury cars to the former USSR.

EFFECTS OF THE NEW POLITICAL PRINCIPLES

The introduction of democratic principles after the breakup of the totalitarian and highly repressive regime resulted in three significant effects:

- less people univocally reject the social reality in which they are immersed, and by extension, less people are prone to emigration, especially to permanent settlement abroad;
- the decision to emigrate is carefully examined and becomes less hasty;
- there has been a significant inflow of people who chose to settle and to pursue a successful professional career in Poland.

One of these effects can be illustrated through the results of sociological studies and public opinion polls. A survey conducted in March and April 1992 indicated that 38 per cent of employees sampled intended to emigrate for work abroad. In 1988 the respective frequency was 63 per cent (Oschlies, 1989; Dyrdol, 1992). In 1992, 10.7 per cent of secondary school graduate students wished to emigrate permanently and 34.0 per cent for a temporary stay. In 1988, the respective proportions were of 13.5 per cent and 52.5 per cent (Górski, 1990; Dyrdol, 1992). Among the Poles who, in 1992, were interested in short-term and long-term emigration, 30 per cent preferred to migrate to Germany, 17 per cent to the USA, 14 per cent to

Canada, and 7 per cent to France. These figures clearly reflect a combination of two factors: the distance of the country of destination from the Polish state border, and the size of Polish diaspora in a given country.

In a remarkably consistent fashion, two nationally representative surveys carried out in the spring of 1991 pointed to a very low frequency (2 per cent) of those who intended to settle abroad permanently. According to the results of one of these surveys, 12 per cent of the respondents stated their interest in working in Germany for a period of a few years. In the other survey, only 4 per cent (in addition to the 2 per cent who were determined to emigrate permanently) were considering whether to leave Poland temporarily within the next three years. The former survey indicated that 85 per cent of the respondents had no intention of emigrating to Germany, while the latter revealed that 89 per cent had no plans to emigrate anywhere (Marek, 1992). These figures are in sharp contrast to the results of the 1987 national survey which disclosed that as much as 30 per cent of the population was contemplating permanent emigration (Górski, 1990).

While the above-mentioned factors did not turn Poland into a country of immigration, they undoubtedly contributed to the ending of a period characterised by the significant exodus of young Poles, and by the desperation and hopelessness induced by the communist rule (Kaminski, 1991).

Three other effects brought about by the recent political change should also be mentioned in relation to migration:

– The first effect is the possibility for dislocated families to reunite. This has put an end to a situation where family members of Polish migrants were, more often than not, treated as *sui generis* hostages.
– The second effect is the possibility for certain members of the intellectual elite and of the anti-communist political opposition to return to Poland and to take part in various sectors of public life.[2]
– The third effect is the liberalisation of international contacts and thus a much faster dissemination of new ideas generated in the most advanced societies, such as effective forms of self-organisation and local government, patterns of modern political relations, more efficient organisation of production, trade and finance, not to mention the role of fashion in mass consumption, and tolerance *vis-à-vis* ethnic, national or language diversity.

ECONOMIC ASPECTS OF RECENT MIGRATION

Among the many consequences of a primarily economic nature, the impact of recent migration on the operation and evolution of the Polish labour market seems particularly important. First of all, foreign migration was likely to contribute to the increase in territorial and occupational labour mobility. Given that the labour market had become more and more inert and inflexible during the last decade of the socialist economy, and given that it was characterized by a weak propensity of employees to change occupation or place of residence (Bednarski and Golinowska, 1991), the recent growth in mostly seasonal emigration and immigration for work has reduced one of the major obstacles to the effective functioning of the labour market. In the regions where foreign guest workers have arrived in large numbers, competition for jobs has been reported, and labour productivity has increased faster than elsewhere.[3]

The second effect is related to economic restructuring and to its most distinctive outcomes: stubborn recession and growing unemployment. Between January 1990 and September 1992, the number of unemployed rose from 55,000 to 2,457,000, while the unemployment rate rose from 0.3 per cent to 13.4 per cent. In some regions, unemployment now amounts to 30 per cent. Certain bilateral agreements on the foreign employment of Polish workers, concluded recently between Poland and a number of other countries, give preference to the unemployed, particularly those coming from the regions most severely affected by the recession. The recent increase in migration for work should therefore be viewed as a means of exporting a portion of the redundant workforce and of alleviating the social burden of unemployment. Finally, migration for work, which is predominantly directed towards the more advanced countries, is likely to upgrade the skills and work ethos of the migrants; this is even more true since international agreements for the training of young Polish workers have also been signed. It is thus believed that not only will the returning migrants work more efficiently than prior to emigrating, but they will also exert a favourable influence on other employees.

The import of foreign capital and managerial skills is another effect of the international migration of Poles. It has recently been claimed that not all segments of the Polish economy were affected by recession; on the contrary, it was argued that the private sector, especially those areas involving the participation of foreign capital, not only did not generate unemployment but actually succeeded in absorbing a considerable portion of the workforce laid off in the public sector (Lubbe, 1992).

As already mentioned, new migration trends have entirely altered the direction of 'brain drain'. The emigrants are generally less educated and possess lower skills than those who emigrated before 1990. On the contrary, immigrants seem to be more educated. This trend, added to the radically decreasing number of emigrants and the increasing number of immigrants, contributed to rendering the net balance of skills neutral, if not favourable, to the Polish economy.

The negative economic effects of foreign migration since 1989 resulted from the high outflow of western currencies (particularly US dollars) to the former USSR, a fact which can be attributed to the overvaluation of foreign currencies in that country. The export of western currency, rather than the purchase of goods and services locally, is in fact a major objective for the millions of Eastern European 'tourists' visiting Poland each year.

SOCIAL CONSEQUENCES

One of the significant effects of growing international population movements in Poland is a noticeable increase in tolerance towards foreigners with different cultural backgrounds, particularly tolerance towards neighbouring nations (especially Germany, Ukraine and Russia) and the ethnic groups established in Poland (more specifically the Belorussians, the Jews and the Germans) (Wilska-Duszynska, 1991). This trend is worthy of note when considering the national resentment and chauvinism which erupted with the collapse of communist rule in other Eastern European countries (e.g. the former GDR, the former USSR, Romania, not to mention the former Yugoslavia). The Polish public opinion's attitudes *vis-à-vis* the mass inflow of visitors from the former Soviet Union is a case in point. While, until recently, the Russians were perceived in Poland as 'outriders of the empire', they are now often seen as hard-working but poor people in need of help, and the Polish population is generally becoming sympathetic to new arrivals from the East (Battiata, 1992). In fact, this evolution of the attitude towards foreign visitors is of a more general nature and concerns all nations (Adamczuk and Walicki, 1992).[4]

On the other hand, due to the fact that visitors from certain Eastern European countries are usually poor but relatively dynamic people who strive to seize the opportunities for immediate financial reward, such visitors are generally reluctant to pay any fee or tax related to their travelling or to their commercial operations. For the same reason, many migrant workers prefer not to apply for a work permit. As a rule, the 'tourists' coming from countries like the former Soviet Union, Romania and Bulgaria avoid spending money on hotels and restaurants, and often 'camp' in city parks, railway stations and other inappropriate places. A large part of them fail to declare imported goods. In order to avoid administrative charges, most of them do not report their arrival to the local authorities.

In addition, and as already mentioned, certain visitors (predominantly from the former USSR) become involved in organised crime including thievery, smuggling, robbery and prostitution. In turn, the visitors from Romania often commit petty crimes and engage in 'professional' beggary. The demand for illegal passage from Poland to Germany is very high among alien visitors, and a network of 'guides' was recently developed with a view to facilitating border-crossings by unauthorized foreigners. The number of people prevented from entering Germany illegally or arrested in Germany after crossing the border illegally (75 per cent of whom are Romanian citizens) has increased considerably. Moreover, it is estimated that only 50 per cent of the attempted cases of illegal crossing are detected.

POLICY CONSIDERATIONS AND IMPLICATIONS

The major principles of migration policy in Poland have remained unchanged since the end of 1989, when the first non-communist government set out the highly liberal policy guidelines for the international migration of people. The right of citizens to change place of residence, to travel abroad, and, eventually, to settle in a foreign country have been recognised, while restrictions on the entry of foreign citizens have been lifted. Over time, however, the parliament and the government have increasingly focused on issues of economic and political transformation, with the result that political debates on migration problems are beginning to be less of a priority.

In fact the first draft of a blueprint for a comprehensive migration policy for the period 1991–5 was never thoroughly discussed within the government, neither was it submitted to the parliament. Consequently, no consistent migration policy has been adopted, and operation of the designated governmental organs is still affected by a lack of coordination and effectiveness. By the end of 1992, at least five governmental organs were entrusted with migration affairs in Poland. The Ministry of Foreign Affairs issues entry visas and is responsible for the consular matters of foreigners in Poland and of Poles abroad. The Ministry is also in charge of migration-related conventions, protocols and agreements. The Office of the Council of Ministers, through local administration, is entrusted with the registration of immigrants and emigrants; it also issues passports to Polish citizens living in Poland. The Ministry of Justice deals with the legal aspects of international tourism, residence, employment, crime, etc. In turn, the major areas of responsibility of the Ministry of the Interior include migration of people across state boundaries; the permanent residence and the temporary stay of foreigners; and refugee matters. Finally, the Ministry of Labour and Social Affairs is in charge of migration for work and related issues (e.g. bilateral employment agreements, work permits for alien workers, recruitment of Polish labour willing to work abroad, etc.). In addition, the Office of the President is in charge of Polish citizenship (e.g. naturalisation of non-Polish nationals). Due to lack of coordination, the competence of each institution is not clearly defined, and in many instances responsibilities overlap.

THE ISSUE OF FUTURE EMIGRATION

In general, the government does not prevent emigration of Polish citizens, and a number of efforts are made to facilitate their migration abroad. In principle, contrary to the situation prevailing before 1989, Polish citizens who settle in a foreign country retain the rights which they enjoyed while living in Poland. The government has been and continues to be engaged in a number of bilateral negotiations aimed at lifting barriers to foreign travel by Polish nationals. Between 1990 and 1992, visa-free entry was granted (on a reciprocal basis) by a large majority of Western European countries, while some other countries have softened non-visa or visa-related restrictions on Poles who wish to travel to their country. A major step forward in this process was made in March 1991 when an agreement on the readmission of people in an irregular situation was concluded with the Schengen co-signatories. At the same time, however, visa requirements have been tightened in Poland for nationals from many developing countries, and, in specific instances (in the case of visitors from Romania for example), non-visa restrictions have been imposed.

Export of redundant labour appears to be one of the most consistently pursued objectives of the current migration policy. This policy is well in line with the expectations and intentions of a large part of the Polish workforce which, following a long tradition, is fully prepared to accept seasonal or long-term employment in neighbouring Western European countries. The cooperation which began in the early 1990s between Poland and the Federal Republic of Germany offers an illustration of this point. In a series of agreements between the two countries, the following principles were agreed:

- Project-tied employment quotas for workers from Poland, particularly in the construction sector and for a maximum duration of two years, were increased to 35,170 people per year.

- A programme of on-the-job-training for young workers (18-34 years) with the appropriate educational background was introduced. The annual quota for this programme is 2,000 people, while the duration of training can vary from 12 to 18 months.
- Seasonal work is allowed for a duration of up to three months; an annual quota was established provisionally at around 50,000 people and will be subject to modifications based on the situation of the labour markets in the regions of Poland affected by high unemployment.
- Employment of commuting frontier workers (living within 50 km of the Polish-German border) was authorised without any quota but subject to an assessment of the situation in the local labour markets in Germany.
- Employment of Polish students during the summer holidays was also authorised.

Similar agreements related to on-the-job-training programmes were also concluded in 1990 with the governments of Belgium and France. In 1992, an additional agreement was signed with the French government regarding the employment of seasonal Polish workers. The agreement restricts the duration of employment to six months within each year and gives strong preference to the unemployed. It does not, however, set any annual quota. During the same year, an agreement was reached between the governments of Poland and Czechoslovakia on the reciprocal employment of citizens of the respective countries. Its clauses are very liberal and assume no quota or time limit, nor any form of discrimination against the guest workers. In addition, negotiations were initiated with the European Community and with more than ten countries with which Poland does not currently have an employment agreement (Okólski, 1992).

With regard to the ethnic minorities in Poland, it is evident that the migratory potential among this group might prove to be enormous. To date, however, the propensity to emigrate among the 200,000–400,000 members of the German ethnic population has been decreasing. This can be attributed to the fact that the basic cultural, educational and religious needs of the German community are officially recognised. A similar trend can be observed with respect to the less sizeable Belorussia and Lithuanian communities, which have not yet shown any significant propensity to emigrate. The only exception is the Ukrainen minority, which amounts to over 100,000 people who in the late 1940s, were displaced to remote areas of Poland. Due to the revival of national identity and aspirations, it can be anticipated that Ukrainens will increasingly solicit the restoration of their past property rights or, in view of favourable developments in the now independent Ukraine, will consider emigrating to that country.

Other factors which might prove important for future emigration from Poland include the reunification of families. Emigration for political reasons, on the other hand, should come to a halt.[5]

THE ISSUE OF FUTURE IMMIGRATION

Among the many obstacles to immigration to Poland, existing legislation is particularly to blame. Though legislative work has already been initiated, it is proceeding very slowly. Between 1990 and 1992, only a few international conventions were ratified, and cosmetic changes were introduced into the so-called alien law, with a view to complying with the Geneva convention and the New York protocol concerning refugees, and with a view to allowing for the deportation of unwanted foreigners.

With regard to return migration, the Polish diaspora all over the world (the so-called Polonia) currently consists of more than 10 million people. The major centres of the Polish diaspora are located in the USA, Germany and the former USSR. The government of Poland, the Episcopate of the Catholic church, and many cultural institutions, actively work to cultivate or revive the Polish national identity and culture among various groups of the Polonia and to strengthen the ties between the diaspora and the motherland. However, no particular activities, which might encourage the members of Polish minority living in diaspora to return to Poland (with the exception, perhaps, of the Polish minority in the former USSR), can be observed.

In addition, the Polish government does not actively promote the return of those nationals who emigrated during the 1980s. Due to the growing scarcity of well-paid jobs for highly qualified professionals and to the deteriorating housing market in Poland, the incentives for well-educated and well-paid emigrants to return home might be insufficient, at least for the time being. The only exception may be certain Polish groups living in the former Soviet Union. These groups did not leave Poland through emigration but through the annexation, during the second world war, of certain parts of Poland (i.e. those parts which presently constitute the territory of Lithuania, Belorussia and the Ukraine) by the former USSR. The majority of Poles in the former Soviet Union have now lost their Polish citizenship and have undergone a gradual 'russianisation'. Recently, however, local cultural initiatives have started to flourish among the Polish population with the strong support of various institutions in Poland, including the Catholic church. In many areas, ethnic, cultural and educational processes were revitalized and the national identity revived.

In certain newly sovereign states with a sizeable Polish minority, on the other hand, ethnic tensions or national conflicts started to surface, and in some cases (e.g. in Lithuania) Poles became involved in these conflicts. The possible repatriation of the Polish communities established in the former USSR is thus gradually being brought to the fore, but the cost of reintegrating such a sizeable community (between 1 and 3 million people according to estimates), has generated a great deal of controversy in Poland (Rzeczypospolita, 1991). Shortly before the recent general elections in November 1991, the organisation of this repatriation was considered by one of the parliamentary commitees and after extensive discussion, the committee agreed to draft recommendations for consideration by the government. Since then, however, there has been no further public debate on this question.

Naturalisation will be another important factor of immigration. Until recently, more people were losing than acquiring Polish citizenship every year. This trend started to change in 1990. Whereas the average annual number of people who were granted Polish citizenship between 1985 and 1989 was 172, the number rose to 478 in 1990, 908 in 1991 and was expected to reach 1,700 in 1992. This increase occurred despite the fact that the existing legislation, which assumes that Polish citizenship can be bestowed in exceptional cases only, remained unchanged.[6] Nonetheless, it appears that the various groups living outside of Poland, such as former Polish citizens (or their children) established in the pre-1939 Polish territories, or Poles who between 1945 and 1989 emigrated to the West and were deprived of their Polish citizenship, have actively become interested in obtaining Polish citizenship.

With regard to asylum seekers, the Polish government collaborates with various international agencies and neighbouring countries in the area of refugee movements (Okólski, 1992). Poland is open to refugees coming from all over the world, and offers humanitarian aid to all foreigners in need. In 1990 and 1991, camps hosting refugees were established, together with provisional facilities to accommodate up to 400,000 refugees from the former USSR.

Until September 1992, only a handful of people who had been affected by ethnic conflicts and regional wars, arrived in Poland from former Yugoslavia and the former Soviet Union. In October 1992, a larger group of some 1,000 homeless people (mostly children) arrived from Bosnia.

The favourable attitude of the Polish government notwithstanding, the present tendency for refugees to settle in Poland permanently seems to be marginal. It could therefore be inferred that Poland is not an easily accessible country for a majority of people, nor is it attractive enough for refugees from certain developing countries. The latter group largely consists of the relatively well-off who strive to settle in the West, and for whom Poland can only be a transitory place on the way to their final destination (Pawelek, 1992).[7]

CONCLUDING REMARKS

Together with the new economic and political reality, migration policy in Poland is still in the making. In the media and on the political agenda, migration by no means occupies a top position and it is hardly surprising that current migration policy is neither comprehensive nor consistent, in fact responding very poorly to the new migration phenomena.

With regard to on-going migration trends, it would be very difficult to determine the direction and magnitude of the future major flows. Although migration will be determined by the on-going transition towards an open, market-driven economy and towards the consolidation of democratic institutions and political freedom, the lack of central guidance and coordination, and the lack of coherent principles or regulations in Polish migration policy make future developments very unpredictable. However, while a further 'appeasement' of migratory movements might be expected, the number of emigrants is meanwhile likely to remain significantly higher than the number of immigrants.

Notes

1. A major breakthrough occurred in 1988, when multi-exit and long-validity passports were introduced by the last communist government, which also abolished exit visas for Polish citizens.
2. In fact between 1990 and 1992 many prominent posts in the government, parliament, diplomacy, mass media and cultural institutions were filled by recently returned emigrants.
3. What characterised the socialist economy was competition for workers among the employers, rather than competition for jobs among the labour force (Kondratowicz and Okolski, 1991).
4. On the other hand, various public opinion polls indicate that the frequency of xenophobic attitudes in Poland is still significant, e.g. many respondents are generally unfavourable to the presence of national or ethnic minorities (Kuczynski, 1991; Glob 24, 1991; Wilska-Duszynska, 1991). In a poll carried out in 1991, 39 per cent of Poles were against receiving any group of refugees from the former USSR in the event of a catastrophe in that country.
5. It is worth mentioning, however, that even after 1989, Polish citizens were seeking political asylum in the West. In Germany, for instance, 9,155 Polish citizens applied for political asylum in 1990, 3,448 in 1991, and 3,447 between 1 January and 31 October 1992.

66   Poland

6.   This refers to the case of applicants who have not resided in Poland for at least five years immediately prior to submitting their application.
7.   It is estimated that among the approximately 2,000 refugees who were registered in Poland in 1990 and 1991, no more than 100 attempted to settle permanently in that country.

References

Adamczuk, L. and R. Walicki (1992). 'Cudzoziemcy: niektorzy z nich beda naszymi sasiadami', *Zycie Warszawy*, 1–2 August 1992.
Battiata, M. (1992). 'Ex-Soviet workers move down the block', *The Washington Post*, 26 January 1992.
Bednarski, M. and S. Golinowska (1991). 'Uwarunkowania polityczno-instytucjonalne podzialu', in Z. Morecka (ed.), *Podzial w latach 80-tych: kontunuacja czy zmiana?*, Warsaw: Warsaw University Publications.
Dyrdol, A. (1992). *Spoleczno-ekonomiczne uwarunkowania emigracji kadr kwalifikowanych w okresie transformacji gospodarczej*, Warsaw: Warsaw University, Department of Economics.
Glob 24 (1991). 'Strach, ciekawosc, respekt: Polacy o Niemcach – Niemcy o Polakach', *Glob 24*, 5 September 1991.
Górski, J. (1991). 'Motywy oraz niektore spoleczne skutki emigracji. Raport przedstawiony Ministrowi Spraw Zagranicznych', Warsaw (unpublished manuscript).
Kamiński, B. (1991). *The Collapse of State Socialism. The Case of Poland*, Princeton, N.J.: Princeton University Press.
Kondratowicz, A. and M. Okólski. 'The Polish economy on the eve of the Solidarity take-over' (Warsaw University) *PPRG Discussion Papers*, No. 4.
Korcelli, P. (1992). 'European Migration – the Polish Example', International Conference on Mass Migration in Europe, Vienna, 5–7 March 1992.
Kuczyński, P. (1991). 'Postawy wobec mniejszosci etnicznych', *Rzeczpospolita*, 18 July 1991.
Lubbe, A. (1992). 'Nie ma wizji przyszlosci (rozmowa z profesorem andrzejem Lubbe, wiceministrem CUP w latach 1990-92)', *Zycie Warszawy*, 13 October 1992.
Lyś, G. (1992). 'Chmury nad budowami', *Zycie Warszawy*, 12–13 September 1992.
Marek, E. (1992). *Emigracja z Polski z uwzglednieniem zatrudnienia pracownikow polskich za granica*, Warsaw: IPiSS and Friedrich Ebert Stiftung.
Okólski, M. (1991a). 'Migratory movements from countries of central and Eastern Europe'. Conference of Ministers, Vienna, 24–25 January 1991 (also in *People on the Move. New Migration Flows in Europe, Strasbourg 1992: Council of Europe Press*).
Okólski, M. (1991b). *Poland: the 1991 SOPEMI Country Report*, Paris: OECD.
Okólski, M. (1991c). 'Poland across the Rio Grande', *The European Journal of International Affairs*, No. 2.
Okólski, M. (1991d). 'Demographic situation, population movements and ethnic minorities in the East European countries. meeting of universities from East and West Europe', 'The Great Europe of Cultures', Rome, 19–22 April 1991.
Okólski, M. (1992). *Poland: the 1992 SOPEMI Country Report*, Paris: OECD.

Oschlies, W. (1989). 'Polnischer "Drang nach Westen": Dynamik und Motive der Juengsten Emigrationswelle aus Polen', *Berichte des Bundesinstituts fuer ostwissenschaftliche und internationale Studien*, No. 30.

Pawelek, E. Uchodzcy. *Zycie Warszawy*, 19–20 September 1992.

Rzeczpospolita (1991). 'W sejmie o reptriacji', *Rzeczpospolita*, 26 July 1991.

Szponar, H. (1992). *Proba rozpoznania zjawiska zatrudniania obcokrajowcow w makroregionie stolecznym oraz wyjazdow do pracy za granica w I polroczu 1992*, Warsaw: Central Planning Board.

Wilska-Duszyńska, B. (1991). 'Od Litwinow do Cyganow: studenci o mniejszosciach narodowych', *Rzeczpospolita*, 27 August 1991.

Van Zon, H. (1991). 'Alternative Scenarios for Central Europe (Poland, Czechoslovakia, Hungary)', *CEC Monitor/FAST Programme, Prospective Dossier*, No. 3.

3 The Baltic States[1]

Luule Sakkeus

Since their incorporation into the Soviet Union, the Baltic States have attracted high levels of immigration from other Soviet republics. Due to their well-developed infrastructure, after World War II the Baltic States hosted, in particular, the development of a number of all-union industries, a process which led to substantial levels of labour migration from other republics. Especially in Estonia and Latvia, immigration primarily consisted of poorly qualified workers recruited by factories in heavy industry and the construction sector. This process naturally determined the considerable increase in the share of foreign-born population in the Baltic States, a population consisting of ethnic groups with few social, historical, cultural or demographic patterns in common with the Baltic States. Since the economic restructuring in the newly independent Baltic States has primarily affected the all-union industries (which had never been integrated into the local economies and which were highly dependent upon the continuous inflow of workers from other republics), a significant proportion of the workers who have been laid-off consists of 'rootless' immigrants who would be prepared to re-migrate to other regions of employment.

The following chapter reviews the main trends in Baltic migration towards the former Soviet Union and Western countries, assessing both the post-war migration dynamics and the new policy determinants after 1989.

IMPACT OF POST-WAR DEVELOPMENTS ON THE CURRENT MIGRATION PATTERNS OF THE BALTIC STATES

The levels of post-war immigration into Estonia and Latvia, and the way such immigration has influenced the formation of the current population of the two states, have often been underestimated, even by the local authorities. This can be explained, to a large extent, by the lack or inaccessibility of appropriate data.

Starting with the forced deportation of native populations, some estimates indicate that in Lithuania, about 10–12 per cent of the total population (230,000–270,000 people) has been deported, while repatriation and emigration involved about 250,000 to 320,000 people (Damushis, 1988; Truska, 1988). In Latvia, deportation during the first years of the Soviet regime involved about 205,000 people, or 10–11 per cent of the total population, while repatriation and forced emigration to Germany involved approximately 100,000 people, in addition to another 100,000 who emigrated to Western countries (*Latvia Today*, 1991: 6).

In Estonia, the population loss between 1940 and 1941 amounted to 104,000 people, and was brought about by factors including: (i) the repatriation of Germans (13,339 people; Raid, 1978), (ii) the deportations of 1941, and (iii) the displacement of some of the population to other regions of the Soviet Union at the beginning of the war. Emigration to the West reached its peak in 1944 with approximately 70,000 people. By 1945, the population of Estonia had been reduced by about 18.5 per cent. According to some estimates (Katus, 1989), about 32,000 of Estonians might have returned since then (eg. Table 3.1).

The second wave of deportations in 1949 involved approximately 53,000–57,000 people (Niinemets, 1989) which, without taking account of those who disappeared during the war, amounts to 12–17 per cent of the total population (Parming, 1972).

Table 3.1   Population of Lithuanians, Latvians and Estonians in the native country and the Soviet Union (in thousands)

	Lithuanians		Latvians		Estonians	
Year	1926	1989	1926	1989	1926	1989
Total number	2230*	3067	1868*	1459	1117*	1113
No. in native-land	(1873)	2924	(1480)	1388	970**	963
Number in USSR	51.1	143	141.4	71	154.6	64
%	2.6	4.7	8.7	4.9	13.5	6.2
Number in rest of world	—	355	—	100	—	86

* By 1.01.1926 = total population.
** By 1922 census.
( ) = Estimate.

Source: Narodnost ..., 1928, s. 24–5; Bromlei, 1988; Nacionalnyi ..., 1991; Tooms, 1927; Kulu, 1992.

MIGRATION WITHIN THE FORMER SOVIET UNION

The Baltic States received large numbers of immigrants from other republics during the first two years after the end of World War II, and in the early 1950s, after the second wave of deportations to Siberia. Towards the end of the 1950s, the importance of forced migration started to decline while those who had survived deportation started to return.

The foreign-born population of Estonia amounts to 411,000 people, or 26.3 per cent of the total population. 42,600 (4.4 per cent of the Estonian population) are foreign-born Estonians. On the contrary, the share of foreign-born people among the non-Estonians is as high as 61.3 per cent. Clearly, this indicator should be kept in mind when assessing the social problems associated with immigrants in the Baltic States (eg. Table 3.2).

The foreign-born population is also characterised by its uneven regional distribution. Most of the immigrants have settled in the cities (over 90 per cent are concentrated in urban areas). As a result, some cities (particularly those which served as Soviet military bases, i.e. Paldiski and Sillamae in Estonia; Daugavpils in Latvia; Snechkus in Lithuania) have become entirely immigrant-dominated, with the native population counting for less than 10 per cent of the overall population.

Attention should also be drawn to the marked differences in the share of foreign-born population according to ethnic group. Common to the three Baltic States is the highest share of foreign-born people among Belorussians and Ukrainens, and the lower share among Russians (the latter is explained by the fact that Russians were among the first to migrate to the Baltic States, and second generation Russians now form part of the native-born population).

Among the 120 ethnic groups composing Estonia's foreign-born population, 10 groups account for 98 per cent of the total foreign-born population (with Russians alone accounting for 65 per cent, and the Slavic groups for more than 80 per cent). It must also be underlined that, in the case of Estonia, the non-Estonian population in most of the 120 ethnic groups residing in Estonia is overwhelmingly foreign-born. The share of the foreign-born population in the total Estonian population is higher in the age group 50–59, and gradually decreases within younger groups. This is due to the fact that Estonia was ethnically homogeneous after the war and the number of native-born non-Estonians was respectively very low.

When analysing differences between the native and foreign-born population of Estonia, comparison of education levels turn up some interesting results (Katus and Sakkeus, 1992). Existing figures show that non-Estonians tend to show higher educational attainments than Estonians.

Table 3.2   Share of foreign-born population in the Baltic States, 1989

(a)   Estonia

	Total	Foreign-born	%
Titular nation	963,281	42,561	4.42
Russians	474,834	271,020	57.08
Ukranians	482,714	380,920	78.91
Belorussians	27,711	21,840	78.81
Jews	4,631	3,062	66.12
Poles	3,008	2,193	72.91
Non-titular	602,381	368,516	61.18
Totals	1,565,662	411,077	26.26

(b)   Latvia

	Total	Foreign-born	%
Titular nation	1,387,757	41,035	2.96
Russians	905,515	409,068	45.18
Ukranians	92,101	74,265	80.63
Belorussians	119,702	82,185	68.66
Jews	22,897	10,755	46.97
Poles	60,416	20,662	34.20
Non-titular	1,278,810	648,279	50.69
Totals	2,666,567	689,314	25.8

(c)   Lithuania

	Total	Foreign-born	%
Titular nation	2,924,231	64,430	2.20
Russians	344,455	172,430	50.06
Ukranians	44,789	35,325	78.87
Belorussians	63,169	46,186	73.11
Jews	12,392	5,415	43.70
Poles	257,994	32,964	12.78
Non-titular	750,571	311,333	41.48
Totals	3,674,802	375,763	10.23

However, this should be related to differences in the definition of educational levels in the former Soviet Union and in Estonia. Whereas in the former Soviet Union, secondary education was completed at the age of 16, in Estonia 16 was usually the age for entry into secondary education. Another indicator relates to the knowledge of the territorial language. In Estonia, the knowledge of the Estonian language is clearly higher among the native-born population, although knowledge declines in younger age groups, a rather surprising trend given that children are better able to assimilate the commonly spoken language. Among non-Estonians, knowledge of Estonian does not vary according to age group: it remains low within all age groups, at around 20 per cent. This evidence thus suggests that second generation immigrants follow behavioural patterns pertaining to their parental home regions, rather than to their regions of residence.

MIGRATORY RELATIONS WITH THE WEST

During the Soviet era, migration to the West remained at very low level due to numerous types of restriction. International migration has had a very low share in overall emigration from the Baltic States, which emigration was mainly directed towards the East. Between 1960 and 1989, the yearly number of people migrating to the West ranged between 500 and 1,500.

Similarly, Western immigration to the Baltic States has been consistently low, the exception being the increase which started to occur during the second half of the 1980s after the initial political changes in the former USSR. At this time, expatriates started to return to their countries of origin, with a view, at least for some, to creating new businesses.

To a great extent, emigration from the Baltic States can be attributed to the significant proportion of people who immigrated to the Baltic States from other Eastern (or former Soviet) regions, and who intended to emigrate subsequently to the West. The analysis of major ethnic groups in Estonia helps to support this argument. Thus in the 1959 census, only 670 Germans were resident in Estonia, while their number had increased tenfold by the 1970 census. Their distribution according to the first language spoken is also revealing: 36 per cent of all Germans speak their own language, while 56.5 per cent are Russian-speakers. Approximately the same holds true for the Polish immigrants, 20 per cent of whom speak Polish and 63.4 per cent Russian (1989 census data) (Katus, 1991).

Gross emigration rates in Estonia, by ethnic group, also confirm the status of the Baltic States as transit countries. In 1989, emigration rates were highest among Poles (17 per cent), Germans (9.06 per cent) and Jews (6.39 per cent), while Finns and Estonians had the lowest propensity to emigrate.

Data for Lithuania reveal the same trends: ethnic migration dominates emigration to the West. The ethnic groups of Slavic origin (particularly Ukrainens), the greatest proportion of whom are foreign-born, show a greater propensity to emigrate than the native-born population.

Table 3.3 (a)   Emigration from Estonia by country of destination, 1984–1991

	1984	1985	1986	1987	1988	1989	1990	1991
Bulgaria	2	4	3	4	0	5	2	3
Afghanistan	4	4	2	4	1	0	0	0
Israel	1	4	0	100	878	782	522	369
USA	3	5	4	7	42	77	27	272
Canada	4	3	7	7	43	22	14	16
Sweden	2	5	5	44	44	42	27	46
Finland	29	386	535	434	173	69	140	289
Hungary	46	36	22	17	22	4	5	5
Czechoslovakia	73	16	30	21	30	13	4	1
Poland	76	60	51	70	399	553	313	148
Mongolia	89	100	44	39	37	3	1	0
Germany	314	279	227	472	497	694	544	499
Other	47	35	67	467	283	101	68	50
Totals	690	938	997	1,368	2,449	2,365	1,667	1,698

Table 3.3(b)   Immigration to Estonia by country of departure, 1984–1991

	1984	1985	1986	1987	1988	1989	1990	1991
Bulgaria	2	5	0	1	2	3	5	3
Afghanistan	4	20	12	25	44	27	9	3
Israel	0	0	0	0	0	4	13	10
USA	1	0	2	1	2	1	4	5
Canada	3	2	0	0	1	1	1	3
Sweden	0	0	1	2	3	0	2	3
Finland	1	1,185	333	85	6	11	11	6
Hungary	36	63	61	68	29	38	22	10
Czechoslovakia	45	67	47	54	41	41	46	23
Poland	69	85	67	145	888	681	342	32
Mongolia	103	146	86	92	72	90	71	22
Germany	365	398	319	304	288	436	217	103
Other	59	60	184	52	232	47	84	14
Totals	688	2,031	1,112	829	1,608	1,380	827	237

Another specificity of the Baltic States is their intermediary role between Eastern European countries and the former Soviet Union. Thus a number of army officers and soldiers who had served in the allied Eastern European countries chose to resettle in the Baltic States, where standards of living are comparable with other Eastern European countries.

Table 3.3 gives an overview of the main countries of destination and departure for Estonian migration. It shows the decreasing importance of Israel and Poland as countries of immigration after 1989, and the consistent role of Germany as the main receiving country. It also shows the emergence of new regions of immigration, such as Sweden, the United States and Canada.

Table 3.4(a)   Distribution of immigration to Baltic States by region of departure in 1990 (%)

	Estonia	*Latvia*	*Lithuania*
Russia	63.4292	71.7855	53.8364
Ukraine	11.1085	9.3023	12.6398
Belorussia	3.2812	2.7869	7.2700
Central Asia	3.5557	3.5364	4.7204
Caucasus	2.6846	2.1910	2.4714
Baltic States and Moldova	6.0733	5.8428	8.5448
Other	9.8676	4.5551	10.5171
Totals	100	100	100

Table 3.4(b)   Distribution of emigration from Baltic States by region of destination in 1990 (%)

	Estonia	*Latvia*	*Lithuania*
Russia	59.2969	45.6981	42.6488
Ukraine	14.5541	13.6518	15.9049
Belorussia	4.8541	15.7201	10.4205
Central Asia	2.3222	2.8482	5.2895
Caucasus	1.8384	0.8731	5.2895
Baltic States and Moldova	3.6930	5.2513	1.8932
Other	13.4414	15.9575	17.3187
Totals	100	100	100

It should not be overlooked, however, that Western countries taken together only represent the third most important destination of Baltic migration (Table 3.4). The levels of migration reviewed in the above sections give account of registered movements only, and do not include all forms of migration. Soviet statistics, in effect, do not register temporary changes of residence, tourist migration, cross-border movements, etc. The statistical system is thus unable to perceive the considerable increase in the illegal population. According to a prognosis made by the Estonian Interuniversity Population Research Centre, based on the births of non-resident parents and deaths of people not registered as resident of Estonia in 1991, the illegal population might amount to a total of 45,000–50,000. The same trend can also be observed in Latvia and Lithuania.

MIGRATION POLICY

So far, no systemised migration policy concepts have been developed in the Baltic States. The initial reaction of policy-makers after the 1989 revolutions mainly consisted of restricting immigration from the East. Estonia was the first to implement such restrictions through the adoption in 1990 of its new Immigration Law. However, the new law failed to determine the criteria and definitions of the populations concerned by the new restrictions, and the new policy has not yet been made operational. Latvia and Lithuania have also adopted restrictions on immigration, but these have mainly consisted of imposing high fees for entry into the national territories (Stankuniene and Sipaviciene, 1989).

Although Estonia was the first to implement restrictions on immigration, Lithuania was actually the first to draft a more comprehensive migration policy. Thus by the end of 1992, Lithuania had already formulated legislation on citizenship, immigration and emigration, and the alien's status. In Estonia, the growing need for an overall emigration policy has not yet been recognised, and in fact it was only at the end of 1992, in reaction to the coming into effect of Russia's free emigration policy, that Estonian policy-makers started to reflect upon the definition of the alien's status in Estonia.

On the other hand, Russia itself is lagging behind in the formulation of an appropriate policy towards those 18 per cent of Russians residing in the newly independent states of the dissolved Soviet Union. The recent Conference on the New Russians Abroad: Problems and Perspectives (Maslov and Osinski, 1992) has called on the Russian government to recognise its citizens in the different regions where there are no grounds for applying for refugee status. Representatives from the Russian communities in the Baltic States and the Ukraine also called for recognition by the Russian authorities of the need to develop education in Russian in the Baltic States and the Ukraine. Only recently have official discussions started with a view to defining the conditions of remigration to Russia, while non-governmental organisations have sprung up in many states to help solve the remigration problem.

The Baltic States have not yet adopted a position on refugees and asylum seekers, even though their Eastern borders are increasingly violated by illegal migrants. Lithuania is faced with growing illegal migration from Pakistan and Turkey, while Estonia is confronted with the problem of Romanians trying to apply for refugee-based entry visas for Finland and with Somalians entering Finland through Estonia. During the second half of 1992, Estonia was also faced with the immigration of Iraqui Kurds and Lebanese. It can be anticipated that these trends will continue to increase until Estonia is able to define its criteria with regard to refugees and to ratify the related UN Conventions.

Due to the lack of an official emigration policy and efficient statistical system, the Baltic States are also unable to register temporary changes in residence of nationals emigrating to the West through the granting of visas or fictious traineeships. Some of the temporary emigrants extend their stay in the West after having found a job or other means of subsistence, and registers in the countries of origin fail to record such emigration (see also Boubnova, 1992).

The trend consisting of applying for work permits and fellowships in Western countries has thus gained momentum over the last few years. In Estonia, the highest proportion of these movements are directed towards Finland. Although information is scattered due to the lack of a centralised system for gathering data, applicants for work permits or scholarships had to apply, until 1991, either to the Ministry of Labour (for work permits) or to the Ministry of Education (for training and further education). It is believed that these two entities have processed approximately half of all applications for either work or training abroad. According to data received from the Ministry of Labour, 2,751 work permits were issued in 1991, of which 2,546 were applications to work in Finland. According to the Ministry of Education in Finland, 500 students were in Finland for the 1991–2 academic year, while the Estonian Ministry of Education has registered another 224 students in other Western countries (excluding those who applied directly to the training institutions abroad). In addition to Finland, major countries of destination include Sweden, Germany and the United States.

FUTURE TRENDS IN BALTIC MIGRATION

To conclude the overview of Baltic migration since 1945, it should again be emphasised that migration in this region has been the main cause of the formation in the Baltic States of a large foreign-born population. While migration to the West remained insignificant until the 1989 revolutions, the foreign-born population has been fed exclusively through migration streams within the regions of the former Soviet Union. These migratory processes constitute a phenomenon which has been exceptional within the territories of the ex-USSR: it can be explained by the difference in the stages of demographic development between the Baltic States (at least Estonia and Latvia) and the rest of the Soviet Union. Estonia and Latvia, which, in their demographic development patterns belonged to Western Europe, have also acted as Western countries in their mobility and migratory behaviour. On the other hand, the Soviet expansive economic policy, supported by its administrative regulations, transformed the Baltic States into enormous labour-consuming regions; during the fifty years of Soviet rule, due to the differences in demographic development, Estonia and Latvia thus acquired the highest share of foreign-born population in Europe, as well as the resulting ethnic and social problems which this situation generated.

Foreign-born populations, whether or not they are citizens of their countries of residence, are receiving increased attention from most European countries. The social and cultural needs of foreigners by birth usually differ from those of the native populations, and social structures are used to meeting the needs of all segments of the populations. The various projects carried out under the auspices of the Council of Europe, the EC (e.g. the COST project), the UN (e.g. the ECE International Migration Project) and different national authorities, demonstrate the need to investigate the new problems arising from intensive migration of people. In the case of the Baltic States, many immigrants entered these states for a short-term period rather than for permanent residence. This is particularly true in the case of families of army officers, or in the case of young people who came to fill the manpower shortages for industrial development projects directly supervised from Moscow. What was previously the common behaviour of many immigrants, i.e. to leave the country after a given period of time, started to change with the new economic and social environment in the neighbouring countries.

In the case of Estonia (and, to a lesser extent, the other two Baltic States), the following two arguments help clarify the singularity of the migratory situation in this region: (i) the foreign-born population and its second generation constitutes a very large proportion of the current population of Estonia, almost the largest in Europe. In some cities, the foreign-born population forms the majority; (ii) in general, the specific needs of the foreign-born population have been ignored by the Soviet ideology preaching the unified characteristics of 'the new people of the communist era'. As a result, the social situation and needs of immigrants are, more often than not, unknown to the national authorities. What is more, due to the unified social organisation practiced in the Soviet Union for decades, institutional changes and new legislation brought about by the independence of the former Soviet republics are increasingly felt by the foreign-born population as a threat to their rights in Estonia or in the other Baltic States.

Another important effect of substantial immigration to the Baltic States, which applies more dramatically to Estonia, is the changing ethnic and linguistic environment of the country. Bearing in mind the loss of its historic ethnic minorities (i.e. Germans left in 1939–40 and Swedes in 1944, while the territories of mixed Estonian-Russian population united with the Russian SFSR in 1945), Estonia was an ethnically homogeneous country after World War II: 97.3 per cent of the total population was composed of Estonians and members of other ethnic groups naturally spoke Estonian (the situation was somewhat different in Latvia and Lithuania, where the titular nationalities formed approximately 80 per cent of the total population).

The future development of the Estonian, and to some extent Latvian, population will thus be continuously determined by the coexistence of the two population groups. The heterogeneity of these communities must be clearly taken into account when assessing the possible migration behaviour of the Baltic States in the near future. It is reasonable to anticipate that migration processes will become the most important factor influencing the formation of the Baltic populations during the twenty-first century.

In this respect, the first issue concerns post-war immigrants, particularly the foreign-born population, but also the non-native population in a wider sense. A number of immigrants will undoubtedly decide to remain in their current country of residence. This group might be composed of the historical Russian minority and other people who have resided in Estonia for decades. It does not, however, exceed 15–20 per cent of the current non-Estonian population. Another group of immigrants, composed in particular of Soviet army officers and their families and Communist Party administrators, might be inclined to leave the Baltic States. This group, however, is even less numerous than the previous one.

Approximately three quarters of the non-native population seem to be faced with different alternatives. The Baltic States are definitely not the ideal homeland for the typical immigrant. Immigrants live primarily in the cities, their knowledge of the local culture and language is poor, and most of their relatives live outside the state. In short, their homeland is somewhere in the former Soviet Union, not in the country of residence. However, once they arrive in the 'Soviet West' (as the Baltic States have been referred to in some circles), immigrants have little motivation to return to their countries of origin. Since the 1989 revolutions, the economic difficulties in the former Soviet Union have reduced the possibility of remigration even further. At the same time, a number of these immigrants would gladly consider the possibility of migrating further West, to the 'real West'. Many of them would prefer the United States, Germany or Finland, but would also consider other destinations such as Argentina. Given this perspective, the migration policy of the developed countries will naturally determine the scale of future out-migration from the Baltic States.

The dynamics of the migratory processes thus suggest that the potential for emigration is quite different between native and immigrant populations. The Parent–Youth Socialisation Survey conducted in 1991 by the Institute of Philosophy, Law and Sociology of Estonia sheds some light on the respective intentions of the two groups (Anderson, Silver, Titma, 1991). Among both groups, only 10 per cent of the respondents stated their intention to migrate. Among natives, 90 per cent intended to move somewhere in Estonia, whereas about 60 per cent of immigrants intended to migrate to the former Soviet Union. With regard to emigration to the West, 3 per cent of the natives were contemplating such a prospect, compared to 28 per cent of non-natives.

Even if to a lesser extent than immigrants, native populations would thus consider migrating in the near future. Indeed, the present disparities in the standards of living in the Baltic States and Western Europe support the likelihood of the above prospect. Nevertheless, it can reasonably be anticipated that native populations contemplating emigration would be more inclined to seek temporary employment in the West, rather than change their residence permanently. This might be in sharp contrast to the migration behaviour of non-native groups, such as the Russians, Ukrainens and Belorussians, who are more inclined to consider long-term emigration to the West. The migration potential among this group would thus replace the substantial, but gradually declining, emigration waves of Germans, Jews, Poles and Finns.

To summarise the above speculations, it can be anticipated that Estonia will probably lose 20–30 per cent of its present population through out-migration. This scenario, however, can only materialise in the event of

Western countries adopting a flexible immigration policy (Soderling, 1991; Iloniemi, 1992). The anticipated outflow could also, in part, be directed towards Eastern European destinations if housing infrastructures were to be properly developed. Under the current economic circumstances, this alternative, too, is to a great extent dependent upon Western policies.

Without contradicting the above speculations, it can also be anticipated that immigration to the Baltic States (particularly Estonia) from the former Soviet Union will gain momentum. The potential levels of such immigration will be conditional upon the number of relatives of current immigrants in the Baltic States. According to a very rough estimate (Katus and Sakkeus, 1992), the number of these future immigrants could amount to 1–1.5 million people in the case of Estonia. This number is nearly equivalent to the current size of the total Estonian population.

The intention of the relatives of the current immigrants to migrate would depend, to a large extent, upon the relative economic development of the Baltic States and Russia (and/or other countries formed on the territory of the former USSR). The possibility of using the Baltic States as a springboard for subsequent out-migration to the West must also be taken into account.

It should also be noticed that the two scenarios for future migration outlined in this section exclude each other to some extent. If large-scale out-migration is to take place from the Baltic States, not many relatives will need to move to the Baltic States. And, conversely, the lower the out-migration during the recent period, the higher the probability of continuous in-migration to the Baltic States in the near future.

With regard to the migratory relations between the Baltic States themselves, it appears that these were insignificant throughout the post-war period. Estonia's migration relations with Latvia are not intensive because both countries are at a comparable stage of mobility transition with no great migration potential. In the case of Lithuania, the situation is quite the opposite. Lithuania's stage of mobility transition should be compared with that of Belorussia, but Lithuania's migration potential has had to compete, on the external labour markets, with migration from bigger countries like Russia and the Ukraine. As a consequence, the potential for migration in Lithuania was contained internally, although it also extended, to some degree, to neighbouring Latvia.

Although net migration rates (as measured by official statistics) in all Baltic States were negative in 1991 and 1992, the number of illegal immigrants, as reflected by calculations using Estonian data, has increased constantly over the recent period. Taking these facts into account, it may well turn out that the Baltic countries are actually gaining in population through migration processes.

CONCLUSIONS

The levels of foreign population in the Baltic States must always be kept in mind when assessing the labour force participation in different economic branches, living conditions, or the future migratory behaviour of the populations in this region. It is also important to underline that the differentiation of the population of these countries did not result from ethnic but from historically different demographic development in the Baltic States and in other former Soviet republics.

The main concern in relation to future migratory movements in the Baltic States should be the behaviour of the foreign-born population, the greatest proportion of which is of Slavic origin. It has frequently been stated by various researchers (Van de Kaa, 1991; Vishnevski and Zayonchkovskaya, 1992) that ethnic migration has its limitations. Taking into account the reduced migration potential attributable to demographic causes, the potential for migration of titular nationalities, especially in Estonia and Latvia, is likely to result in mainly temporary moves aimed at obtaining special education or at gaining temporary benefits from differences in the standards of living. As these differences are declining, migration could gradually be stabilised at levels prevailing between Western European countries themselves.

The potential for future Slavic ethnic migration will largely depend upon bilateral or multilateral agreements between the states involved. Economically, much could be accomplished through joint ventures with the regions most interested in repatriating their expatriate communities. For the Baltic States, these regions could consist of the Pihkva (Pskoff) and Novgorod regions in Russia, and Vitebsk in Belorussia.

The main concern of the Baltic States at the present time is also to build up a proper data-recording system, as the current system does not cover all types of movement in the region and thus 'produces' a high number of 'illegal' residents. In order to take stock of movements which are currently not registered, the Baltic States would certainly gain by joining existing all-European projects carried out in this field (e.g. the International Migration Project carried out under the auspices of the UN Economic Commission for Europe). The reorganisation of the existing system would allow for further investigation into the categories involved and the main regions of destination, and could assist in the formulation of an appropriate migration policy for the Baltic States.

Note

1. The author gratefully acknowledges the kind cooperation of Ms Marta Vavere and Mr Uldis Ushatskis from Statistics Latvia and Ms Marite Karoliene and Ms Irena Mazuriene from Statistics Lithuania in preparing material for this chapter.

References

Anderson, Barbara, Brian Silver and Mikk Titma (1991). 'Motivations for Migration Among Long-term Residents of Estonia: An Exploratory Analysis of Survey Data', Paper presented at the Conference on Prospective Migration from the USSR, November 17–19, Santa Monica, California.

Bengtsson, Tommy and Mats Johansson (1992). 'The Slow-down of Internal Migration in Post-industrial Sweden', Paper presented at the conference 'Mass Migration in Europe: Implications from East and West', Vienna, March 5–7, Vienna.

Boubnova, Helena (1992). 'East–West Commuting', Paper presented at the conference 'Mass Migration in Europe: Implications from East and West', Vienna, March 5–7, Vienna.

Bromlei, J.V. (ed.) (1988) 'Narody mira. Istoriko-etnograficheskii spravochnik', *Sovetskaja Enciklopedija*, Moskva.

Chesnais, J.-C. (1991). 'Migration from Eastern to Western Europe, Past (1946–1989) and Future (1990–2000)', Paper presented at the Conference of Ministers on the movement of persons coming from Central and Eastern European Countries, January 24–25, Vienna.

Coquin, Francois-Xavier (1969). 'La Sibérie. Peuplement et immigration paysanne au XIX siècle. *Collection historique de l'Institut d'Etudes Slaves.* – XX, Paris.

Damushis, A. (1988). *Lietuvos gyventoju aukos ir nuostoliai antrojo pasaulinto karo ir pokario 1940–1959 metais*, Chicago.

Iloniemi, Jaakko (1992). 'Change in Economic Life', in *Proceedings of the International Population Conference 'Revival of Ageing Societies'*, Espoo, Finland, September 2–4, pp. 89–101, Helsinki.

Kaa van de Dirk, J. (1991). 'The Future of International Migration in Europe', Paper presented at the European Population Conference, October 21–25, Paris.

Katus, Kalev (1982). 'Dolgosrotchnye tendencii razvitija i upravlenija demografitcheskoi sistemoi', PhD thesis, Moscow.

Katus, Kalev (1989). 'Demographic Development in Estonia through the Centuries', *Working Papers of Estonian Interuniversity Population Research Centre/EKDK*, Series B, EKDK, RU No. 9, 43pp, Tallinn.

Katus, Kalev (1991a). 'Estonian Fertility in the European Context', Paper presented to Estonian – Swedish Demographic Seminar, Viljandi, September 13–15. RU No. 12, Series B, EKDK, Tallinn.

Katus, Kalev (1991b). 'Mitmerahvuseline Eesti', EIPRC Working Paper, Series B, RU No. 16, Tallinn.

Katus, Kalev and Toomas Kümmel (1989). 'Demograficheskoje razvitite stolic stran Baltiiskogo basseina', in *Demografi tcheskoje razvitie Litvy*, pp. 60–83, Vilnius.

Katus, Kalev and Allan Puur (1990). 'General Mortality Trend: the Case of Estonia 1897–1989', Paper presented to the Conference 'Health, Morbidity and Mortality in Europe', Vilnius.

Katus, Kalev and Luule Sakkeus (1984). 'Demographic Factors in Transition towards the Stabilization of Urbanization', Paper presented at the meeting of the working committee RC No. 21 of the International Sociological Association, Bratsk-Irkutsk.

Katus, Kalev and Luule Sakkeus (1992). 'Foreign-Born Population of Estonia', Paper presented at the Academy Colloquim 'Population of the Former USSR in the 21st century'. September 29–October 2, Amsterdam.

Kaufmann, V. (1967). 'Rahvastiku dünaamika ja seda mõjutanud seaduspärasused Eestis XX sajandi esimesel poolel (1897–1959)', PhD thesis, Tallinn.

Kulu, Hill (1992). *Eestlased maailmas: demograafiline ülevaade. Diplomitöö*, Tartu, TÜ.

Kümmel, Toomas (1986). 'Proportsioonid Eesti linnade arengus', *Geograafia rakendusprobleeme Eestis*, Tallinn.

Latvia Today (1991). 'Brief socio-economic overview', State Committee for Statistics of Latvia. – Riga.

Maiste, Margus (1988). 'Rahvaarv ja tema dünaamika aastail 1881–1934/Number of Population and its Dynamics in 1881–1934', EIPRC Working Paper, Series B, RU No. 6, Tallinn.

Maslov, V.A and Osinski, V.G. (ed.) (1992). 'Novoje possiiskoje zarubezhe: problemy i perspektivy', *Proceedings of the Conference in St Petersburg*, November 27–29, St Petersburg.

Mihhailov, Dmitri (1990). Mitteeestlastest, ennekõike venelastest, Eestis', *Aja Kiri*, No. 58, 1990, Stockholm.

Nacionalnyi sostav naselenija SSSR (1991). '*Po dannym vsesojuznoi perepisi 1989 g. Goskomstat SSSR. Finansy i statistika*, Moskva.

Narodnost i rodnoi jazôk naselenija SSSR (1928). *Vsesojuznaja perepis naselenija 17 dekabrija 1926, kratkie svodki, vôp. IV*, Moskva.

Nigol, Andres (1918). *Eesti asundused ja asupaigad Wenemaal*, Tartu.

Niinemets, Asta (1989). 'Võimu kuriteod', in *Edasi*, No. 131. – Tartu.

Paadam, Katrin (1990). 'Naiste sotsiaalse käitumise erisused Tallinnas', *Linna sisestruktuurid III*, LUI, Tallinn.

Palli, Heldur (1988) *Otepaa rahvastik aastail 1716–1799*, Valgus, Tallinn.

Parming, Tônu (1972) 'Population changes in Estonia, 1939–1970', in *Population Studies*, vol. 26, pp. 53–78.

Parviainen, Seija (1992). 'European Integration and the Finnish Labour Market', Paper presented at the conference 'Mass Migration in Europe: Implications from East and West', Vienna, March 5–7, Vienna.

Pavelson, Marje (1992). 'Naised ja tööturg', Paper presented to the Estonian–Finnish Seminar on Women, May 14–15, Tallinn.

Pullat, Raimo (1981). *Peterburi eestlased*, Tallinn.

Puur, Allan (1989) 'Female Labour Force Participation in Estonia,' EIPRC Working Paper, RU No. 8, EKDK, pp. 30, Tallinn.

Puur, Allan (1991). 'Life Cycle Differences in Economic Status of Families in Estonia,' Paper presented at the 2nd Finnish–Estonian Demographic Seminar, August 27–29, Helsinki.

Puur, Allan (1992) 'Labour Force Participation Trends in Baltic States', Paper presented at the 10th Nordic Demographic Symposium, August 12–14, Lund.

Raid, J. (1978). *Pribaltiiskije nemtsô v burzhuaznoi Estonii*, Tallinn.

Recent Demographic Developments in the member states of the Council of Europe and Yugoslavia (1990). Council of Europe, Strasbourg.

Reinans, Sven Alur (1985). 'Balterna i Sverige – nagra demografiska aspekter', in *De första batflyktinarna – en antologi om balterna i Sverige. Statens invandrarverk 1982–1985*.

Reuderink, Ronald and Peteris Zvidrinsh (1992). 'De Baltische staten demografische gevolgen van de 'russificatie', in *Demos*, No. 9, October, NIDI.

Rhode Barbara (1991). 'East–West Migration/Brain Drain. Mapping the Available Knowledge and Recommendations for a European Research Programme', Brussels.

Sadik, Nafis (1992). 'Where is Our Planet Going To?', in *Proceedings of the International Population Conference 'Revival of Ageing Societies'*, Espoo, Finland, September 2–4, pp. 9–26.

Sakkeus, Luule (1991a). 'Stabilization of migrational interregional relationships of Estonia (the example of Tallinn)', in *Espaces et Sociétes. L'Est Européen: Sociétés àrefonder, espaces à reconquérir* No. 64, 1/1991, pp. 97–112, Paris.

Sakkeus, Luule (1991b). 'Post-war Migration Trends in Estonia: Formation of the Foreign-Born Population', EIPRC Working Paper, RU No. 15, Series B, EKDK, Tallinn.

Sakkeus, Luule (1992). 'Migration Trends in Estonia: Formation of Foreign-Born Population', Paper presented at the conference 'Mass Migration in Europe: East–West Implications', March 5–7, Vienna.

Sipaviciene, Audra (1989). 'Razvitie migracionnych processov v Litve', in *Demografitcheskoje razvitie Litvy*, pp. 117–147, Vilnius.

Sipaviciene, Audra and Vladislava Stankuniene (1989). 'Problemy izucheniya i regulirovaniya mezhrespublikanskoi migracii naseleniya na urovne soyuznoi respublikoi', in *Demografitcheskoje razvitie Litvy*, pp. 148–169, Vilnius.

Sipaviciene, Audra (1990). 'Razvitie selsko-gorodskoi migracii naselenija i puti ejo regulirovaniya v usloviyah perehoda k urbanizirovannomu obschestvu', PhD thesis, Moscow.

Sipaviciene, Audra (1992). 'Migration Development against the Background of Recent Changes in Lithuania', Paper presented at the 10th Nordic Demographic Symposium, August 12–14, Lund.

Socialnoye razvitie Litvy v 1990 godu (1991). Department of Statistics of Lithuania, Vilnius.

Stankuniene, Vladislava (1989) 'Vosproizvodstvo naseleniya Litvy', in *Demografitcheskoje razvitie Litvy*, pp. 22–59, Vilnius.

Söderling, Ismo (1991). 'Suomi siirtolaisuuden kohdenmaana', Paper presented at the 2nd Finnish–Estonian Demographic Seminar, August 27–29, Helsinki.

Tooms, A. (1927). Quelques comparisons entre les Etats baltes 1920–26. I. (Vôrdlusandmeid Balti riikest 1920–1926). Recueil Mensuel du Bureau Central de Statistique de l'Estonie. Pour l'année 1927, No. 62(1)–73(12), pp. 629–634 (in Estonian), Tallinn.

Truska, L. (1988). 'Baltos demes' karo bei pokario metu Lietuvos demografijoje', in *Komjaunimo tiesa*, No. 124, birzhelio 28d, Vilnius.

Vikat, Andres (1991). 'Non-Marital cohabitation in Estonia: Differences by Ethnicity, Country of Birth and Education', Paper presented at the 2nd Finnish–Estonian Demographic Seminar, August 27–29, Helsinki.

Vishnevski, Anatoli and Andrei Volkov in Andrei Volkov (ed.) (1983). *Vosproizvodstvo naselenija SSSR*, Moscow.

Vishnevski, Anatoli and Zhanna Zayonchkovkaya (1992). 'Emigration from the USSR: the Fourth Wave', Paper presented at the conference 'Mass Migration in Europe: Implications from East and West', Vienna, March 5–7, Vienna.

Vitolinsh, E. and Z. Matule (1986). 'Izmenenija v pazmeschenii naselenija i razvitie urbanizacii', in *Naselenie Sovetskoi Latvii*, ed. by P. Zvidrinsh, pp. 34–47, Zinatne, Riga.

Vôime, Lembit (1975). 'Estonskije poselenija na Tchernomorskom poberezhje Kavkaza', PhD thesis, Tallinn.

Zelinsky, Wilbur (1971). 'The Hypothesis of the Mobility Transition', *Geographical Review*, vol. 61, pp. 219–249.

Zvidrinsh, Peteris (1986). 'Osobennosti razvitija naselenija v Latvii do 1940 g', in *Naselenie Sovetskoi Latvii*, ed. by P. Zvidrinsh, pp. 6–28, Zinatne, Riga.

4 Hungary
Maria Redei

Migration does not affect all Eastern European countries in the same way. Due to topological factors, some countries, such as Romania and Poland, have acted as transit countries. Others, such as Hungary, can be considered as recipient countries. In the context of Central and Eastern European migration, a distinction also needs to be made between safe (Hungary, Czechoslovakia, Poland) and unsafe (the former Soviet Union, Romania, Albania, Serbia) migratory fronts. The levels of migration can be attributed to a combination of ethnic and economic push effects.

For both topological and functional reasons, Hungary has had the highest level of transit migration and is gradually becoming a new host country. The government is now increasingly aware of the effects of its liberal admission policies, in terms of uncontrolled and unplanned immigration pressures, and is gradually implementing measures to reduce false expectations held by potential immigrants.

This chapter reviews various stages in Hungary's migratory trends after World War II and analyses the effects of policy developments after 1989 on Hungary's new immigration features.

HUNGARIAN MIGRATION IN A HISTORICAL PERSPECTIVE

Historically, due to inter-regional disparities, internal and international population movements have always occurred from East to West, and Eastern European regions contributed significantly to inter- and intra-continental migration until the second World War. In this case migration was characterised by outflows of lowly skilled nationals, on the one hand, and by internal migration (from peripheral to core regions) of nationals with even lower skills, on the other.

These past trends tend to be reproduced within current migration. Eastern Europe has been one of the major sources of migration in Europe during the past 100 years, even though population movements have been extremely varied in their socio-economic, political and cultural aspects. What is more, government interventions have also heavily influenced the migration process in this region of Europe: While in the interwar period, the recipient countries imposed restrictions on immigration, for four decades after 1949 the countries of origin themselves created legal obstacles to emigration.

Hungary has played a pioneering role in the continental migration stream because of its geographic location and because of a combination of several other features, such as its relatively liberal policy for ethnic and cultural relations, a higher standard of living, stable relations with the West, and sensitivity to change. All these features have had a clear effect on both emigration and immigration trends. Functionally and topologically, Hungary has always been at the cross-roads; indeed streams in the European migration network actually converged here. Up to the autumn of 1991, Hungary acted as a transit country and was in a similar situation to Austria. After this date, due to the restrictive measures to protect the Austrian border, Hungary became a proper recipient country and a sort of European Ellis Island.

Like all former COMECON countries, since World War II Hungary has been engaged in a policy of hermetical isolation. Nationals who succeeded in leaving the country illegally could not return without facing punitive consequences. At the same time, tourist travel to the West was almost completely restricted.

Within Eastern Europe, Hungary was the first country to open its borders in 1956 and the Hungarian emigration wave of 1956 was significant not only in terms of Hungarian demographics, but also because it represented the first mass refugee flow in Eastern Europe and the first after the Spanish Civil War. The main characteristics of the 1956 refugee wave were:

- The high proportion of young people, a fact which contributed to Hungary experiencing the lowest fertility rates in Europe throughout the 1960s;
- The high proportion of refugees from the western part of Hungary and from Budapest, where frustration was higher and information on how to cross the border more readily available;
- The bipolarisation of flows into two streams: the first one directed towards the overseas countries (USA, Canada), which lifted their admission quotas during the revolution; the second one directed, in a more traditional way, towards the German-speaking countries. At present, a large proportion of those returning to Hungary come from these countries. The direction of movement followed, in part, the direction of earlier traditional migration (with the exception of the Scandinavian countries which also received a smaller number of emigrants).

After the 1956 exodus, Hungarian migration followed two major patterns which were quite distinctive from other Eastern European countries:

1. Hungary's participation in international migration was among the highest, while ethnic German migration was among the lowest.
2. Hungary continued to implement a comparatively more liberal legislation on migration and a more liberal economic policy.

After the events of 1956, Hungary experienced a negative migration balance. In the mid-1970s, however, the balance became positive. During this period, the right to free movement was limited and migration was possible only for family reasons, a restriction which led to several *pro forma* events, such as marriage. The ratio of 30–40 year old females immigrating to Hungary through 'passport marriages' grew substantially.

During the past three decades, the number of migrants has been far less important than the changing structure of, and differences between, immigrants and emigrants. As a general rule, emigrants consisted of qualified males from the Western part of Hungary. Those who arrived were younger, with lower qualifications, limited experience, and had emigrated from neighbouring countries. Over a long period, the unbalanced composition of immigrants and emigrants resulted in sporadic ethnic and political tensions.

From 1956 to 1987, between 2,000 and 4,000 Hungarians emigrated on average every year. Illegal emigration during the same period is estimated at 4,000–5,000 departures every year. German-speaking countries comprised the major destination of Hungarian emigration. The only way to leave the country was under a legal emigration passport, given for family reasons. Those who left the country without a valid passport or prolonged their stay abroad after expiry of their visas, had no opportunity to return. The year 1989 thus gave rise to a new situation with regard to return migration. Although many Hungarians had received political refugee status abroad, Hungary had no experience of receiving refugees, apart from some Chileans and Greeks who were admitted in the 1960s and 1970s.

Immigration to Hungary originated primarily from neighbouring countries such as the former Soviet Union, Romania and East Germany. The arrivals from Romania started to increase in the 1980s, and became massive after the Romanian revolution (Table 4.1). Although a major proportion of immigrants originated from the former socialist countries, immigration to Hungary during the same period also consisted of non-European (4 per cent) and non-socialist European (12 per cent) flows. At the same time, a significant decline in the number of Soviet immigrants occurred. The reason for immigration was mainly attributable to marriage, family

Table 4.1 Labour migration to Hungary

Year	Number of labour permits issued	Of which Romanian workers
1989	24,759	16,456
1990	48,751	39,593
1990	33,352	22,944

Source: Ministry of Labour, Budapest.

reunion and repatriation. During the past decade, the repatriation process involved 3,000–4,000 people annually.

THE TURNING POINT IN 1989

Historically, a high proportion of Hungary's population has possessed the same language and culture and assimilation has never been a real problem. Due to ethnic conflicts in other countries, however, approaches to Eastern European migration are gradually shifting towards cultural rather than policy-related issues.

The border-crossings in Hungary amounted to 14 million in 1980 and to over 100 million in 1991. In 1990, 40 million foreigners came to Hungary. Most arrived from Europe, 75 per cent of whom had migrated from Central Europe. 600,000 were non-Europeans. Hungary's cultural, economic and political mediating functions have become increasingly important for other European countries. Despite having advocated free movement of people for over four decades, the West developed restrictive immigration policies after the 1989 revolutions. Not realising, at first, the extent of the change brought about by the 1989 revolutions, Western European countries were clearly taken by surprise and no particular strategy to resist massive post-1989 migration had been conceived. By helping first-asylum countries such as Hungary, the West was able to protect its Eastern European borders. Until today, Western European countries, which have experienced marked difficulties in distinguishing between economic and political migrants, have tried to discourage their Eastern European partners from deregulating national migration. It is also noticeable that the Eastern European countries themselves do not make any legal distinctions between tourists, asylum seekers and immigrants. This is not simply due to a lack of information, but also to a lack of generally agreed legal definitions of the various categories of population mobility.

Following the adoption of liberal passport laws, an increasing number of Central/East Europeans expressed their intention to 'enjoy the forbidden fruit', i.e. the achievements of the developed market economies. More and more people started to realise that spatial mobility was the quickest, most accessible channel to achieve better standards of living within their own lifetime. Just as in the case of internal, rural to urban migration, East–West migration was seen as a chance to benefit from better redistribution of wealth. On their way to, or once in, their new host countries, many immigrants had to concede, however, that their freedom of movement was now being restricted not by the country of origin, but by the Western European potential host countries. This has been a painful discovery for the newly democratic countries and for the individuals most affected by the structural unemployment and social antagonism which have resulted from economic and political reforms.

Clearly, Western European countries have been slow to understand the actual dynamics of ethnic and social relationships in Central and Eastern Europe. One of Western Europe's major mottos has consisted of promoting the ideal of European unification as a means of preventing the revival of nationalism. Hungary's decision to admit East German refugees marked a turning point in the European unification process. The situation was rather confusing, since it was the inter-German frontier that crossed the population, rather than population crossing the frontier. The definitions of nations, as is well known, have been endlessly discussed and there have been problems in interpreting these definitions, which are border-dependent. Thus in mid-1991, the Bosnian border was not recognised internationally, and Bosnians were not able to seek refugee status in any neighbouring country. Hungary was the first country to grant asylum to Bosnians.

The problem of ethnic populations is an important factor, and one which is well rooted in the history of a region with permanent ethnic conflicts. Eastern Europe produces convincing evidence of the direct correlation between the phenomena of conflict and migration, supporting the idea that future migration policy will aim to resist 'cultural threats' and will increasingly consist of positive or negative discrimination towards ethnically driven movements. In this context, Hungary's current foreign policy is faced with a conflict between two principles: the first aims to offer a safe haven to all Hungarians fearing persecution or experiencing discrimination; the second aims to safeguard the survival of the Hungarian communities in the surrounding countries (Tóth, 1991).

Hungary signed the Geneva Convention in October 1989 but excluded the provision of refugee status to non-European applicants. However, according to the Hungarian minister for Home Affairs, Hungary was to consider signing this provision by the end of 1992. As a result, news of Hungary's relatively liberal policy have spread rapidly over the Asian region and non-European migrants seeking longer term residence began to shift their focus from the West, to Hungary (estimates of non-European applications in 1992 range between 40,000 and 100,000).

Another special aspect of Hungary's approach to migration is the country's active role in facilitating the movement of Soviet Jews to Israel. This started at the end of 1989, and the flow of emigrants from the Soviet Union en route to Israel reached significant proportions in March 1990. The flow gained new impetus after the end of the Gulf war, particularly after the opening of a large temporary facility run by a Jewish agency on the outskirts of Budapest. While no data has yet been published on the number of Jews travelling to Israel via Hungary, estimates predicting that 50 to 60 per cent of the (350,000) new arrivals in Israel have transited through Budapest would seem to be quite acceptable. (Szôke 1991).

HUNGARY AS A 'SAFE' COUNTRY

In 1990, during the gradual removal of all visa requirements with Western countries, Hungary was officially identified as a 'safe' country. In addition, Hungary also became 'safe' for those wishing to settle anywhere in the country, whether they came from the region, were in transit, or were of non-European origin.

Now that Hungarians only need a valid passport to travel abroad, there is no procedure to identify overstayers. Indeed, statistical evidence of the population leaving the country has decreased although the 1990 Hungarian census presented an opportunity to estimate the number of nationals who were not at home at the time of the survey. While taking into account some margin of error, the difference between the statistics for 1989 and the census data indicates that the Hungarian expatriate population amounts to approximately 200,000 people.

POLICY DEVELOPMENTS AFTER 1991

In August 1991, the Hungarian government established a Committee on Migration, the role of which is to advise the central authorities on legal, social, educational and cultural issues related to new migration.

1991 was characterised by rising immigration, an explosive illegal population movement, a sudden refugee wave, and by the repatriation of Hungarian nationals. As from October of the same year, immigration regulations became more restrictive. Due to rising unemployment (15 per cent in 1992, with some parts of the country reaching a rate of 20 per cent), severe restrictions were imposed on obtaining a work permit. Since October 1991, residence in Hungary is granted to those who deposit *per diem* funds, who provide a letter of invitation guaranteeing accommodation, or who can prove to benefit from a minimum amount of capital or permanent income. Western Europeans are subject to the above conditions, a fact which demonstrates a degree of discrimination against those who are not in possession of hard currency. During the last three months of 1991, more than 200,000 people were refused entry at the borders for failing to meet these conditions. In 1992, this number rose to approximately one million. This restrictive approach has proved to be essential. Hungary's Eastern, Northern and Southern borders are not heavily protected and there is a high level of illegal crossings, particularly by Romanians and Chinese. Hungary has also been subject to significant levels of illegal migration from Vietnam, Pakistan, Somalia, and Iraq. During 1992, border crossings of the Romanian frontier were four times higher than in 1991; such an increase can in part be attributed to clandestine migration, which itself is based on pendulum flows related to seasonal and casual employment.

In addition, Hungary's approach to political migrants differs from that of other European countries in that it does not distinguish between asylum seekers and refugees. The rate of admission of recognised refugees in Hungary is around 5 per cent, which is similar to the overall European rate. However, the Hungarian government provides the same level of support to asylum seekers and to refugees. This approach is due to the high proportion

Table 4.2   Refugees and asylum seekers in Hungary

Year	Registered asylum seekers	Citizenship	Ethnic Hungarians	Illegal arrivals	Refugee status
1988	13,173	Romanian 99%	90%	48%	0
1989	17,448	Romanian 98%	85%	79%	185
1990	18,283	Romanian 95%	85%	7%	1561
1991	54,693	Yugoslav 80% Romanian 7% Soviet 1%	21%	5%	434
1992*	9,297	Yugoslav 91% Romanian 5%			

* First seven months.

Source: Ministry of Home Affairs Office for Refugees, Budapest.

of ethnic Hungarians involved in such migration and to the fact that from 1988 to 1989, during the first wave of political migration, Hungary had had no legal experience in distinguishing between asylum seekers and refugees. The first refugee wave started in 1988 and peaked in December 1989. A second, higher, wave occurred in March 1990 after the events of Tirgu Mures. Romania tried to solve its domestic ethnic conflicts by opening its borders and issuing more than 4 million passports. In 1990, after the withdrawal of the Red Army troops, some Soviet nationals sought asylum in Hungary. The number of refugees from Yugoslavia increased after June 1991 (Table 4.2).

Table 4.3   Number of applicants for Hungarian citizenship, 1990–2*

Year	Applicants	Ethnic Hungarians	Repatriation	Applying to reclaim citizenship
1990	12,650	8,000	1,500	2,150
1991	18,600	10,800	6,009	7,500
1992†	11,700	6,000	4,170	4,700

*Before 1990 the annual number of applicants was under 1000.
†First part of the year.

Source: Ministry of Home Affairs, Department of Citizenship.

Table 4.4   Major differences between immigrants and refugees, 1987–91

Feature	Immigrants	Refugees
Sex ratio	1150.0	456.4
Average age for whole period	33.9	29.3
Place of residence: Budapest	23.6	47.1
Urban	36.7	32.3
Rural	39.5	20.6
By region		
Central Hungary	36.0	54.8
Western Hungary	22.8	5.4
Proportion of non-manual workers	44.1	15.0
Highly qualified proportion	20.5	6.2
Rate of arrivals from Romania	63.0	99.3
Proportion of inactive population	35.3	14.3
Average age of non-manual workers	35.3	32.3

Source: Authors' own calculations.

Some estimates are also available with regard to Chinese asylum seekers. Hungary, the former USSR and Romania are the only European countries which have no visa agreements with China. Of those Chinese who intend to migrate to Europe, a high proportion wishes to settle in Hungary. In 1992, more than 2,000 Chinese joint ventures were established in Hungary and it is anticipated that between 40,000 and 100,000 Chinese would consider Hungary not as a transit country but as a country of residence (see Table 4.3 and 4.4).

CONCLUSIONS

The major reasons behind the emigration of Hungarian nationals relate to such factors as the newly acquired freedom to travel following the removal of legal and other restrictions; exaggerated expectations about the West, most significantly the desire to achieve the same levels of income as Western European nationals; and the difficulties in utilising in Hungary highly professional skills because of the lack of appropriate infrastructure and career opportunities.

Another set of causes derives from regional tensions brought about by the difficulties of transition to a market economy, and by social stress generated by unemployment, itself caused by restructuring, low labour productivity, a weak social security system, and an overall decline in the standard of living.

The migration map of Europe was redrawn by the Dublin and the Schengen agreements. The traditional Western European receiving countries shifted the borders of free movement and the burden of migration towards the 'safe' Eastern European countries. Poland, Czechoslovakia and Hungary were particularly affected. The topological situation of these countries, with regard to the neighbouring potential sending countries, is also a determining factor. What is more, those countries which are not members of a treaty system do not contribute to decisions and are dependent on the system. The consequences of such a system are already reflected by the rapidly increasing number of immigration applications and illegal flows in these three countries. Such flows are also encouraged by the lack of consistent migration policies in these new immigration countries and by their lack of legal experience in regulating the wide spectrum of in-coming flows.

Although leaving a country is a basic human right, admission into another country should be regulated by a set of clearly-defined priorities. Regulating migration is not a purely negative discrimination; it can also be determined by positive objectives, such as to serve domestic interests and to contribute to national economic and social stability.

Positive objectives, however, need to rely on a set of pre-existing conditions, such as:

- regular and reliable data sources;
- restrictions on transit migration;
- assistance in return migration of nationals;
- assistance in emigration of nationals for short periods of time, with a view to upgrading their skills and professional experience (this, however, pre-supposes that attractive conditions for the reintegration of expatriate professionals are prepared well in advance);
- legal distinctions between humanitarian and economically motivated admissions of immigrants;
- development of technical and scientific infrastructures and career opportunities in order to absorb highly qualified nationals;
- emergency measures to resist unexpected, massive immigration.

Positive objectives also imply the development of a policy of prevention for certain types of migration. There is, in particular, a need to achieve regional stability at the level of the state and of the individual, in order to moderate the effects of un-planned migration.

Regional stability is based on individual well-being. The opening up of Eastern Europe has given East European nationals a different idea of what constitutes well-being. Because of the youthful age structure of the East European population, motivations are strong and the ability to migrate high. While migration is a selective process mostly on the sending side, on the receiving side it is mainly a harmonising factor. The majority of new immigrants in Western Europe are able to accept, for example, lower living and working standards. Being admitted into an advanced country with the hope of future prospects is much more important than living and working at a level where skills and potentials are not fully utilised.

With a view to reducing false expectations and unnecessary emigration of qualified nationals, however, there is a need to increase the information available in Hungary on the real work opportunities and living conditions in Western Europe. Information in Eastern Europe on the new opportunities in Western Europe is mainly disseminated through informal channels, as distrust of centralised media sources is still high. The Hungarian government, nevertheless, has recently established an information centre the role of which will be to disseminate regular and practical information on legal, labour market and social immigration policies in Western Europe.

Given the importance of human capital in promoting regional development, there is a need to establish domestic conditions which are stimulating and rewarding enough to retain highly qualified professionals and the skilled labour force, or to induce those abroad to return, particularly through the return migration programmes promoted by international organisations. Hungary is affected by both the positive and negative consequences of brain drain. The well-educated and highly trained have more opportunities, which means that their residence choices are wider, and their adaptability to the business cycle more adequate. At the same time, qualified nationals have started to realise that in order to be competitive in the new European economic order, they will need to acquire skills that are marketable abroad. For decision-makers, a major step forward should thus consist of developing conditions locally to induce the voluntary return of expatriate nationals.

References

Baehr, R. and Tessényi, R.G. 'The New Refugee Hosting Countries: Call for Experiences – Space for Innovation', SIM special No. 11. 1991, Netherlands Institute of Human Rights.

Dövényi, Z. 'Social and Regional Aspects of Residents', Research Paper Hungarian Academy of Sciences Geographical Research Institute, 1990.

Nagy, B. 'Refugees and Asylum Seekers', *Külpolitika*, 1989, 16/21, 114–42 pp.

Rédei, M. 'Does Hungary Remain a Sending Country?', paper presented to NIAS conference on 'Demographic Consequences of International Migration', Wassenaar/The Netherlands, 27–29 September 1990.

Rédei, M. 'The Composition of the Stay Permit holders in Hungary – An Overview on the Basis of the Stock of Foreign Population from Aliens Controlling Department Data', in Endre Sík (ed.) *Menekülôk, vándorlók és szerencsét próbálók* – (Refugees, Immigrants, Adventurers), – MTA Politikai Tudományok Intézete Budapest, 1992. (This book contains a brief review of Hungarian research activity in this field.)

Rédei, M. *Trends of International Migration*, – SOPEMI report, 1991, OECD, Paris. (An occasional report about the past 35 years international movement in Hungary.)

Rédei, M. 'International Migration and the Impact of the Labour Force', *Munkaügyi Szemle* (*Labour Review*) June, 1992.

Rédei, M. 'The past 100 years of Hungarian Flow: The Demographic Impact of this Movement', in Adelman-Sìk-Tessényi, (ed.) *Refugees in Hungary*, York Lanes, Toronto Publishers Ltd, 1991.

Regio 91/4, a thematical report about the EC migration, Budapest – Teleki Foundation.

Rhode, B. 'East–West migration/Brain-Drain' – COST pilot seminar in Vienna, 13–15 June 1991, Mapping the Available Knowledge and Recommendations for a European Research Programme published in Brussels, October 1991, by CEC.

Sìk, E. *Report on the Transylvanian Refugee Wave*, TARKI Report, Budapest 1989.

Szoke, L. *Hungarian Perspectives on Emigration and Immigration in the New European Architecture* – Turin, November 25–27, 1991.

Tòth, J. *Draft on Immigration Administration and its Future Tasks*, Magyar Közigazgatás, 1990, September.

Tòth, J. *Main Demographic and Occupational Data of the Refugees who Entered Hungary between January 1, 1988 and May 31, 1990*, HCSO, Budapest.

Tòth, J. 'The Development of Hungarian Refugee Policy', – Paper presented in Turin, November 25–27, 1991, Conference on the New Europe and International Migration.

5 Russia and the CIS
Valentina Bodrova and Tatjana Regent

Migration has always been a characteristic trend within the Russian Federation. The yearly number of internal population movements often reached
several million. Due to the highly centralised nature of the economy, state
bodies have traditionally controlled all forms of migration as a way of
securing inter-industrial and interregional distribution of the workforce.
Some economic factors, such as the lack of balance between existing or
planned jobs and the labour force, contributed to this practice.

Up to Perestroika, two successive concepts of migration dominated in
the ex-USSR. In the 1960s, in the absence of any deficit of manpower, the
ruling idea prescribed that the intensity, levels and directions of migration
should follow the geography of the centres of production in different
regions of the country. In the 1970s, when, contrary to this theory, people
migrated not only to the new regions of construction, such as Siberia and
the Far East, but also to other areas of the USSR with a labour surplus (i.e.
Southern regions of Russia, Ukraine, Kazakhstan, Middle Asia), a new
conception of migration was elaborated. This theory took account of the
differences in the social and economic development of the regions, and, as
a result, of the comparative advantages of regions in terms of their standards of living.

It soon became apparent, however, that neither concept took into consideration the entire diversity of factors which are critical to internal economic
migration, and in the 1980s both concepts were criticised for their one-
sided interpretation of factors determining economic migration.

In the 1990s, with the breakup of the USSR and the formation of the
CIS, with the coming into play of economic relations between the republics
of ex-USSR and the launching of radical reforms to develop a market economy, new forms of, and a new attitude towards, migration gradually
emerged. Recession, coupled with growing unemployment and political
instability, led to movements of three broad categories of migrant: economic migrants; refugees and forced migrants; emigrants.

This chapter addresses current trends in internal migration in the ex-
USSR and in today's Russia, as well as trends in emigration to Western
Europe.

TRENDS IN INTERREPUBLIC AND RUSSIAN MIGRATION

The natural increase in the population of the Russian Federation has traditionally been lower than other republics in the ex-USSR, especially the Middle Asian republics. Migration, however, has been higher. In 1991, 43 per cent of the increase in the population of the Russian Federation was due to migration.

Up to the mid-1970s, emigration from the territory of the Russian Federation surpassed immigration from other republics. Since 1975, the number of migrants arriving in Russia exceeded the number of those leaving the Russian territory. The most intensive migration during the 1970s was directed towards Siberia and the Far East, especially to Tyumen, Tomsk, Khabarovsk, the Krasnoyarsk regions, Kamchatka, Primorye and Yakutia. To a great extent, these trends were determined by the geography of production centres (e.g. the development of oil and gas plants in Western Siberia, railways in Baikal-Amur, etc.). The cities and regions of Moscow and Saint Petersburg (formerly Leningrad) were the most attractive destinations for internal migrants. From 1979 to 1988, the

Table 5.1   Interrepublic migration in the Russian Federation in 1991

	Arrived	*Left*	*Growth*
Ukraine	210,121	276,196	–66,075
Belorussia	45,618	50,272	–4,654
Uzbekistan	69,149	33,276	35,873
Kazakhstan	128,906	99,380	29,526
Georgia	42,863	14,115	14,115
Azerbaijan	47,951	27,215	20,736
Lithuania	10,044	5,665	4,379
Moldavia	29,534	27,052	2,502
Latvia	13,035	7,197	5,838
Kirgizstan	33,703	15,962	17,745
Tadjikistan	27,808	10,249	17,559
Armenia	12,006	7,942	4,964
Turkmenistan	13,118	8,617	4,501
Estonia	8,176	4,012	4,164
Migration in total	692,056	587,150	104,906
Migration to and from foreign countries	113,960	145,067	–31,107

Source: State Committee for Statistics of the RSFSR, 1991.

Table 5.2   Directions of migration of the population of the Russian Federation, 1970–1990

Region	Migration balance, thousand of people			Migration intensity for 10,000 people		
	1970–8	1979–88	1989–90	1970–8	1979–88	1989–90
Russia	147	1819	247	1	13	8
incl. countryside	−7663	1–3910	−346	−187	−98	−44
Nechernozemye	479	1180	151	9	19	12
incl. countryside	−3132	−1343	−130	−220	−102	−52
Siberia and Far East	231	1191	−55	10	40	−9
incl. countryside	−1273	−479	−100	−162	−58	−59
Economic regions						
Northern	23	39	−23	5	7	−18
North-Eastern	516	450	32	78	56	19
Central	634	1006	162	25	34	27
Volgo-Vyatsky	−348	−224	−10	−47	−27	−6
Chernozemye	−346	−138	36	−49	−18	23
Povolzhye	153	−119	61	11	−1	18
North Caucasus	156	68	98	11	4	29
Ural	−879	−562	−63	−51	−28	−15
West Siberia	−97	814	4	−9	58	1
East Siberia	−66	43	−49	−9	5	−27
Far East	394	334	−10	70	45	6

Source: State Committee for Statistics of the RSFSR, 1991.

average annual migration balance exceeded 180,000 due to inflows from Ukraine, Kazakhstan, Belorussia, Azerbaijan and Moldova. At the same time, Russia had a negative migration balance with the Baltic republics. Another example shows that in 1989 alone, 396,000 Russians arrived in the Russian Federation from other Soviet republics, while 334,500 people left the Russian territory, thus contributing to an increase in the Russian population of 61,500 people (see Table 5.1 and 5.2).

Until recently, the intensity of the migration of Russians from other Soviet republics was mainly determined by employment-related factors. With the aggravation of the social, economic and political situation, and the development of international conflicts in various regions of the country, new migration processes appeared. First, migration of Russians from other republics, to Russia, increased, while migration of Russians to other republics decreased (in 1990, the balance of interrepublic migration to Russia

was + 199,900). In 1990, for example, 36,200 people of Russian nationality arrived in the Russian Federation from Tadjikistan (10,500 in 1989),
48,800 from Azerbaijan (16,600 in 1989), 25,000 from Kirgizstan (14,100
in 1989), and 55,200 from Uzbekistan (34,900 in 1989).

In 1991, a survey on the reasons for migrating was administered by the
State Committee of Statistics of the Russian Federation and the Ministry of
Internal Affairs. The survey covered a sample of 91,900 respondents aged
above 16 in 23 territories of the Russian Federation.

The survey showed that 80 per cent of the respondents had moved within
the Russian territory (52 per cent of whom had migrated within their regions,
and 48 per cent from other territories of the Russian Federation), while 20 per
cent had migrated from other republics of the ex-USSR (mainly from the
Ukraine, Kazakhstan, Uzbekistan, Georgia, Azerbaijan and Belorussia).

More than half of the migrants who moved to Russia from other republics were of Russian nationality. Other nationalities included Ukrainians
(15 per cent), Armenians (4.2 per cent), Belorussians (4.2 per cent), Tatars
(3.2 per cent) and Azerbaijanians (2.5 per cent) (see Table 5.3).

Table 5.3   Immigration to 23 territories of Russia from other republics of the
ex-USSR in 1991

	No. of respondents	*Came from*		*%*		
		Town	*Countryside*	*Total*	*Town*	*Countryside*
Totals	18,138	13,045	4,742	100	100	100
Came from						
Ukraine	5,038	3,510	1,427	28	27	30
Kazakhstan	2,727	1,595	1,043	15	12	22
Uzbekistan	1,971	1,632	313	11	13	6.6
Georgia	1,748	1,312	413	9.6	10	8.7
Azerbaijan	1,654	1,299	335	9.1	10	7.1
Belorussia	1,208	820	365	6.7	6.3	7.7
Tadjikistan	818	744	64	4.5	5.7	1.3
Kirgiztan	778	435	318	4.3	3.3	6.7
Moldova	557	338	203	3.1	2.6	4.3
Turkmenistan	420	352	60	2.3	2.7	1.3
Armenia	386	291	92	2.1	2.2	1.9
Latvia	316	269	42	1.7	2.1	0.9
Lithuania	290	253	36	1.6	1.9	0.8
Estonia	227	195	31	1.3	1.5	0.7

The survey identified the following reasons for migration *within* the Russian Federation: family circumstances (particularly family reunion); studies; employment; international conflicts; ecological reasons. The motivations of migrants who moved from other republics were less contrasted and only included family circumstances (39 per cent) and international conflicts (61 per cent). International conflicts were most frequently cited by respondents from Azerbaijan (70 per cent mentioned this reason), Tadjikistan (64 per cent), Georgia (63 per cent), Lithuania (53 per cent), Uzbekistan (51 per cent), Armenia (50 per cent), Kirgizstan (47 per cent), Latvia (46 per cent) and Moldova (36 per cent). Migrants from Estonia mentioned international conflicts as frequently as family circumstances.

The survey also showed that the educational level of migrants closely reflected the average educational level in Russia: 14 per cent of migrants had studied at tertiary level and 58 per cent at secondary level (this second figure is higher than the Russian average); 24 per cent had received secondary specialised education, and 5 per cent primary education or no education at all.

FORCED MIGRATION AND THE NEW LEGISLATION

According to official statistics from the Ministry of Internal Affairs, the number of forced migrants in the ex-USSR was close to 800,000 people at the end of 1991, including 230,000 in Russia alone. In June 1992, 315,000 refugees were officially registered. However, due to the fact that the Ministries of Internal Affairs of the ex-USSR have only registered forced migrants from the zones of conflict defined by governmental decrees, it is estimated that the actual number of refugees is considerably higher.

In 1989, the first refugees appeared in the Russian Federation, when more than 20,000 Meskhetian Turks came from Uzbekistan. 13,000 were provided with jobs and dwellings. In 1990 more than 90,000 people arrived from Baku, the majority of whom were Russian-speakers. In 1991, more than 100,000 Ossets migrated to North Osetia from Georgia.

Since the former Soviet Union had passed no laws on refugees, citizens who came to the Russian Federation received aid (as refugees) through special decrees of the Russian government. In 1991, 37 per cent of refugees officially registered in the Russian Federation were Ossets, while 20 per cent were Armenians, 20 per cent Meskhetian Turks, and 23 per cent Russians. Refugee movements predominantly affected such regions as North Caucasus, Krasnodar, Stavropol and Rostov. Indeed, these regions gradually became buffer zones between the Caucasian republics and regions of Central Russia. A favourable climate and proximity to places of previous residence also made these regions attractive for a significant proportion of refugees (40 per cent of all registered movements).

Another problem of a similar dimension relates to so-called forced migration to Russia. The main causes of forced migration are social and ethnic tensions, laws on citizenship and language adopted by the republics of the former Soviet Union, and nationalistic tendencies in daily life. It is anticipated that the increase in nationalist sentiment over the next five years will exert considerable pressure on Russians living in the republics of the former Soviet Union. Migration of first and second generation Russians will probably be more pronounced from the republics with an 'alien culture' (Turkmenistan, Kirgizstan, Tadjikistan, Azerbaijan, Uzbekistan, Kazakhstan), while migration from republics with fewer cultural differences (Moldova, Lithuania, Latvia, Estonia, Georgia, Armenia) will be less intense. Migration will be even less significant from republics such as the Ukraine and Belorussia. According to an investigation conducted in 1991 by the Russian Center of Public Opinion and Market Research, 37 per cent of the Russian population in the first group of republics of the ex-USSR are planning to move to Russia (18 per cent from the second group and 10.5 per cent from the third group). According to these predictions, from 400,000 to 2 million people (about one-third of the Russian population in the other republics of the ex-USSR) would plan to move to Russia because of discrimination based on language or nationality. Furthermore, the aggravation of international relations has also produced forced migration within the territory of the Russian Federation itself. Examples of such migration recently included movements from the Tuva republic and from Checheno-Ingushetia.

Combined with the unsolved problems of the populations who have already moved to Russia, the anticipated increase in Russian migration is clearly posing a threat to the development of political and economic reforms in the Federation of Russia. In effect, the problem of refugees in Russia contains one specific aspect unknown to other states. According to world tradition, refugees make no claim on the receiving state. On the contrary, Russian refugees have clearly claimed that they were not properly protected by the Russian President, the Supreme Soviet and the government of the Russian Federation in the new states/republics of the ex-USSR. The Russian authorities have thus come to believe that such resentment could eventually be used by social-chauvinist circles in their current battle against democracy and in favour of the return of Russia to its borders of 1913.

Despite the above, forced migration to Russia has also yielded positive effects for the Russian Federation. The increase in the labour force, including the supply of highly qualified specialists, clearly brings favourable opportunities for the improvement of demographic trends in Russia and for economic development in some of the territories faced with a labour deficit. However, the positive effects of migration will only occur if proper reception and integration schemes for future migrants are organised in advance.

Against this background, in 1992 the Supreme Soviet of Russia approved a new law on the legal status of forced migrants and refugees in the territory of the Russian Federation. The new law aimed at setting out the mutual obligations of forced migrants, the state, governmental bodies and non-governmental organisations. As well, it introduced for the first time the terms *refugee* and *forced migrant*. A citizen of the Russian Federation is recognised as a forced migrant if he was forced to leave his permanent residence in another state or in the territory of the Russian Federation because violence or other forms of persecution were exerted against him or members of his family, or because of a real threat of persecution on account of his race, nationality, religion, language, political convictions, etc.

Any person without Russian citizenship can be recognised as a forced migrant if he was forced to leave his permanent residence in the territory of Russian Federation for the same reasons. A person moving or wishing to move to the territory of the Russian Federation can be recognised as a *refugee* if he does not possess Russian citizenship and was forced to leave his permanent residence in the territory of another state because of the above-mentioned types of persecution or threat.

The granting of refugee status is decided by the migration services of the corresponding republic or region of the Russian Federation, or by the central migration service of the Russian Federation, on the basis of applications submitted to the diplomatic or council delegations of the Russian Federation.

In brief, the new law introduced:

- definitions of the terms 'refugee' and 'forced migrant';
- the rights and duties of a person applying for one of the two status;
- procedures for the granting of refugee or forced migrant status;
- procedures for appealing against decisions taken by the corresponding bodies;
- additional obligations of the state *vis-à-vis* forced migrants;
- compensations paid to forced migrants;
- duties of the Federal Migration Service of Russia;
- duties of state and administrative bodies, particularly as regards their collaboration with non-governmental organisations;

- prohibitions regarding the *refoulement* of refugees or forced migrants to their previous place of residence;
- naturalisation procedures.

INTERNATIONAL MIGRATION

The levels of international migration from the former Soviet Union and the attitudes towards it have traditionally been governed by political motives. The democratisation of social and administrative structures, policy openness, and transition towards a market economy contributed to the liberalisation of emigration in the early 1990s. Liberalisation was characterised by the gradual lifting of administrative restrictions and by the development of new possibilities for departure abroad.

In 1990, 454,000 people received permits for permanent emigration (in 1986 the corresponding number was 6,000), most of whom came from Russia, the Ukraine and Kazakhstan. The largest number of emigrants from Russia was from the cities of Moscow and Saint Petersburg, or from the regions of Moscow and Leningrad (36 per cent), from the region of Omsk (8 per cent), from Altai (6 per cent), and from the region of Orenburg (5 per cent). Jews, Germans, Armenians and Greeks constituted the majority of emigrants, confirming the idea that emigration from the former Soviet Union throughout the 1980s and early 1990s has been primariliy ethnically-driven. Nearly 98 per cent of emigrants in 1990 moved to Israel (59 per cent), Germany (30.6 per cent), Greece and the USA (see Table 5.4).

Soviet emigration has been characterised by the high educational and professional levels of emigrants. Social scientists, scientists, engineers, highly skilled workers constituted a significant group of people who left the country. It is estimated that one fifth of current emigrants are professionals with higher education.

Table 5.4   Structure of emigration according to its destinations, 1980–90 (%)

Years	Total	Emigrated to				
		Israel	*Germany*	*USA*	*Greece*	*Other*
1980	100	53.6	17.6	14.0	0.9	13.9
1985	100	19.4	8.5	3.2	2.4	66.5
1990	100	59.0	30.6	2.9	5.2	2.3

In 1991, the Law on Employment in Russia, which set out the possibilities for working abroad on a contract basis, was adopted. According to the Ministry of Labour and Employment of the Russian Federation, about 1.5 million people would be prepared to work abroad. Findings of a survey carried out by the Russian Centre of Public Opinion and Market Research in 1991 in the republics of the ex-USSR show that emigration is more popular among residents of large cities, and among people with a comparatively high income.

According to this survey, more men than women wish to work abroad. On the contrary, more women than men wish to migrate for permanent residence abroad. In both categories, respondents aged 20 to 39, with higher or secondary technical education, are predominant. According to the same survey, no

Table 5.5 Socio-demographic characteristics of potential emigrants (%)

Groups of respondents	Wish to work abroad for a long period of time	Wish to migrate for permanent residence abroad
Total	100	100
Sex		
Men	58	47
Women	42	53
Age		
Up to 20	13	28
20–29	38	37
30–39	29	18
40–49	14	7
50–54	2	1
Over 54	4	9
Education		
Higher (partial or completed)	23	21
Secondary – technical or specialized	44	43
General secondary	21	17
Foreign language proficiency		
Fluent	2	6
Can read and speak	42	40
No knowledge at all	56	54

Source: Russian Centre of Public Opinion and Market Research (VCIOM), 1991.

more than 2 per cent of those who wish to work abroad and 6 per cent of those who wish to reside permanently abroad possess at least one foreign language (See Table 5.5). The investigation also identified preferences with regard to the countries of destination. As mentioned above, in the late 1980s/ early 1990s, most emigrants moved to Israel and Germany. The investigation by the Russian Centre of Public Opinion shows that the USA and Israel are not particularly attractive destinations, which can be explained by the strict immigration regulations applied by these two countries on the basis of nationality or religion. Potential emigrants thus prefer European countries, primarily because of their geographic and cultural proximity.

Potential emigration for work or permanent residence depends on a range of domestic and external factors, e.g. the economic situation in Russia, the normalisation of international relations, and immigration restrictions in the receiving countries. It was nevertheless expected that emigration through the contract system would increase after January 1993, when the Law on immigration and emigration will came into effect.

External migration brings about both positive and negative effects. Negative effects mainly consist of social and economic problems associated with brain drain, illegal employment, difficulties of adaptation, and problems linked to the social security of emigrants in foreign countries. On the other hand, economic migration can be expected to contribute to the improvement of professional skills, to acquaintance with progressive technologies, and to experience with business, administration and market economy. Furthermore, external migration will allow expatriate professionals to remit hard currency to their family members, thus improving their standards of living and enhancing national investment in foreign currency.

It is against this background that the Ministry of Labour and Employment of the Russian Federation decided to establish a special state body, the responsibility of which will be to regulate external labour migration and to set out a special programme to resolve any economic and political problems associated with migration.

THE NEW MIGRATION POLICY

Migration policy in Russia is still in the making. The need to create appropriate conditions for the integration of migrants from other republics of the former Soviet Union has clearly become a priority. Given the increased momentum of forced migration within the ex-USSR, in June 1992 the government of the Russian Federation established the Federal Migration Service of Russia. The main responsibilities of this new organ consist of:

- Advising on new migration policy and on its implementation.
- Organising the reception, temporary housing and economic assistance of refugees and forced migrants in accordance with the legislation of the Russian Federation and international law.
- Allocating financial and technical aid for programmes of assistance to refugees and forced migrants.
- Assisting in the adaptation and naturalisation of migrants from other states.
- Promoting cooperation with international government and non-government organisations engaged in solving the problems of refugees and forced migrants;
- Assisting public organisations in helping refugees and forced migrants, and in organising researches into the problems of forced migration;
- Developing contacts with the United Nations High Commissioner for Refugees, the International Organization for Migration, and other international institutions.
- Assessing current and future levels of migration, and identifying suitable measures to integrate refugees and forced migrants;
- Organising and coordinating the work of the local migration services.

In addition to the establishment of the above federal body, special groups will also be created, or officers appointed in local employment agencies, with a view to assisting with issues of forced migration. In the territories where immigration is substantial, migration services will be set up to act as the local representatives of the Federal Migration Service.

Finally, in May 1992, the government of the Russian Federation adopted its long-term programme on migration. Based on the fundamental principles and requirements of international law, on the practice of different states, and on concrete political, social and economic specificities of the Russian Federation, this programme describes a range of activities designed to implement the new policy regarding, in particular, refugees and forced migrants.

GENERAL CONCLUSIONS

1. Migration plays a significant role in the population growth of Russia. The significance of migration within the next few years is expected to grow.
2. In the 1990s, rural migration in Russia decreased. This can be explained by social and economic instability, shortages of food and

other consumer goods in the cities (particularly in Moscow and St Petersburg), the decreasing demand for labour, and the ageing of the rural population.

3. In the 1990s, new forms of migration, consisting of refugees, forced migrants and emigrants, appeared in the former USSR.

4. Contrary to the situation in other countries, refugees arriving in Russia claim that they are not sufficiently protected by the new authorities of the Russian Federation. Experts believe that the discontent of the new refugees is likely to be used by Russian social-chauvinists in their battle against democracy.

5. Due to aggravation of the social, economic and political situation, and to conflicts in various regions of the former USSR, migration of Russians, from other republics to Russia, is increasing. This migration stream is expected to last for at least another four or five years.

6. Due to democratisation and the lifting of administrative restrictions, new possibilities for emigration have appeared. While migration throughout the 1980s was primarily ethnically driven, it is expected that after January 1993 (when the new law on free emigration will come into effect) the number of Russians who will consider emigrating for work abroad will increase considerably. On the other hand, it is expected that the risk of national dictatorships in Azerbaijan, Georgia and the Middle Asian states will exacerbate political emigration from these states until 1995.

7. The attitude of foreign countries towards future migration from the ex-USSR is increasingly negative. A system of barriers to Soviet migration is gradually being put in place, particularly in Central and Eastern European transit countries which are situated between the CIS and Western Europe. These transit countries limit the issue of entry visas to former Soviet tourists and impose other restrictions, notably in terms of the availability of currency. Western states, in turn, have introduced more rigid immigration regulations after the collapse of the Soviet Union (Shevtsova, 1992).

8. According to some estimates (Shevtsova, 1992), emigration of intellectual and highly skilled personnel from the CIS will result, in the near future, in an economic loss worth one trillion rubles. This figure exceeds the Commonwealth's current annual national income.

References

Problems of Higher Effectiveness of Exploitation of the Labour Force in the USSR, Moscow, 1983, pp. 214–16.

Shevtsova, L. 'Post-Soviet Emigration Today and Tomorrow', *International Migration Review*, XXVI, 2, 1992, pp. 252–255

Shkolnikov, V. 'Comparative Research in Brain Migration. Implications for the Former Soviet Union', Rand (*Report on the Conference on the Population of the Former USSR in the 21st Century*, 29 September–2 October 1992, Amsterdam).

6 Former Czechoslovakia
Zdenek Pavlik and Jarmila Maresova

Former Czechoslovakia consists of two relatively different territories which became independent in January 1993: The Czech Republic (CR) and the Slovak Republic (SR). The CR is geographically closer to Germany, a country towards which emigration of Czechs had already started before 1880 (together with emigration to Ireland, the United Kingdom, the Netherlands, Belgium, France and the Scandinavian countries). As a part of great Hungary, the SR experienced large emigration flows only after 1880, mainly towards the United States, Canada, Argentina, Brazil, Australia and New Zealand, all countries which were affected by considerable shortages of manpower.

Using population census statistics and other survey data, this chapter briefly retraces major migratory trends in former Czechoslovakia after World War II and following the Velvet Revolution. It also examines new forms of immigration to the territory of former Czechoslovakia, particularly immigration of an illegal character.

MIGRATION BETWEEN WORLD WAR II AND 1989

According to official data, the compulsory transfer of Germans or their expulsion from Czechoslovakia in the aftermath of World War II involved 2,916,000 people; 2,256,000 were transferred in an organised manner from May 1945 to the end of 1946, and 80,000 Germans were expelled in 1947. Only 204,000 Germans stayed in Czechoslovakia after May 1947. A rather significant proportion of former emigrants (approximately 200,000 according to official estimates) returned to Czechoslovakia during the first two years after World War II.

Between the population censuses of 1961 and 1970, it is estimated that 80,000–100,000 people emigrated from Czechoslovakia illegally, while total emigration amounted to 190,000. Illegal emigration increased considerably after the Soviet invasion of August 1968. The number of illegal emigrants between the 1970 and 1979 population censuses is estimated at 51,402, while legal emigration, on the basis of passports issued, did not exceed 24,000 people.

Net migration data in Table 6.1 represent the official statistics published by the Federal Statistical Office and the Federal Ministry of the Interior. They reflect a much lower level of emigration than other estimates based on population censuses and vital and migration statistics.

Table 6.1   Emigration from and net migration in Czechoslovakia between 1950 and 1979 (in thousands)

Year	Net migration	Number of passports issued	Total emigration
1950	+2.3		
1951	+0.7		
1952	+0.7		
1953	+0.4		
1954	−0.7		
1955	−1.0		
1956	−0.9		
1957	−0.3	18,221(a)	21,251(a)
1958	−0.7		
1959	−1.0		
1960	−1.6		
1961	−0.7		
1962	−1.0		
1963	−1.0		
1964	−3.5	5,633	7,040
1965	−3.2	4,630	6,359
1966	−3.2	8,237	10,368
1967	−9.7	8,016	10,152
1968	−6.4		
1969	−6.0	21,780(b)	71,910(b)
1970	−8.8	4,413	8,995
1971	−2.6	3,670	4,960
1972	−0.3	1,532	2,650
1973	+1.8	1,392	2,372
1974	+0.3	1,385	2,340
1975	−1.0	1,694	2,435
1976	0.0	1,723	2,604
1977	−0.8	2,053	3,374
1978	−1.3	2,453	4,308
1979	−1.3	3,365	7,517

(a)   1952–63
(b)   1968–69

Source: Federal Statistical Office and Federal Ministry of the Interior.

Zdenek Pavlik and Jarmila Maresova   113

Table 6.2   Emigration from and net migration (in thousands) in Czechoslovakia
between 1980 and 1989

Year	Net migration	Passports issued	Total emigration
1980	-1.3	3,568	10,712
1981	-2.4	3,710	10,986
1982	-2.0	2,644	9,547
1983	-1.9	2,825	8,136
1984	-1.5	2,061	7,606
1985	-1.1	2,436	7,662
1986	-1.3	2,412	7,108
1987	-1.0	2,399	7,460
1988	-1.0	2,741	7,533
1989	-1.3	2,998	8,513

Source: Federal Statistical Office and Federal Ministry of the Interior.

According to the results of the 1991 population census, emigration increased during the 1980s, reaching 80,000 people between 1980 and 1989. Again, official data considerably underestimate the magnitude of the flow (Table 6.2), although assessment of both legal and illegal migration is closer to reality than in the previous decade.

Emigration from Czechoslovakia during this period was directed predominantly towards the Federal Republic of Germany: more than 28 per cent of all legal emigrants between 1981 and 1989 opted for this destination (Table 6.3). The second most important country of immigration was Greece, which received almost 12 per cent of the out-flow. The relative importance of Greece as a country of destination can be explained by the fact that several thousand Greeks came to Czechoslovakia as political emigrants in the 1950s. Some are now returning to Greece. Similarly, the majority of emigrants to Germany consists of people with German nationality. North America, Austria, Asian states, Yugoslavia and Hungary received more than 1,000 Czechoslovakian emigrants each during the same period.

Consistency in the choice, by legal emigrants, of countries of destination is not very surprising. It reflects, in fact, one of the main causes of emigration, i.e. marriage. The sex structure of legal emigration (Table 6.4) clearly underlines this finding, which is also reflected by the fact that the majority of woman emigrants choose a destination in Europe (or in other developed countries), while men prevail only among emigrants to African and Asian immigration countries.

Table 6.3   Legal emigration from Czechoslovakia, 1981–9

Country	1981	1982	1983	1984	1985	1986	1987	1988	1989
FRG	1,264	1,023	982	750	481	593	619	653	936
Greece	482	655	445	261	232	341	201	222	159
Austria	194	498	151	130	142	161	207	111	161
Yugoslavia	217	197	178	136	113	137	117	115	82
Hungary	153	144	213	160	116	116	119	98	71
Italy	103	112	106	117	90	104	104	118	128
GDR	100	74	87	93	95	71	46	75	66
Sweden	71	68	77	57	50	54	46	75	66
Switzerland	73	67	54	43	40	32	53	60	81
France	64	64	71	60	46	44	41	28	40
Poland	48	37	46	68	53	43	61	46	47
UK	65	49	41	56	43	35	37	51	49
Holland	54	30	31	40	40	43	47	55	49
Bulgaria	43	37	35	36	47	46	33	20	15
W. Berlin	54	38	18	23	21	26	28	20	26
Other EC	63	55	49	39	75	50	47	48	35
Europe total	3,048	2,848	2,584	2,069	1,684	1,896	1,830	1,766	2,004
Asia	135	251	303	314	204	150	84	76	75
America	295	324	251	257	252	248	283	271	324
Australia	93	65	103	75	77	73	93	77	130
Africa	142	104	114	211	106	29	30	29	34
Soviet Union	19	33	49	66	76	29	16	22	33
Totals	3,733	3,625	3,404	2,992	2,399	2,425	2,337	2,241	2,590

Source: Federal Statistical Office.

Table 6.4   Legal emigrants from Czechoslovakia by sex, 1981–9

Continent	Male	Female	Total
Europe	7,155	12,574	19,729
Asia	951	641	1,592
N. America	981	1,524	2,505
Africa	600	199	799
Australia	380	406	786
Soviet Union	162	171	333
Totals	10,231	15,515	25,746

Source: Federal Statistical Office.

Table 6.5 Immigrants to Czechoslovakia by sex, 1981–9

Continent	Male	Female	Total
Europe	2,644	3,289	5,933
Asia	1,370	396	1,766
Africa	750	149	899
America	381	368	749
Australia	48	33	81
Soviet Union	857	1,880	2,737
Total	6,053	6,118	12,171

Source: Federal Statistical Office.

With regard to immigrants to Czechoslovakia, their number before November 1989 can be measured with great accuracy (Table 6.5). Statistics on immigration by gender are also interesting in that they clearly reflect the prevalence of women from Europe and the former Soviet Union, and the predominatly male structure of immigration from Africa and Asia.

Table 6.6 Immigrants to Czechoslovakia by sending country, 1981–9

Country	1981	1982	1983	1984	1985	1986	1987	1988	1989
Poland	351	350	272	288	298	296	255	219	191
Yugoslavia	34	54	67	92	82	50	69	88	88
GDR	63	76	80	64	34	62	80	41	41
Bulgaria	89	64	54	43	40	43	51	76	60
Hungary	59	47	60	59	52	48	39	55	44
FRG	18	22	31	33	34	35	43	37	50
Greece	31	10	38	21	18	9	33	18	19
Romania	11	11	25	17	19	21	13	22	34
Austria	22	14	14	9	25	15	30	19	23
Italy	5	1	7	8	9	14	32	20	21
Other EC	26	24	24	39	36	34	44	37	40
Europe	709	673	672	673	647	327	689	632	311
Asia	206	385	218	233	147	119	150	175	133
N.America	41	72	63	83	68	71	79	121	151
Africa	71	82	173	10	4	9	10	8	22
Australia	3	2	13	10	4	9	10	8	22
Soviet Union	314	369	338	315	240	273	293	264	331
Total	1,344	1,583	1,477	1,451	1,302	1,174	1,296	1,266	1,278

Source: Federal Statistical Office.

The stability in the number of immigrants between 1981 and 1989 is very surprising. The levels of immigration do not appear to be affected by the economic or political situation in Czechoslovakia and are only partially affected by the situation in the countries of origin (Table 6.6).

AFTER THE VELVET REVOLUTION

With its low level of mortality and fertility and decreasing regional disparities, contemporary Czechoslovakia, before its dissolution, belonged to the demographically developed countries. Differences between the CR and SR are much smaller than they were 74 years ago, when the history of a common state began. The main demographic characteristics of former Czechoslovakia during 1990 and 1991 are summarised in Table 6.7. This table shows that the natural increase in population was close to zero, the total fertility rate already below 2, and the crude marriage rate starting to decrease in 1991 (this rate is likely to continue to decrease in line with the continued reduction in fertility levels).

The last population census carried out in March 1991 estimated the total population of former Czechoslovakia at 15,576,550, with a relative proportion of 10,302,215 in the CR, and 5,274,335 in the SR. The size of the population as measured by the latest census is slightly lower than the one indicated in Table 6.7, which can be explained by the levels of unrecorded emigration.

Free emigration from former Czechoslovakia effectively started in December 1989, although the corresponding legislation was only approved

Table 6.7   Main demographic characteristics of former Czechoslovakia, 1990–1

	1990	*1991*
Population on 1 January in thousands	15,675	15,559
Populaton increase in per cent	0.16	0.21
Natural increase in per cent	0.17	0.19
Net migration in per cent	–0.01	0.02
Crude marriage rate	8.4	6.7
Total fertility rate	1.96	1.92
Infant mortality rate	11.3	11.5
Life expectancy at birth – males		67.3
– females		75.8

Source: Federal Statistical Office.

at a later stage. The Charter of Rights and Freedom, which grants the freedom of migration and residence to every person legally established in the country, was adopted by the parliament on 9 January 1991. Another law on travel documents, which guarantees the freedom to emigrate from and return to Czechoslovakia, was approved on the 15 May 1991.

The nature of migration changed after the Velvet Revolution of 1989. While political emigration before 1989 was directed towards Western European and other democratic countries and was, more often than not, of a permanent nature (given the impossibility of returning to Czechoslovakia), current emigration is primarily composed of people travelling abroad for relatively short periods with the sole intention of taking up better paid jobs or improving their professional experience or qualifications.

In a survey carried out in 1991 by the Institute of Social and Political Sciences of Charles University, one in six respondents expressed an interest in working abroad, at least for a short period of time. Even assuming that the conditions for such migration would not be acceptable to many of those who expressed such an interest, it is reasonable to say that the potential for labour migration from former Czechoslovakia is nevertheless enormous. As expected, the interest of respondents in working abroad varied greatly according to age and gender. The greatest interest appeared among respondents below 25 and decreased among older respondents. Among women, the interest in external migration was also lower. Germany, Switzerland, Austria, Sweden and the USA were the most frequently mentioned countries of destination.

The adoption of the new legislation in the field of migration has not yet led to any improvement in the collection of data. Table 6.8 thus only gives account of registered migrants in the period 1990–1.

Around one quarter of all emigrants moved to Germany, followed by Switzerland, Australia, Canada and Austria. Similarly, among immigrants

Table 6.8   External migration from Czechoslovakia, 1990–1

Year	Emigration			Immigration		
	Males	*Females*	*Total*	*Males*	*Females*	*Total*
1990	2,602	2,378	4,980	1,865	1,417	3,282
1991*	1,773	1,464	3,237	4,032	3,360	7,392

*Provisional data

Source: Federal Statistical Office.

to Czechoslovakia, the majority came from Germany (approximately 15 per cent), the former Soviet Union (around 10 per cent), Poland, Austria, the United States and Canada. The relatively significant share of immigrants coming from Western countries indicates that the main reason for their move is that it offers them the possibility of asking for the restitution of their former possessions. The Act of Extra-Judiciary Rehabilitation has been in effect since April 1991, and according to data released by the Czech Ministry of the Interior, 1030 foreigners were naturalised in the CR in 1991. 28.1 per cent were former citizens of the Soviet Union, 21.8 per cent of Greece, 17.7 per cent of Poland, 7 per cent of the United States and 6.3 per cent of Syria. Other states with a share lower than 5 per cent included Iraq, Bulgaria, Vietnam, Indonesia, Iran, and Jordan. Among immigrants from Poland and the former Soviet Union, family reunification is one of the main reasons for emigration to Czechoslovakia.

FOREIGNERS AND COMMUTERS

The number of foreigners with a permanent or long-term stay-permit in Czechoslovakia increased slightly during 1990 and 1991 (Tables 6.9, 6.10 and 6.11). The share of each nationality within the foreign resident population is usually in line with the share of nationalities among foreign workers

Table 6.9   Foreigners in Czechoslovakia with a permanent stay-permit

Country	31.12.1989	31.12.1990	31.12.1991
Poland	14,666	14,249	14,449
Former Soviet Union	8,514	8,678	9,135
Bulgaria	4,310	4,183	4,468
Greece	3,408	3,005	2,665
Hungary	1,656	1,656	—
Former Yugoslavia	1,258	1,368	1,593
Germany	1,102	1,128	1,111
Romania	744	1,022	1,757
Austria	570	547	—
Vietnam	329	451	535
Other	1,800	2,230	—
Total	37,957	38,517	40,907

Source: Federal Ministry of Interior (unpublished data).

Table 6.10   Foreigners in Czechoslovakia with a long-term stay-permit

Country	31.12.1989	31.12.1990	31.12.1991
Vietnam	920	923	968
Former Soviet Union	774	793	1,188
Poland	714	605	1,172
Bulgaria	369	484	237
Germany	406	364	377
Syria	339	334	—
USA	24	300	—
Mongolia	269	276	—
Former Yugoslavia	160	239	821
Iraq	200	232	—
Other	6,703	6,282	—
Totals	10,878	10,832	(12,135)

Source: Federal Ministry of Interior (unpublished data).

Table 6.11   Number of people in former Czechoslovakia (females in parenthesis) from selected countries obtaining a permit for permanent residence or long-term stay from 1.1.1992 to 30.6.1992

Country	Permanent stay	Long-term stay
Former Soviet Union	317 (209)	1,188 (315)
Poland	122 (56)	1,172 (103)
Vietnam	205 (25)	968 (182)
Former Yugoslavia	228 (13)	821 (146)
Gemrany	78 (28)	377 (65)
Bulgaria	45 (16)	237 (515)
Romania	31 (16)	159 (53)
Greece	21 (5)	19 (5)

Source: Federal Ministry of the Interior (unpublished data).

and with the cultural proximity to Czechoslovakia. Thus the highest proportion of foreigners with a permanent residence permit (37 per cent) is of Polish origin and corresponds to the higher share of Polish citizens among foreign workers (57 per cent in 1990). On the contrary, the proportion of workers from the former Soviet Union is low while their share among foreigners with a permanent stay permit (22 per cent) is second only to Polish

Table 6.12   Foreign workers in Czechoslovakia

Country	31.12.1990	31.12.1991	30.6.1992
Poland	54,813	16,777	7,168
Vietnam	33,970	9,908	5,483
Former Yugoslavia	2,983	1,899	1,307
Cuba	1,111	100	24
Mongolia	1,013	151	37
Hungary	799	283	96
Bulgaria	305	279	106
Angola	213	0	0
Former Soviet Union	58	308	193
Other	185	236	80
Totals	95,450	29,841	14,494

Source: Federal Ministry of the Interior (unpublished data).

citizens. The opposite trend can be observed among foreigners from Vietnam, who account for 36 per cent of the foreign workers but for only 19.5 per cent of the holders of a permanent stay permit.

The number of foreign workers decreased considerably after 1989. Foreign workers were employed mainly in the construction industry on the basis of commercial agreements.

The number of citizens from former Czechoslovakia working abroad on a permanent basis before 1989 was limited, as citizens are allowed to work abroad on the basis of intergovermental agreements or commercial contacts only. Their number was estimated at around 1,000. The number of people working for Czechoslovak organisations abroad has not been recorded but could reach much higher levels.

On the contrary, the situation of commuters evolved considerably after 1989. Many cross-border workers commute daily to neighboring Bavaria and Austria. Precise data on these flows are not available but it can reasonably be estimated that approximately 1,000 people commute every day from former Czechoslovakia. Frontier workers are not registered as such and some might be considered as unemployed in their country, hence benefiting from unemployment allowances in former Czechoslovakia.

The situation is quite different as regards seasonal workers; agreements have been concluded with Germany (i.e. Agreement of 1991 between the Czech Ministry of Labour and Social Affairs and the Federal Labour Office in Nuremberg) and Poland (i.e. Agreement of 1992 on the mutual employ-

Table 6.13 Number of seasonal workers from the Czech Republic who obtained a 'work promise' in Germany between April and July 1992, by age and economic sector

Age	−20	21–30	31–40	41–50	51–60	61–	n.a.	Total
Number	2,313	6,937	6,319	3,390	750	138	572	20,959

Economic Sector	Agriculture	Services	Construction	Other
Number	3,452	3,231	7,900	6,376

Source: Czech Ministry of Labour and Social Affairs (unpublished data).

ment of Czechoslovak and Polish citizens). Workers from the CR moving to Germany, who were registered by the Czech Ministry of Labour and Social Affairs, amounted to 20,000 between April and July 1992 (see Table 6.13). They were predominantly men (80 per cent) and were mainly employed in the construction industry. The majority of them was in the age group 21–40.

REFUGEES AND ASYLUM SEEKERS

A special group of immigrants who can be considered as refugees consists of people of Czech or Slovak descent returning from the Ukraine. The decision to resettle these compatriots living primarily in the most affected regions close to the Tchernobyl nuclear power station was taken at the beginning of 1990 by Czechoslovak humanitarian organisations. During 1991, almost 900 refugees resettled into 34 communities. It is estimated that the same number of people resettled in 1992. Discussions have also begun on the possibility of resettling Czechs and Slovaks from other parts of the former Soviet Union, particularly Moldavia and Belorussia.

Available data on refugees and asylum seekers originates from the Secretariat of the Representatives for Refugees. It only refers to those refugees who have transited through refugee camps and applied for a legal refugee status. A rather significant number of foreign 'tourists', however, extend their stay beyond the authorised 30 days without applying for any legal status. These overstayers, who take advantage of the open-border policy implemented between former Czechoslovakia and all Eastern European countries and the former Soviet Union,[1] are often involved in a variety of

Table 6.14   Refugees in former Czechoslovakia from selected countries received by refugee camps from August 1990 to 4 February 1992

Country	Males	Females	Total
Romania	1,611	518	2,129
Bulgaria	596	218	814
Former Soviet Union	371	200	571
Angola	182	31	213
Albania	80	32	112
Vietnam	76	12	88
Afghanistan	44	26	70
Iran	30	16	46
Zaier	18	8	26
Other	280	82	362
Totals	3,288	1,143	4,431

Source: Federal Ministry of the Interior (unpublished data).

illegal economic, or even criminal, activities. Their aim is to emigrate to Germany or Austria, although some are more interested in saving enough money to return to their countries of origin. Although it is difficult to assess their exact number, it is believed that up to 100,000 'false tourists' are currently established in the territory of former Czechoslovakia.

Looking at the official data, it can be said that the problem of refugees has not yet become a major issue in former Czechoslovakia. Refugee camps were established in August 1990, and by the beginning of February 1992 they had received a total of 4,431 refugees (Table 6.14).

Table 6.14 shows that almost half of the refugees came from Romania. Romanians also represented the most sizeable group of refugees in February 1992 (38 per cent) (Table 6.15). On the other hand, around 15 per cent only of Romanian refugees expressed a desire to stay in former Czechoslovakia permanently. A similar attitude was observed in the case of refugees from Bulgaria, who constitute the second largest group of refugees in former Czechoslovakia. The third largest group, with 13 per cent of all registered refugees who transited through refugee camps, came from the former Soviet Union; only 28 per cent were still living in the camps in February 1992, although they showed a higher tendency to remain in Czechoslovakia than Romanians and Bulgarians. The number of refugees from other countries has been far less significant.

Table 6.15   Refugees present in camps on in former Czechoslovakia 4 February 1992

Country	Males	Females	Total
Romania	196	119	315
Former Soviet Union	84	75	459
Bulgaria	60	40	100
Vietnam	54	7	61
Albania	18	12	30
Afghanistan	13	11	24
Angola	16	3	19
Zaire	14	4	18
Other	76	27	103
Totals	531	298	829

Source: Federal Ministry of the Interior (unpublished data).

Athough the number of officially registered refugees from former Yugoslavia is negligible, numerous groups of 'tourists' came from this country with a view to escaping war conflicts. Some are about to apply for refugee status in Western European countries. While living in former Czechoslovakia, they are in most cases granted a 'temporary protection status'.

Former Czechoslovakia grants refugee status in line with international recommendations, i.e. the 1951 UN Refugee Convention and the 1967 New York Protocol, both of which it ratified in October 1991. Altogether, 3,139 applications had been filled by the end of 1991. Refugee status was granted to 711 applicants (and 113 of their dependents), i.e. 22 per cent of all applications, most notably to Romanians and former Soviet nationals.

After 1989, Czechoslovakia became a country to which people come with various objectives: either to stay, or, more frequently, to continue on their way to some Western European country. The number of those coming to Czechoslovakia illegally, or with falsified documents, together with those who alone or with the help of smugglers, attempt to enter Germany or Austria illegally, has increased dramatically. Thus among the 10,291 people who tried to cross the Czechoslovak borders illegally during the first half of 1992, only 887 were planning to stay in Czechoslovakia, while 8,782 intended to cross the border to Germany (Table 6.16).

Table 6.16   Number of illegal crossings of Czechoslovak borders by various nationals in the first half of 1992

Country	January	February	March	April	May	June	Total
Romania	620	813	1,048	1,179	1,130	1,177	5,967
Bulgaria	100	208	346	267	327	453	1,701
Vietnam	91	60	51	43	71	71	387
Turkey	29	18	24	46	102	76	295
Philippines	81	134	61	10	0	0	286
Sri Lanka	16	67	26	33	43	35	220
Afghanistan	33	14	17	50	20	24	158
Czechoslovakia	15	16	24	33	12	23	123
Albania	10	10	29	38	14	18	119
Yugoslavia	20	22	9	20	33	13	117
China	12	19	18	7	9	46	111
Poland	6	30	15	12	12	19	94
Former Soviet Union	16	4	27	15	12	20	94
Other	74	45	66	74	69	80	408
Total	1,163	1,489	1,892	1,829	1,857	2,061	10,291

Source: Federal Ministry of the Interior (unpublished data).

CONCLUSIONS

During the last three years, Czechoslovakia became a transit country in terms of migration. Since the 1st of October 1992, the conditions under which foreigners may stay in and depart from Czechoslovakia has been regulated by the law of 4 March 1992. This law applies to all those who do not possess Czechoslovakian nationality, with the exception of those foreigners who have applied for or who were granted refugee status. The law defines three categories of stay permit:

1. a short-term permit, which is granted for up to 180 days;
2. a long-term permit, which is granted for the period necessary to achieve a given purpose (e.g. studies, medical cure, business etc.), and is renewable for a period of up to one year;
3. a permanent stay permit which can be granted for specific reasons, e.g. family reunification (if relatives hold a permanent stay-permit in former Czechoslovakia), and humanitarian reasons.

The problem of refugees and asylum seekers, at least in comparison with some neighbouring States, has only affected Czechoslovakia in a marginal manner. For the majority of refugees from Eastern Europe, Czechoslovakia is not yet an attractive state. Emigration from Czechoslovakia, on the other hand, which was at a reasonable level until 1992, is expected to increase. The labour migration potential is enormous and the on-going economic transformations, which generate increasing numbers of unemployed, are likely to stimulate it further. The December 1991 Agreement of Association between the European Community and the Czech and Slovak Republic, which will be transferred to the successor States, i.e. the Czech Republic and the Slovak Republic, is also likely to increase selected forms of labour emigration, albeit of a temporary nature.

Note

1. Until 1992, citizens of the former USSR intending to visit former Czechoslovakia had to obtain a personal invitation from a Czechoslovak national.

7 Former Yugoslavia
Vladimir Grecic

INTRODUCTION

Yugoslavia, before the outbreak of civil war, was in many ways similar to the other countries of Central and Eastern Europe. It was also very different, however, the most important difference being that it was the only former socialist country which allowed its citizens to leave the country without any restrictions. As a South-East European country with a tradition of emigration, it has therefore played a special role in European migration over the past 30 years. Migration of Yugoslav workers to Western Europe reached its peak in 1973–4. Since the first oil crisis of 1973–4, when restrictions on the inflow of foreign workers were imposed by Western European countries, the number of Yugoslav workers has stabilised at around one million (Grecic, 1989). According to official statistics, 1,062,388 Yugoslavs were established in the European OECD countries in 1990–1. The largest number (61.6 per cent) was in the Federal Republic of Germany, followed by Switzerland (13.3 per cent), Austria (11.8 per cent) and France (4.9 per cent).

Since mid-1991, the latest phase of population movements from former Yugoslavia has been marked by the migration of displaced people and refugees. This has included the massive displacement of 'minorities' within the affected areas.

THE YEARS OF FORCED YUGOSLAV MIGRATION: 1991–2

During the last few years, Western Europe has been confronted with an increasing inflow of former Yugoslavs migrating to the West for a variety of economic, political and other reasons. In spite of immigration restrictions in many countries of destination, the number of former Yugoslavs employed abroad grew in 1990 to lead to the biggest increase in their presence in European immigration countries since 1973 (SOPEMI, 1992: 88). The total number (over half of which were in Germany) rose by 11 per cent between 1989 and 1990, to reach 716,000 people. The largest growth in the number of workers took place in Switzerland, with a stock of 132,900 former Yugoslavs, 44,500 of whom were seasonal workers (SOPEMI, 1992: 88). Emigration of workers increased by a dramatic 160 per cent between 1989 and 1990 (from 26,400 to 69,600). Return migration (mainly of 'political' emigrants who felt safe to return home) also rose from 13,300 in 1989 to 17,300 in 1990. The net outflow in 1990 was thus 52,300, four times that of the previous year (SOPEMI, 1992: 88).

The civil war in Yugoslavia, which began in 1991, forced a greater number of people than ever before to try to escape, primarily to Western Europe. The main group of migrants from former Yugoslavia is now composed of refugees, and some figures estimate that more than 2.5 million people have had to leave their homes over the last two years (*'The Economist'*, September 19, 1992). In the context of this mass migration, resettlement of 'minorities' has played a significant role.

The number of Yugoslav refugees outside former Yugoslavia was estimated at 531,412 in August 1992 (*'The Economist'*, September 19, 1992), the largest proportion of which was established in the Federal Republic of Germany (220,000), followed by Switzerland (70,450), Austria (57,500), Hungary (50,000), Sweden (47,600), Italy (17,000), and Turkey (15,000). The majority of the refugees is young and well educated and hence exerts an additional pressure on Western European labour markets.

Most of the 'Yugoslavs' have fled no farther than the neighbouring Yugoslav republics. According to data released by UNCHR, 1,979,476 Yugoslav refugees were in former Yugoslavia in September 1992 (Table 7.1).

Table 7.1 Yugoslav refugees in former Yugoslavia, September 1992

Present location	*From:*		
	Croatia	*Bosnia-Herzegovina*	*Total*
Croatia	271,798	335,985	638,109
UN-patrolled areas	87,000	—	87,000
Serbia	162,337	252,130	414,467
Bosnia-Herzegovina	93,000	588,000	681,000
Montenegro	6,743	50,857	57,600
Slovenia	1,000	69,000	70,000
Macedonia	2,500	28,800	31,300
Totals	624,378	1,324,772	1,979,476

THE MAIN CAUSES OF THE RECENT YUGOSLAV MIGRATION

From 1990 to 1992, international migration was dominated by political uncertainty and war. With the breakup of the Yugoslav state, the distinction between internal and international migration disappeared. Conflictual relations between the republics also affected the collection and publication of official data, thus compromising any attempt to present an aggregate picture of international movements (SOPEMI, 1992: 88).

The war, which began in the immediate aftermath of the Slovene and Croatian declarations of independence on 25 June 1991, progressively reduced the chances for co-existence of the main Yugoslav nations. At the same time, it presented the international community with a seemingly intractable problem, involving complex issues of ethnicity, sovereignty, self-determination, borders and diplomatic recognition (Zametica, 1992: 3). In this sense it may be said that the Yugoslav crisis has two dimensions – one internal and one international – which largely coincide with the development of the crisis over time (Simic, 1992a). On the internal level, the civil war in Yugoslavia is the result of the long-lasting crisis in Yugoslav communism and rivalry between the republics' political nomenclatures, which for decades systematically used nationalism and unsolved ethnic and border conflicts between the Yugoslav nations as the main instrument of political mobilisation and legitimacy of their power. On the international level, the Yugoslav crisis coincided with profound changes in Europe after 1989, which soon brought about the internationalisation of this crisis. Consequently, the war in Yugoslavia presented the first opportunity for leading political actors to redefine their interests and policy in the New Europe, above all towards the Balkan region (Simic, 1992a). The former division of the European continent between the East and the West was gradually replaced by a new three-unit division consisting of Central, Eastern and South-East Europe (Simic, 1992a). Under such circumstances, the attitude of certain international political actors towards the Yugoslav crisis was strongly influenced by their new security agenda and geopolitical interests. Hence in Yugoslavia, the European Community endorsed the Slovene and Croatian secessions which changed the map of South-Eastern Europe. Yet at the same time, it insisted on the inviolability of Yugoslavia's internal boundaries, with the provision – somewhat meaningless in the current Yugoslav context – that boundaries could be modified by agreement. What is more, by condemning the use of force to redraw frontiers within Yugoslavia while recognising Slovenia and Croatia, the EC retrospectively legitimised the force used by the secessionists to break-up the country (Zametica, 1992: 78). The prevention of armed conflicts therefore constituted the weakest aspect, by far, of international responses to the Yugoslav crisis.

The Republic of Slovenia, which is considered the richest republic of former Yugoslavia (with a GNP per capita of $12,520, more than 8 times that of Kosovo, the poorest part of Yugoslavia) has not experienced too great an emigration of its nationals, nor has it been significantly affected by ethnic conflicts and movements of displaced persons. In fact, 88 per cent of its population is composed of Slovenians, with the rest made up of Croats, Hungarians, Italians, and, to a lesser extent, Germans and Serbs. The Republic has an area of 20,251 km² and 1,974,000 inhabitants. Most of its inhabitants are Catholics, with less than 5 per cent adhering to the Orthodox faith. Slovenia proclaimed independence on 25 June 1991.

Croatia is the second republic which seceded from former Yugoslavia. The Republic of Croatia occupies an area of 56,538 km² (22.1 per cent of the territory of former Yugoslavia) with a population of 4,763,900 inhabitants (according to the 1991 Census). 78.1 per cent of the population is composed of Croats, 12.2 per cent of Serbs, 2.2 per cent of 'Yugoslavs' (a group from various national backgrounds which appears in all republics and which considers itself as a new ethnic group promoting the unity of Yugoslavia), and 7.5 per cent of various other ethnic groups. Croatia, like Slovenia, is mainly a Catholic republic, with the exception of Serbs, who are Orthodox, and a small number of Muslims. The Republic of Croatia is, together with Slovenia, one of the richest ($7,110 of GNP per capita) and most industrialised republics of former Yugoslavia. It is also, however, the republic with the strongest tradition of emigration. According to the 1991 Census, 38 per cent of all Yugoslav citizens employed abroad came from this republic, and the outbreak of war in mid-1991 generated further substantial flows of refugees from Croatia.

The Republic of Bosnia-Herzegovina is the least homogeneous part of former Yugoslavia. It is a multi-ethnic state consisting of Muslims (43.5 per cent of the total population), Serbs (31.3 per cent), Croats (17.2 per cent) and other nations and minorities (8 per cent). It occupies an area of 51,129 km² and is considered to be very poorly developed (its GNP per capita in 1990 was estimated at $3,590, one-third that of Slovenia). The Republic of Bosnia-Herzegovina has been further affected by the civil war and by hundreds of thousands of Bosnians fleeing abroad.

Macedonia, which is not yet fully recognised by the international community, is the least developed republic of former Yugoslavia. It occupies a total area of 25,713 km² with a population of 2,033,964 consisting of groups such as: Macedonians (1,314,283), Albanians (427,314), Turks (97,416), Serbs (44,159), Gypsies (55,575) and others (95,218). Macedonia is an emigration region by tradition. Today, the causes of emigration are mainly economically-driven and the majority of emigrants left for overseas countries.

The Federal Republic of Yugoslavia was proclaimed on April 26, 1992. It is composed of only two of the former Yugoslav republics – Serbia and Montenegro – and covers an area of 102,173 km². According to the 1991 Census, its population totals 10,406,742 people or 42.5 per cent of the total population of former Yugoslavia. Today, this number is probably higher, since ethnic conflicts and civil war in Croatia and Bosnia-Herzegovina have prompted a large number of people to seek shelter on the territory of the Federal Republic of Yugoslavia. In late September 1992, UNCHR had registered in the Federal Republic of Yugoslavia 414,467 refugees from other republics, in addition to those who were not registered but had found shelter with relatives. A large number of these refugees aim to settle permanently in the Federal Republic of Yugoslavia.

According to the 1991 Census, approximately 251,000 people from the Federal Republic of Yugoslavia were living and working mainly in Western European countries (figures for Kosovo are only estimates as Albanians boycotted the Census). The Federal Republic of Germany accepted almost 61.6 per cent of the total number of 'Yugoslavs' who migrated to fifteen receiving countries, as migration from former Yugoslavia had played an important role for the Federal Republic of Germany even before the recent political developments.

Contemporary migration from former Yugoslavia can thus be attributed to substantial push factors which reflect the dramatic ethnic conflicts. The sharp aggravation of inter-ethnic tension over the last three years has resulted in tragic events in many regions of what was formerly Yugoslavia. On the other hand, transition towards a market economy has also created high unemployment in the individual republics, and it is very likely that growing unemployment will induce many workers from these regions to emigrate. Finally, demographic factors do not appear to play any significant role in movements of people from the republics of former Yugoslavia (except for Kosovo), given that the overall increase in the size of the population of working age is rather moderate.

Table 7.2 Population of former Yugoslavia according to ethnic nationality (thousands and percentages)

Nationality	1921	1948	1953	1961	1971	1981
Serbs		6,547.1	7,056.9	7,806.2	8,143.2	8,140.5
%		41.5	41.7	42.1	39.7	36.3
Croats	8,911.5*	3,784.4	3,975.6	4,293.8	4,526.8	4,428.0
%	74.7*	24	23.5	23.1	22.1	19.8
Muslim	—	808.9	998.7	973.0	1,729.9	1,999.9
%	—	5.1	5.9	5.2	8.4	8.9
Macedonians	—	810.1	893.2	1,045.5	1,194.8	1,341.6
%	—	5.1	5.3	5.6	5.8	6.0
Montenegrans	—	425.7	466.1	513.8	508.8	579.0
%	—	2.7	2.8	2.8	2.5	2.6
Slovenes	1,020.0	1,415.4	1,487.1	1,589.2	1,678.0	1,753.6
%	8.5	9.0	8.8	8.6	8.2	7.8
Albanians	439.7	750.4	754.2	914.7	1,309.5	1,730.9
%	3.8	4.8	4.5	4.9	6.4	7.7
Germans	505.8	55.3	60.5	20.0	12.8	8.7
%	4.2	0.4	0.4	0.1	0.0	0.0
Hungarians	467.7	496.5	502.2	504.4	477.4	426.9
%	3.9	3.2	3.0	2.7	2.3	1.9
Romanians	231.1	64.1	60.4	60.9	58.6	55.0
%	1.9	0.4	0.4	0.3	0.3	0.2
Turks	150.3	98.0	259.5	183.0	127.9	101.3
%	1.3	0.6	1.5	1.0	0.6	0.5
Slovakians	115.3	83.6	85.0	86.4	83.7	80.3
%	1.3	0.5	0.5	0.5	0.4	0.4
Czechs	—	39.5	34.5	30.3	24.6	19.6
%	—	0.2	0.2	0.2	0.1	0.1
Yugoslavians	—	—	—	317.1	273.1	1,219.0
%	—	—	—	1.7	1.3	5.4
Romanians	—	72.7	84.7	31.7	78.5	168.2
%	—	0.5	0.5	0.2	0.4	0.7
Other	143.4	320.8	208.6	179.3	295.3	375.1
%	1.2	2.0	1.2	1.0	1.4	1.7
Totals	11,984.9	15,772.1	16,935.6	18,549.3	20,523.0	22,427.6

* Serbs, Croats and other nationalities were accounted for together.

Source: F. Glatz: *Die Regelung von Nationalitaten und Minderheitenkonflinkten in mittel Osteuropa* (Europa Institut, Budapest, 1992).

THE EFFECTS OF YUGOSLAV MIGRATORY FLOWS

If ethnic tension continues, it may result in waves of migration from former Yugoslavia. Political, economic, religious and cultural factors all combine to motivate an increasing number of people to leave the Yugoslav area. There are many minorities in former Yugoslavia with a strong ethnic consciousness and a feeling of belonging to a geographical area other than the one in which they are currently established.

Ethnic minority problems have produced at least two effects:

- Unemployment in the ethnic motherlands is rising under the pressure of minorities from other countries.
- The number of asylum seekers and refugees in the EC countries is growing.

However, following decisions taken at the Maastricht Council, asylum seekers and immigrants will face tougher rules on entering the European Community. Moreover, the Conference on Security and Co-operation in Europe (CSCE) neglected the new migratory processes and only reaffirmed the protection and promotion of the rights of migrants who are already established in countries of immigration (See: CSCE Documents from Copenhagen 1990, Paris 1990, and Moscow 1991).

The effects of migration on Yugoslav republics consist, primarily, of both a decrease in unemployment and an increase in remittances in convertible currencies (Grecic, 1990). Although remittances can be seen as an effective response to market forces providing a transition to an otherwise unsustainable development (Keely, 1989), there is a general feeling that the net balance of positive and negative consequences may be unfavourable (Okolski, 1990). In the case of Yugoslavia, the 'brain drain' effects of increased migration are quite obvious, together with family separation, hard work, xenophobia and unfavourable living conditions in Western Europe (Grecic, 1992).

Negative effects on receiving countries can also be identified in the case of immigration of the labour force in the shadow economy. The shadow economy and clandestine immigration often nourish each other (Golini, 1990).

FUTURE POLICY CONTEXT

1. The new European migration policy explicitly supports all forms of organised movement of labour force, particularly that from the East.

The basic motivation behind this policy lies in the fact that European immigration countries are interested in engaging cheap, skilled labour as well as highly educated people from the countries of Central and Eastern Europe.

2. The new states of former Yugoslavia all share the same interest in employing their workers abroad. They all wish to participate in an organised way in the European labour market, on the basis of the principles of the new migration policy.

3. The new states of former Yugoslavia are also interested in financing projects and programmes as a way of assisting in the elimination of some of the causes of migration, and as a way of opening new economic perspectives in the regions of emigration.

4. Even after the disintegration of Yugoslavia, the newly emerged states are still interested in implementing the interstate agreements concluded between former Yugoslavia and the countries of immigration. These agreements not only form a basis for future cooperation with Western European countries, but also guarantee the employment and protection of former Yugoslavs abroad.

5. The newly created states perceive the importance of education, vocational training, and the dissemination of information and social services as a way of protecting the cultural identity and the labour competitiveness of their citizens. These states have thus developed teaching programmes in their mother tongue, together with other activities aimed at safeguarding the national and cultural identity of their youth. They have also organised various channels of information for their citizens in the countries of immigration. This information refers primarily to the conditions of employment upon return to the countries of origin, and also aims at keeping the ties with the homeland alive.

6. The position and protection of citizens of former Yugoslavia in Western Europe have evolved since 1991 due to changing living and working conditions in the countries of immigration (particularly after the unification of the two Germanies), and due to political developments in former Yugoslavia. The countries of immigration have accepted increased responsibility for the protection of migrants, including the teaching of their mother tongue and their culture, thus reducing the possibilities for direct action on the part of the countries of origin. On the other hand, the position of citizens of former Yugoslavia is still insecure as a result of increased xenophobia in Western Europe.

7. The sanctions imposed by the UN against the Federal Republic of Yugoslavia have produced adverse effects on the employment of workers from this republic in the countries of immigration. However, it can

be expected that the countries of immigration will shortly take political decisions to define the position of about half a million citizens from former Yugoslavia who are civil war refugees and who exert pressure on the Western European labour markets.

8. Participation of former Yugoslavs in the Western European labour market implies the reciprocal creation of conditions for free circulation of foreign labour in former Yugoslavia, together with measures to prevent the illegal employment of foreigners and to protect asylum seekers and refugees. Slovenia, Croatia and other newly created states are in fact on the point of considering the position of citizens of the Federal Republic of Yugoslavia established on their territory.

All of these challenges call for a combination of actions which take account of the interests of both the receiving countries and the newly created states of former Yugoslavia. Such actions might consist of:

– Mitigating the root causes of the refugee crisis and the mass population movements through UN or bilateral cooperation, including cooperation on a humanitarian level.
– Increasing economic and other assistance with a view to reducing the burden of the states of former Yugoslavia. This should include the peaceful settlement of Yugoslav regional conflicts, creating the conditions for economic growth by abolishing economic sanctions and trade protectionism, and alleviating poverty. Although all of the newly created states of former Yugoslavia are in dire need of foreign investment, these economies must be stabilised and the restructuring process brought to completion before investment can be increased. This process of economic restructuring has currently reached very different stages in the individual states. Official capital flows will be necessary in order to support the adjustment process and ease the social cost of transition toward a market-oriented economy. Private flows, particularly foreign direct investment that could entail technology transfer, are also needed, although, until the reforms gain credibility and output begins to increase, private external flows are unlikely to increase significantly (particularly given the debt situation of some of the states).

While not sufficient in itself, Western assistance will be crucial in helping former Yugoslavia to overcome the obstacles it faces. Reform strategies will be developed and implemented more easily through a structured dialogue within each state and with the assistance of multilateral institutions, including the International Monetary Fund (IMF) and Islamic sources, the

World Bank, GATT, the Organization for Economic Cooperation and Development (OECD), the UN Economic Commission for Europe, the Conference on Security and Cooperation in Europe (CSCE), the European Community (EC), and the Council of Europe.

CONCLUSION

Migration from the Yugoslav area is a phenomenon which affects all Western European countries, particularly receiving countries. Accordingly, peaceful action to resolve the Yugoslav crisis should be taken jointly by all countries concerned. There are many important reasons for examining the complex issues related to asylum seekers, refugees, economic refugees, illegal migrants and migrants as a whole. Although priority should be given to economic factors, it would be a grave mistake to believe that non-economic issues (such as the protection of the rights of all migrants and the protection of minorities) do not constitute major elements of a policy aimed at reducing migration pressures in former Yugoslavia.

In the light of current determinants, it can be anticipated that migration from former Yugoslavia over the near future will be characterised by:

-   The continued ethnic emigration of certain national minorities who are dissatisfied with their position in the republics of the former Yugoslavia;
-   The continued emigration mainly of skilled labour, which will aggravate the brain drain from the former Yugoslav republics. This flow will run in parallel to the emigration of lesser skilled labour, which labour will be affected by the growing poverty in the majority of the newly created states of former Yugoslavia.

References

Brunner, G. (1992). 'Minority Problems and Policies in East-Central and South-East Europe', Universitat zu Koln (mimeo).

Council of Europe (1991). *Recent Demographic Developments in Europe*, Council of Europe Press, Luxembourg.

Glatz, F. (1992). 'Die Regelung von Nationalitaten und Minderheitenkonflikten in Mittel und Osteuropa', Europa Institut, Budapest (mimeo).

Golini, A. *et al.* (1990). 'South–North Migration with Special Reference to Europe', *International Migration*, 29 (2).

Grecic, V. (1992). 'Mass Migration from Eastern Europe: A Challenge to the "West"?' in *The Geography of European Migrations*, ed. Russell King, Belhaven, London, pp. 135–51.

Grecic, V. (1991). 'East–West Migration and Its Possible Influence on the South-North Migration', *International Migration*, 29 (2).

Grecic, V. (1990). 'The Importance of Migrant Workers' and Emigrants' Remittances for the Yugoslav Economy', *International Migration*, 28 (1).

Grecic, V. (1989). *The Migration and Integration of the Foreign Population in the Countries of Northern, Western and Central Europe*, IIPE, Belgrade.

Keely, Ch. B. (1989). 'Remittances From Labor Migration: Evaluations, Performance and Implications', *International Migration Review*, 23 (Fall).

Kussbach, E. (1992). 'European Challenge: East–West Migration', *International Migration Review*, 26 (2).

Heisbourg, F. (1991). 'Population Movements in Post-Cold War Europe', in *Global Responsibilities: Europe in Tomorrow's World*, ed. Werner Weidenfeld and Josef Jannings, Bertelsmann Foundation Publishers, Gutersloh.

Mesic, M. and Hersak, E. (1992). 'Certain Socio-Political Circumstances which may affect East–West European Migration (with the case of Croatia)', Paper presented at the International Conference on Mass Migration in Europe: Implications in the East and West, Vienna, March 5–7.

Okolski, M. (1990). 'Migratory movement from countries of Central and Eastern Europe', Council of Europe, Strasbourg (paper).

Rhode, B. (1991). *East–West Migration/Brain Drain*, COST Social Science, Brussels.

Salt, J. (1991). 'Current and Future International Migration Trends Affecting Europe', paper presented at the *4th Conference of European Ministers Responsible for Migration* affairs, September 17–18, Luxembourg.

Simic, P. (1992). 'Civil War in Yugoslavia: From Local Conflict to European Crisis', in *The Political and Strategic Implications of the State Crisis in Central and Eastern Europe*, ed. Armund Clerse and Andrei Kutanov, Luxemburg, Institute for European and International Studies, pp. 190–234.

Simic, P. (1992a). 'Civil War in Yugoslavia: From Local Conflict to European Crisis' (mimeo).

SOPEMI (1991). *Continuous Reporting System on Migration (SOPEMI) 1990*, OECD, Paris.

SOPEMI (1992). *SOPEMI. Trends in International Migration*, OECD, Paris.

Zagar, M. (1992). 'Local Government and Minorities in Different Parts (Republics) of the Territory of (Former) Yugoslavia', *ToD Newsletter*, 5.

Zametica, J. (1992). 'The Yugoslav Conflict: An Analysis of the Causes of the Yugoslav War, the Policies of the Republics and the Regional and International Implications of the Conflict', *Adelphi*, paper 270.

Part III
Western Europe

Introduction
Solon Ardittis

Part III is divided into five chapters devoted to Germany, Austria, Italy, the United Kingdom and Switzerland and the EFTA countries. In the absence of a coordinated European immigration policy, the analysis of the way in which major Western European receiving countries currently approach new migration from the East helps to anticipate both the levels and nature of future immigration from Central and Eastern Europe.

The Western European countries reviewed in this section can be divided into three groups.

The first one is composed of Germany, Austria and Italy. Since the 1989 revolutions, Germany has had to manage the effects of both the reunification and the substantial levels of ethnic German immigration; Austria, and to a lesser extent Italy, have experienced substantial levels of immigration of former Yugoslavia and other Eastern European, mostly illegal, labour migrants.

In all of these countries, new East–West migration has signified a process of policy revisions characterised, in particular, by:

- The adoption or discussion of new legislation to increase restrictions on immigration;
- The adoption or discussion of new measures to curb growing illegal immigration;
- The adoption or discussion of new measures to confront growing xenophobic sentiments and decreasing economic competitiveness caused by significant levels of migration from the East.

The United Kingdom, which constitutes the second group, illustrates the rationale of an immigration policy which is quite distinct from that implemented in other EC member states. The British ambivalence over European unity and the signing of the Maastricht Treaty are duly analysed. In particular, the chapter on the UK analyses the way in which the British Home Office is resisting the idea that immigration policy should be subsumed under a European policy, and is pressing EC ministers to force asylum seekers to find protection from within their own countries of origin.

The third group is composed of Switzerland and the EFTA countries. Despite Switzerland's rejection, by public referendum, of European integration, the current negotiations between EC and EFTA member states on the mechanics of the European Economic Area (EEA) help to anticipate the contours of the future coordinated immigration policy at the EURO-19 (or 18) level. In particular, the chapter on Switzerland and the EFTA countries analyses the way in which the restriction of free movement of labour to EEA citizens only, by preventing the improvement of welfare in Eastern Europe and by creating barriers to trade from non-EEA countries, will increase migratory pressures in Eastern Europe and affect, in the long term, the EEA economies.

Part III thus provides the main policy parameters of East–West migration from the point of view of the receiving countries. It allows the identification of both the singular national characteristics of immigration pressures in Western European countries (according to the policy traditions of each country *vis-à-vis* immigration) and the areas for which needs for better European coordination of migration-related measures and long-term policies have become pressing. The specific areas and tenets for policy coordination at the European level are then addressed in Part IV.

8 Germany
Elmar Honekopp

Since World War II, Germany has accepted millions of fugitives and immigrants from different ethnic origins and nationalities, from all parts of Europe and the world. Since the political upheavals in Eastern Europe, Germany has once more been the target of large-scale immigration movements: Between 1989 and 1992, four million people migrated to Germany at a rate of one million per year.

This chapter describes and analyses immigration trends in Germany before and after the 1989 revolutions; it discusses the economic effects and the political reactions which such sizeable population movements have generated and assesses their likely evolution over the near future, taking into account the foreseeable needs of the German economy for additional foreign labour.

IMMIGRATION TO GERMANY BEFORE THE POLITICAL CHANGES IN EASTERN EUROPE: A SHORT SURVEY

The present-day difficulties and the political discussions which the pressure of large-scale immigration from the East have generated in Germany can only be understood in the light of traditional immigration movements since World War II. Six major immigration phases can be identified:

The first one, from 1945 to 1950, is composed of movements of refugees and displaced persons from the former German Eastern regions. Approximately eight million refugees migrated to Germany during this period.

During the second phase, from 1950 to 1961 (the year in which the Berlin wall was erected), large numbers of fugitives and *Ubersiedler* migrated from the German Democratic Republic to the West. This period also witnessed the first immigration movements of *Aussiedler* from the Soviet Union, the result of special arrangements concluded by Chancellor Adenauer with the Soviet authorities.

Whereas immigration during the first two phases was mainly composed of people of German origin, the third phase, from the end of the 1950s to 1973, was characterised by high levels of immigration of foreign workers.

These 'guest-workers', as they came to be called, moved to Germany within the framework of bilateral recruitment agreements with Italy, Greece, Yugoslavia, Turkey, Spain, Portugal, Morocco and Tunisia. These agreements came to an end after the outbreak of the oil crisis in 1973.

The fourth phase, which lasted until the late 1970s, was determined by the consequences of the recruitment ban, which witnessed the emergence of new forms of immigration, i.e. that of the family members of migrant workers. Family reunion flows naturally contributed to extending the stay of guest-workers in Germany.

The fifth phase, which lasted from the beginning of the 1980s until 1988, was characterised by two very different developments: firstly, by a consolidation of immigration flows of *Aussiedlers*, mainly from Poland, the former Soviet Union and Romania; and secondly, by a marked increase in the number of asylum seekers from Turkey, Poland and Romania.

The last phase, which has been in effect since 1988, has so far consisted of a series of events, i.e.: an increasing influx of *Aussiedler* from Eastern Europe; extremely large migration movements of *Ubersiedlers* from the former GDR; even larger movements of foreigners mainly from Poland and the former Soviet Union; and increasing numbers of asylum seekers from former Yugoslavia, and from Africa and Asia.

In short, between 1950 and 1992, about 4 million *Ubersiedler* from the former GDR and 2.7 million *Aussiedler* from Eastern European countries migrated to Germany. This is in addition to the 4.5 million foreigners who migrated to Germany between 1960 and 1992.

This brief account amply demonstrates that immigration from Eastern Europe has always played an important role in Germany and is not a feature of the recent political changes. What has changed, however, is the political reactions to such sizeable immigration. Whereas immigration during the cold war era was consistently approved of from a political standpoint, movements after the 1989 revolutions, as the next sections will show, have gradually generated increasing discontent among the German population and a new political thinking among the German authorities.

PRESENT-DAY IMMIGRATION AGAINST THE BACKGROUND OF THE POLITICAL UPHEAVAL IN EASTERN EUROPE AND ITS EFFECT ON POPULATION AND EMPLOYMENT

Germany was in fact affected by numerous changes in Eastern Europe far earlier than 1989. Above all, the situation in Poland at the beginning of the 1980s and the struggle between Solidarnosc and the communist establishment led to waves of emigration to Germany as well as to other Western European and non-European countries. As far as Germany is concerned, the migrants of that time included ethnic Germans as well as non-German Poles. For example in 1981, migration reached its first peak with 46,000 ethnic Germans. However, in that same year, about 93,000 non-German Poles also came to Germany, mostly as fugitives.

Throughout the early 1980s, about ten thousand migrants came from Romania, two-thirds of whom were ethnic Germans and one-third non-German Romanians. The German government paid around 10,000 DM per ethnic German to the Romanian government which claimed back its investment costs in educating these ethnic Germans. During the second half of the 1980s, with the beginning of the liberalisation process in Poland, immigration from that country also started to increase, primarily involving Polish nationals, then ethnic Germans.

Despite the steady East–West migration movements before the revolutions in Eastern Europe, 1989 brought about new migratory phenomena: first, more and more Poles came to the West, mainly to sell and re-sell their goods on the so-called Polish markets, or to seek – legally or illegally – employment; second, hundreds of thousands of people from the former GDR came to Germany via Hungarian and Czechoslovakian borders, and later on by crossing the German borders directly; third, immigration of ethnic Germans started to double from one year to the next; finally, the number of asylum seekers from Eastern Europe, Turkey and non-European areas (especially from some countries in Asia and Black Africa) reached unprecedented levels. In 1989, in short, almost one million more people immigrated to Germany than left it (including *Aussiedlers* from Eastern Europe, *Ubersiedlers* from the GDR and all foreigners with different statuses) and figures for all the following years until 1993 show similar levels of net immigration.

From a non-German standpoint, the distinction between immigration of ethnic Germans and foreign immigrants from Eastern Europe may seem pointless. In reality both groups of immigrants until recently benefited from various advantages which other groups did not have: Eastern European foreigners who came to Germany could, until 1993, enter Germany on the grounds of political persecution, whether or not they were actually granted formal refugee status. Until a few years ago, these immigrants were also allowed to look for employment straightaway. In a way, people immigrating from Eastern Europe as *Aussiedler* were sure of being immediately recognised as Germans and, by extension, of accessing the German labour market and social benefits. Indeed, over 90 per cent of *Aussiedlers* who immigrated to Germany were definitively recognised as Germans.

Statistics, however, show that the increase in emigration to Eastern Europe from Germany has paralleled the increase in immigration from Eastern Europe to Germany. This indicates a high turnover among migrants, which itself points to the fact that immigration to Germany is often of short duration. Emigration towards Eastern Europe can be explained by the difficulty in finding employment in Germany, by the rejection of certain asylum applications, but also by the desire of some old-time Eastern European immigrants to return to their countries of origin after the liberalisation process of 1989 (this is particularly true of Poles, whose relative share among the Eastern European immigrant population in Germany is decreasing).

THE EFFECTS OF RECENT IMMIGRATION ON GERMANY'S DEMOGRAPHIC AND INTEGRATION ISSUES

Although the natural increase in the resident population of Germany continues to be negative (for example in 1992 the population decreased by 75,000 people if we include the new German Länder), the population effects of post-1989 migratory movements cannot be assessed without comparing the Eastern and the Western parts of Germany. Given the fact that the trend towards permanent migration from the former GDR to West Germany is persisting and that only a few of the new immigrants (*Aussiedlers* and Eastern European foreigners) choose to migrate to Eastern Germany, most of the burden of new immigration from the East rests on the Western part of Germany. Thus in 1992, the population of Western Germany was estimated at around 65.5 million, with a growth rate of about 1.5 per cent over the last few years.

Although a detailed analysis of the effects of recent migratory processes from Eastern Europe and elsewhere in terms of integration policies should obviously look at the specific sub-groups of the new German and foreign immigrants, official statistics do not keep separate records of *Aussiedlers* once they are recognised as Germans. What official statistics show, however, is that the foreign population increased markedly after 1989: it represented 10 per cent of the population of Western Germany in 1992, compared with a proportion of 8 per cent in 1989. In absolute figures, the Eastern European segment of the foreign population in Germany increased from 400,000 in 1989 to 720,000 in 1992.

Even though the effects of such large-scale immigration on different sub-systems of German society have been considerable, the restless political discussions which such immigration has generated (and continues to generate) in the German parliament, among political parties and in the public opinion indicate that policy-makers in Germany have not yet succeeded in mastering and alleviating the adverse effects of growing immigration waves. Of course, mastery of this phenomenon is also greatly influenced by the financial burden which reunification has inflicted upon West Germany's national budget. Thus large-scale immigration from the East has created an enormous demand for housing, additional school classes and special language and 'cultural' courses, in addition, of course, to additional jobs and special labour market-related integration measures. But the lack of housing is increasing, the school budget is about to be reduced and competition in the labour market is extremely tough. Even the budget for language courses destined for *Aussiedlers* is now being reduced. Xenophobic sentiments among certain segments of German society are, of course, not indifferent to such budgetary cut-backs.

THE NEW MIGRANTS IN GERMANY'S LABOUR MARKET

As in most other types of international migration, recent immigration from Eastern Europe is mainly economically driven, although civil war and ethnic tensions in former Yugoslavia and specific areas of the former Soviet Union have also acted as powerful push factors. But because of the overall economic and social situation prevailing in Eastern Europe since 1989, the pressure to work abroad, at least for a limited period of time, has been very high. Although emigration can often relieve pressure on the labour markets of the countries of origin, immigration to West Germany has to a great extent involved the young and highly qualified East European nationals. The loss of the most active and qualified people, if it were to continue and expand, would clearly contribute to reducing the potential for development of the native countries. This is particularly true since the knowledge and competence of the brightest nationals are increasingly required to support the development of new enterprises and structures.

Among the Western European countries, Germany has by far provided the largest number of jobs for new Eastern European migrants. In most other countries, and if we except clandestine migrants, employment of Eastern Europeans has not influenced in any significant way the functioning of national labour markets. In the Federal Republic of Germany, there was an increase of 1.9 million people (or 9 per cent) in total employment between 1989 and 1992. The increase in employment of foreigners was 20 per cent, while the increase related specifically to Eastern European workers was 260 per cent during the same period. And these figures probably do not include a significant portion of the Eastern European active population: in particular, they do not include a number of seasonal workers in agriculture and tourism, who are recruited during the summer (employment statistics are only collected in June each year) and who do not always contribute to the social security system; similarly, these statistics do not include project-tied workers. It can thus be estimated that the actual Eastern European workforce in Germany is double the size shown by official statistics.

The Federal Republic of Germany has concluded treaties with almost every Eastern European country, which treaties have allowed, to a limited extent, temporary employment possibilities and migration for education and on-the-job training. These treaties have touched, in particular, upon the following employment categories:

- Project-tied work (i.e. execution of a project by foreign companies employing their own workers): the total number of foreigners who are allowed to work within this category is, currently, 100,000, with different quotas for each sending country. In 1992, there were some 95,000 workers employed under this category, but political pressure in Germany is likely to decrease this number in the near future.
- Seasonal work: foreigners can work in Germany for up to three months per year subject to the agreement of the respective labour administrations. More than 200,000 people, mainly from former Czechoslovakia, Hungary and Poland were employed as seasonal workers in 1992 (the number will be similar in 1993). However, the levels of seasonal workers are due to decrease since this type of work will soon be restricted to specific sectors (e.g. agriculture and restaurants).
- Work in border areas: in the border areas (i.e. within a distance of up to 50 km), workers from Poland and former Czechoslovakia are allowed to work in Germany (with the agreement of the respective labour administrations) if they return daily to their normal residence in their countries of origin or if they do not work in Germany for more than two days per week. In 1992, there were about 12,000 border workers in the Bavarian-Czechoslovakian border areas.
- Guest-Worker agreements: the aim of this fourth category is to enable Eastern European workers to improve their vocational skills (occupational or language) through short stays in Germany of up to one-and-a-half years. The beneficiaries must have completed a given vocational training cycle in their countries of origin and have a basic knowledge of German. They must be between 18 and 40 years of age. The following national quotas have been established: 1,000 guest-workers from the

Czech republic and Slovakia together, 1,000 from Poland, 1,500 from Hungary, and other quotas for a number of other countries. In 1992, no more than 3,600 workers benefited from this scheme.
- Finally, there is a small programme on the employment of nurses, which in 1992 enabled 1,500 nurses to come and work in Germany.

The effects of some of these schemes, particularly the seasonal and project-tied contracts, have often been perceived as negative. There have been indications of illegal lending of workers or of illegal prolongations of stay. There are also fears that these schemes might produce negative effects on wages because of the low wages which are offered to these workers and because of the concentration of seasonal workers in specific industries. These fears are also justified by the regional concentration of border workers and by the concentration of project-tied workers in the construction sector.

From the standpoint of the German authorities, however, the fundamental aim of such schemes has been to help relieve the pressure on the Eastern European labour markets and, at the same time, to channel the growing, and to some extent illegal, migration flows. It can be said that these aims have in part been achieved in Germany.

However, the example of guest-worker agreements in Germany also confirms the difficulty in implementing political measures which attempt to link migration with the development of the countries of origin: the idea of using temporary migration as a means of improving the vocational qualifications of migrants who are meant to return to their countries of origin has so far only rarely produced the expected results. The qualified migrant workers who, from the start of their migratory process, will agree to return to their countries of origin after only a short stay in the country of employment are few and far between. On the contrary, most of the qualified workers will be prepared, with a view to extending their stay in Western Europe, to accept jobs which do not correspond to their qualifications. These lessons had already been drawn within the framework of bilateral agreements concluded in the 1970s with Southern European countries, and they have again been confirmed in the context of East–West temporary migration agreements.

The qualification levels of employment taken up by Eastern Europeans in Germany very much differ according to nationality. In the case of Poles, who have contributed more than any other nation to the increase in Eastern European employment in Germany, the growth in employment mainly affected low-level jobs. The same trend can be observed in the case of Czechs and Slovakians. Within the Hungarian population, on the contrary, the increase in employment has been directed towards qualified jobs. But looking at the absolute figures, the number of new qualified jobs is similar for each of the three nationalities. This suggests that Eastern European qualified workers are recruited along the general structure of available jobs, independent of the nationality.

Until 1992, due to the favourable economic climate in Germany which considerably increased manpower requirements, the economic integration of new Eastern European workers did not pose any significant problems, even considering the sizeable increase in the supply of labour comprising ethnic Germans and workers from the former GDR. But since 1992, the labour market situation in Germany has changed dramatically. The unemployment rate increased rapidly in Western and Eastern Germany, affecting German, but above all foreign, workers. Long-term unemployment is also growing. In addition, Germany is affected by the new conditions in the international division of labour, i.e. the participation of Eastern European countries in international trade and in the international movements of capital. Orders for goods which used to be directed to Germany are now extended to Eastern European countries. Direct investment is increasingly targeted towards the Czech Republic, Hungary or Poland. For these countries, this is clearly a valuable means of achieving their restructuring process. But given the current economic downturn in Germany, these developments have intensified the economic difficulties in certain branches and regions and have made the unemployment problem within certain groups more severe. As a result, there is increased pressure to reduce the possibilities for foreign newcomers to work in Germany, and it is likely that job openings foreseen under the above-mentioned agreements will gradually decrease.

FUTURE MIGRATORY PRESSURES: WILL THERE BE DEMAND FOR FOREIGN LABOUR IN THE MEDIUM AND LONG TERM IN GERMANY?

International political and economic perspectives suggest that migratory pressures will increase rather than decrease in the near future. In the countries of the former Eastern Block, the process towards democracy and towards integration into the international division of labour has only recently begun. Income differentials between Eastern and Western Europe will remain high. Unemployment will continue to grow. If it is likely that Germany's eastern neighbours, especially the Czech Republic but also Poland and Hungary, will make substantial progress results in the medium-term, its effect on the labour market will only be apparent at a later stage. Other countries, such as Russia and other parts of the former Soviet Union, have yet to start upon a radical economic liberalisation. Labour market problems in those countries, needless to say, have not yet begun. The potential for migration from Eastern Europe is therefore still considerable. Several opinion polls demonstrate the willingness of the population to migrate to the West. Naturally, current and future levels of unemployment in the East should not be equated with the scale of future migration. Nor is the potential for migration equivalent to actual migration. But Western Europe clearly cannot ignore the likelihood of significant levels of migration from the East, and also from the South, in the future. The discrepancy between demographic explosion and slow economic growth in many developing countries of the South is a clear determinant of South-North migration, not to mention pressures exerted by war and ethnic tension.

Alongside these considerations, it should also be asked whether, and to what extent, Western economies are likely to be faced, in the future, with an additional demand for foreign labour. In Germany, as in almost all other EC countries, the population is ageing. Whereas in countries of Northern Africa children under 15 make up about 50 per cent of the population, in Germany the proportion is around 15 per cent (compared to 18 per cent in the European Community as a whole). Conversely, in Northern African countries only 4 per cent of the population is older than 64, whereas in Germany the proportion reaches 15 per cent (14 per cent in the EC). Population forecasts in Germany predict a decline from 61.3 million today to 60.7 million in the year 2000.

Even if, in global terms, a decline in population need not necessarily be seen as a misfortune, such demographic trends cannot but influence the evolution of certain economic and social indicators:

- A decline in population means that the economy loses consumers. This could be partially offset, however, by the higher capacity to consume brought about by more rapidly increasing incomes, and by an increased focusing on export production.
- The social expenditure ratio for the active population will increase steadily in the medium term, given that the declining working population will need to finance the pension incomes of a growing population of elderly people.
- Finally, the labour market will be faced with an ever declining pool of active workers. Quantitatively, this could easily be offset by measures affecting such indicators as

- development of productivity;
- economic growth;
- working hours;
- pension age;
- duration of military service;
- the length of education and training;
- the relationship between paid work and family work;
- migration policy.

Lengthening working hours, raising the age of retirement, making it easier for women to work and shortening the period of compulsory military service, are all measures which, by increasing the labour supply, can have a positive effect. But actions of this type can only have limited results for limited periods of time: participation rates cannot be raised above a certain level, training periods cannot be drastically reduced without impairing the competitiveness of the economy, the age of retirement cannot be delayed *ad infinitum*.

It is also important to note that the effects stemming from the above measures are mainly quantitative, whereas qualitative aspects are also of great significance in this context. The most important point here is that a decline in new entrants to the labour market implies that the renewal and up-dating of knowledge cannot be fully secured through the normal school and university channels, and that greater reliance must be placed on training the existing workforce. This increases the costs for employers and, at the same time, reduces the number of hours worked.

The present and forthcoming levels of unemployment must also be considered when discussing the possible needs for foreign labour in the future. In 1993, there were 2.3 million unemployed in Western germany and 1.2 million in the Eastern Länder. In the year 2000 the number of unemployed in Germany is likely to be 5.9 million (3.4 registered unemployed and 2.5 million of hidden labour force).

Nevertheless, it can be assumed that there will be some need for additional foreign manpower. Until recently, West Germany witnessed a significant increase in employment alongside persistently high unemployment. This indicated that structural rigidities among the unemployed impaired the immediate availability of jobs. Age, state of health and lack of qualifications often prevent jobs from being matched to job-seekers.

We can assume that there will be a need for immigration into Germany after the year 2000. Without immigration, the labour market would soon be placed under considerable strain, and the financial burden on the working population and businesses would rise significantly. However, it is not possible to predict precisely the additional number of immigrants that might be required, as this would depend upon the objectives in mind. Aiming to maintain the potential labour force over the long run would appear to be a sensible objective. Taking this objective as a reference, and assuming an increase in labour market participation rates, the number of new immigrants would need to total 200,000 at an initial stage and then as many as 800,000. These figures, however, are lower than the levels of immigration which Germany has experienced over the recent past; they are also lower than existing estimates of the likely levels of future migration from the East. In addition, because of the changing age structure and the changing qualifications required by jobs of the future, the demand for foreign labour will be increasingly directed towards qualified personnel.

PERSPECTIVES AND CONCLUSIONS: THE NEED FOR AN IMMIGRATION CONCEPT AND INTERNATIONAL COOPERATION

Previous sections have shown that, during the last four or five years, Germany has been confronted with what can be referred to as mass immigration. Germany has now become one of the most important countries of immigration in the world, with figures comparable to those experienced by the United States (including illegal immigration). Despite its recent and long-standing experience in receiving large numbers of migrants and refugees, Germany has not yet given itself recognition as a country of immigration. The major concepts of Germany's migration policy have so far consisted of halting the recruitment of new foreign labour; promoting the integration of legal immigrants; and promoting the return to countries of origin. During the last three years, some typical immigration control measures were also taken, consisting of:

- The conclusion of specific bilateral agreements to allow the employment of certain groups (and quotas) of immigrants, and at the same time to control, in part, the illegal streams of migration and to help the countries of origin to transform their economies.
- The establishment of a yearly quota of 215,000 for the admission of ethnic Germans from Eastern Europe.

In the recent past, however, the government and political parties have held major discussions on issues related to migration. These discussions led the German government to revise, in part, its position regarding the need for EC member states to regulate immigration on a national, sovereign basis.

Thus at the Paris Summit of June 1991, the German government launched a proposal which aimed at giving the European Commission more competence in the field of migration. Although this proposal was not fully retained in the Maastricht Treaty, the Commission is now officially allowed to participate in discussions on Schengen and TREVI, and can also take certain initiatives to address specific migration issues.

Since early 1993, the idea of conceiving a proper immigration law in Germany is also under discussion publicly and among political parties. It is obvious that, at the very least, Germany needs to develop an immigration concept, thus acknowledging its status as a country of immigration. Discussion of such a concept would also enable Germany to more systematically address the consequences of immigration on different subsystems of society and to devise ways of controlling immigration which would recognise the need to accept certain groups of immigrants in the future.

These discussions should also allow German institutional actors to realise that immigration pressures cannot be controlled purely from the receiving end: international cooperation on the political and economic fronts is a *sine qua non* to reduce migration push factors in the countries of origin themselves. International cooperation targeted towards Eastern Europe could consist of promoting political stability and equal participation in the international division of labour (through international trade and direct foreign investment). The latter is, of course, a sensitive issue which requires the richer countries to share some of their wealth with their poorer neighbours. Such a redistribution will be difficult to accept, as some of the EC agreements with Eastern European countries already tend to indicate. Borders between the East and the West are thus still in force: if the Iron Curtain of old no longer exists, it has however been replaced by economic borders. An increase in the wealth of all the nations involved will only be achieved if these new borders are successively dismantled.

References

Blaschke, D. 'Aussiedler und Ubersiedler auf dom beundesdeutschen Arbeitsmarkt', *Wirtschaftsdienst* , V/1990.
Blaschke, D. 'Sozialbilanz der Aussiedlung in den 80er und 90er Jahren', in Baumeister, H.P. (ed.); *Integration von Aussiedlern*, Weinheim, 1991.
Chies, L. and Honekopp, E. 'La Germania Occidentale di Fronte a Nuovi Flussi di Lavoro?', *Economia e Lavoro*, 1/1990.
Commission of the European Communities. *Central and Eastern European Barometer*, no. 2, January 1992, and no. 3, February 1993.
Fuchs, R. 'Arbeitskrä ftewanderungen', *Bundesarbeitsblatt Heft*, 9/1990.

Ghosh, B. 'East–West Migration: The European Perspective – Current Trends and Prospects Beyond 1992', *IOM/Greek Government Regional Seminar on Prospects of Migration in Europe Beyond 1992*, Athens, October 1991.

Heyden, H. 'South–North Migration', *Ninth IOM Seminar on Migration*, Geneva, 4–6 December 1990.

Hof, B. 'Arbeitskr ftebedarf der Wirtschaft, Arbeitsmarktchancen für Zuwanderer', in Friedrich-Ebert-Stiftung (ed.); *Zuwanderungspolitik der Zukunft, Gesprächskreis Arbeit und Soziales*, no. 3, Bonn, February 1992.

Hoffmann-Nowotny, H.-J. *Weltbevölkerung und Weltmigration – Eine Zukunftorientierte Analyse*, Zurich, 1990.

Hönekopp, E. 'Arbeitskräftezuwanderung aus Osteurop', in *Ausländer in Deutschland*, 1/1992.

Hönekopp, E. *Einwanderung aus Osteuropa – Ursachen und Auswirkungen aus die Arbeitsmarktsituation in der EG und in Deutschland*, SYSDEM Paper no. 6, Brussels, February 1992.

Hönekopp, E. 'The Effects of the Turkish Accession to the EC on population and the Labour Market', *Intereconomics*, March/April 1993.

Hönekopp, E. 'East–West Migration: Recent Developments concerning Germany and some Future Prospects', in *The Changing Course of International Migration*, Paris, OECD, 1993.

International Organization for Migration (IOM). *Profiles and Motives of Potential Migrants – an IOM Study undertaken in four countries: Albania, Bulgaria, Russia and the Ukraine*, Geneva, IOM, January 1993.

Koll, R., Ochel, W. and Vogler-Ludwig, K. 'Uswirkungen der Internationalen Wanderungen auf Bevölkerung, Arbeitsmarkt und Infrastruktur', in *IFO-Schnelldienst*, 6/1993.

Koller, B. 'Aussiedler nach dem Deutschkurs: Welche Gruppen Kommen rash in Abeit', in *Mittab*, 2/1993.

Kommission der EuropäischenCominschaften. 'Tabilisierung, Liberalisierung und Kompetenzverlagerung nach unten – Eine Bewertung der Wirtschaftlichen Lage und des Reformprozesses in der Sowjetunion', *Europäische Wirtschaft*, no. 45, December 1990.

Layard, R. *et al. East–West Migration: The Alternatives*, MIT Press, Cambridge, London, 1992.

Oberg, S. and Wils, A.-B. 'East–West Migration in Europe – Can Migration Theories help Estimate the Numbers?', in *POPNET*, 22, Winter 1992.

Polyakov, A. 'Labour Emigration from the Former USSR – Challenges for the European Labour Markets and Cooperation', Paper prepared for the European Labour Market Conference, Glasgow, November 1992.

Polyakov, A. and Ushkalov, I. 'Labour Migration from the Former USSR – Causes, Forecasts, Implications', draft (1991).

Prognos, Franzen, D. *et al. Die Bundesrepublik Deutschland 2000–2005–2010 – Entwicklung von Wirtschaft und Gesellschaft*, Prognos Deutschland Report no. 1, Basel, 1993.

Straubhaar, T. 'Allocation and Distributional Aspects of Future Immigration to Western Europe', *International Migration Review*, no. 98, Summer 1992.

Thon, M. 'Neue Modellrechnungen zur Entwicklung des Erwerbspersonenpotentials im bisherigen Bundesgebiet bis 2010 mit Ausblick auf 2030', *Mittab*, 4/1991.

Vichnevski, A. and Zayontchkovskia, J. 'Emigration from the Former Soviet Union', *Revue Européenne des Migrations Internationales*, 3/1991.

Watrin, C. 'Liberale Toleranz auf dem Prüfstand', *Sozialwiisenschaftliche Studien des Schweizerischen Instituts fur Auslandsforschung*, 20/1991.

Withol de Wenden, C. 'Les Politiques migratoires européennes face à la double pression venant de l'Est et du Sud', *Séminaire international sur le travail clandestin*, Paris, 16/17 May 1991.

9 Austria
Rainer Baubock

Since the second world war, Austria's peculiar position with regard to international migration has been characterised by six distinctive stages, consisting of (i) an inflow of a large number of ethnic Germans in the immediate postwar period; (ii) three major waves of refugees from Hungary in 1956/57, Czechoslovakia in 1968/69 and from Poland in 1981/82; (iii) substantial labour migration of Austrians to Germany and Switzerland; (iv) the recruitment of foreign workers from Yugoslavia and Turkey since the mid-1960s; (v) the stabilisation of the resident foreign population in the 1980s at a level of 4 per cent of the total population, after waves of remigration and family reunification; (vi) the marked increase of labour and refugee immigration from Central and Eastern Europe after the 1989 revolutions and the Yugoslavian crisis.

Since 1989, Austria, together with Germany, has been a major destination for Eastern European migrants. Particularly since the outbreak of war in Yugoslavia, substantial unorganised migration has prompted the Austrian government to revise and expand its previously embryonic asylum and immigration legislation. This has also coincided with the development of a powerful anti-immigrant sentiment in Austria, promoted to a great extent by the so-called Freedom Party.

This chapter aims to introduce the main legislative and political revisions adopted in Austria in the light of new migration determinants in Central and Eastern Europe and in view of Austria's forthcoming integration into the European Economic Area and the European Community. After a short review of the main migratory trends after 1945, the chapter will successively address the levels of new immigration since the 1989 revolutions, the effects of such migration in terms of legislative revisions and new policy issues, and the extent to which new migration from Eastern Europe will determine Austria's role within an integrated Europe.

LEVELS AND CHARACTERISTICS OF IMMIGRATION TO AUSTRIA FROM 1945 TO 1989

At the end of World War Two, a large number of ethnic Germans from different parts of Central and Eastern Europe was already established in

Austria. Mass expulsions, which followed the formation of the Warsaw Pact, rapidly increased this number. In 1951, an official count showed that 250,000 refugees of German origin and 58,000 other refugees were established in Austria, in addition to another 30,000 people from the pre-war German Reich and from South Tyrol (UN 1951: 63ff.). In fact according to an overall estimate by demographers, about 400,000 post-war refugees might have integrated into Austria by 1950 (Fassmann/Münz 1992: 9), and substantial numbers of ethnic Germans had already been naturalised by the early 1950s.

This first, and exceptional, wave of refugee immigration initiated a pattern that would become dominant in the following years: Due to its geographic location, neutral status and Western democratic system, Austria emerged as a haven for first asylum from countries under Stalinist rule. This does not however mean that Austria was perceived as a country of permanent immigration and settlement. Rather, it was considered as a transit station from which point subsequent migration to larger Western countries could be organised.

The next big immigration wave, of a level comparable to the massive post-war inflows, followed ten years later. After the military intervention in the Hungarian revolution, several hundred thousand Hungarians fled to Austria in 1956 and 1957. Most of those who stayed were granted refugee status, bringing applications for asylum to a total of 228,500 during 1956 and 1957 (BMI). In 1968 and 1969, after the Soviet occupation and the suppression of the reform movement, an estimated 162,000 citizens of the CSSR left their country via Austria. In spite of traditional Czech immigration to Austria (at the beginning of the century, one quarter of the Viennese population had been born in Bohemia or Moravia), this was primarily a transit flow. Only a very small percentage of these refugees stayed in Austria and no more than 12,000 claimed political asylum. After General Jaruzelski's coup against the Solidarnosc movement in Poland in 1981, about 120,000 to 150,000 Poles fled temporarily to Austria, a quarter of whom applied for asylum (Münz/Fassmann 1992: 9). This higher number, compared with the previous movement from Czechoslovakia, was the first indication that traditional oversea target countries had become more reluctant to take in unlimited numbers of refugees from Eastern Europe. It also demonstrated that many among those who had fled hoped to return, in the not too distant future, and wished to stay in contact with family members in their countries of origin.

The model of refugee transit was more successfully applied to Jewish emigration from the Soviet Union. Between 1976 and 1989 about a quarter of a million Soviet Jews came to Austria as the first stop on their way to Israel or the USA (Münz/Fassmann 1992: 10), and only recently has there been an increasing number of Jews who have stayed in Vienna with a view to settling with the aid of Vienna's small Jewish community (Jews from the former Soviet Union are generally classified as *de facto* refugees and, therefore, do not have access to public assistance).

In terms of East–West migration, Austria has not only been a receiving country, but also a sending one; in fact both movements almost match each other in quantitative terms. Austrian migration to neighbouring regions of Switzerland and Germany has been primarily determined by substantial wage differentials. In the Western province of Vorarlberg, in particular, Austrians employed in Switzerland are frequently daily or weekly cross-border commuters, and in Austria there seems to have been a causal relation between outmigration of nationals and the need to import foreign labour.

Contrary to other Western European states, Austria only started to import foreign labour in 1961, when an agreement for a first contingent of 47 000 was reached. The threshold of 50 000 was only exceeded in 1966, in part due to the fact that after 1945, the gradual dismantlement of the vast agricultural sector provided enough indigenous labour during the reconstruction period. This can also be explained by the fact that during the Second Republic, labour market policies were regarded as the exclusive domain of trade unions and employer federations. During that period, the trade union federation was very reluctant to give in to employers' urgent demands for immigrant labour, as long as wages in Austria lagged behind. The 1961 agreement was based on a package deal which increased the unions' role in national economic policy decisions (Wimmer 1986: 7f.). Finally, the main reason why recruitment was generally lower than the contingents agreed upon by the social partners was that economic growth had been rather slow in the 1960s and most immigrants preferred to move to countries offering higher wages.

In the early 1970s, what had begun as an organised recruitment by employment agencies turned into a large scale spontaneous inflow of Yugoslavian and Turkish citizens, who came to Austria as tourists but who subsequently found access to legal employment. A record number of 227,000 foreigners employed, i.e. 8.7 per cent of total employment, was thus reached in 1973.

Largely due to family reunifications, the number of foreign residents stabilised in the 1980s at an average of about 285 000. A survey carried out in 1983 showed that more than 50 per cent of families of immigrants had already been reunited in Austria (Bauböck 1986: 216 and 219).

LEVELS OF POST-1989 IMMIGRATION TO AUSTRIA

The estimated foreign population in Austria increased from a level of 299,000 in 1988 to 323,000 in 1989, 413,000 in 1990 and 518,000 in 1991. In 1990 alone, net immigration was estimated at 129, 000 people which brought the share of foreign citizens in the total population from 3.9 per cent in 1988 to 6.7 per cent in 1991. That is to say that, among OECD countries, Austria has experienced the largest increase in immigrants, relative to the size of its population, during this period (ÖSTZA, SOPEMI 1992: 131).

The resulting dramatic changes in the labour market have mostly been interpreted as a supply shock due to the fall of the Iron Curtain. However, inflows from former Warsaw Pact countries have been much smaller than expected. During the very first wave of migration, Austria mainly acted as a transit country. When the Hungarian government opened its Western border in autumn 1989, about 45,000 GDR citizens came to Austria. Although they would probably have been welcomed as permanent immigrants in Austria, virtually all of these Germans subsequently moved to the Federal Republic of Germany where they were recognized as German citizens and were entitled to substantial integration assistance.

Since 1990, there has been a large increase in border crossings of Czecho-Slovak and Hungarian citizens. Most, however, came as short term visitors and window-shopping tourists. Poles were the first large group to arrive as temporary economic migrants. Some tried to make a living as street vendors until open air markets were closed down by the local authorities in Vienna. Many more have entered illegal employment. But initially, even economic immigration was intended to be, and was, in fact, for most migrants, purely temporary. Both illegal traders and workers tried to benefit primarily from the high purchasing power their small earnings in Austria had in their home country. With monetary stabilisation and steep rises in consumer prices in these countries, this incentive has now become less significant. Temporary visa requirements for Poland also helped to curb the inflow. Nevertheless, in spite of being denied access to legal employment, a significant number of new Polish immigrants succeeded in establishing themselves in Austria, adding to the refugees of 1981.

A second group, which came to Austria on a longer term basis, comprised Romanian citizens, particularly members of the Hungarian and Roma minority. The German speaking minority, which has been virtually extinguished by emigration, opted for emigration to Germany, although some of their ancestors had come from what is now Austrian territory. Unlike Polish migrants, who were practically excluded from claiming political asylum by new 'accelerated procedures', many Romanian immigrants applied for refugee status. In 1988, Poles were still the largest group of asylum seekers (6,670), followed by Hungarian and Romanian citizens. In 1989 this distribution was reversed: Romanians became by far the largest group of refugees (7,932 applications in 1989 and 12,199 in 1990). During the same period, Poles virtually disappeared from asylum statistics, together with citizens of Czechoslovakia, 3,307 of whom had tried, in 1989, to gain refugee status in Austria. In 1989 most Romanians were still recognised as refugees according to the Geneva Convention: 69 per cent of the 2,663 decisions taken on Romanian applicants were positive in that year, by far the highest rate for refugees of Eastern European origin. Most, however, had applied for refugee status before the toppling of the Ceausescu dictatorship. Since then, Austrian officials have generally considered Romania as a safe country. In 1991, the recognition rate for Romanian asylum seekers consequently dwindled to a mere 11 per cent (BMI). The inflow was further curtailed by visa requirements reintroduced in 1990 and by ordering the army to assist in controls along the Austrian-Hungarian border, which had traditionally been crossed illegally by many Romanian immigrants.

As is well known by now, the widely expected mass emigration from the former USSR has not materialised. Migratory movements have been much stronger inside the CIS than beyond the former Soviet borders, and their main causes have owed more to ethnic tensions than to economic instability. Soviet migration to the West has been mainly directed towards non-OECD neighbouring countries.

Although detailed statistics of inflows from Eastern European countries are not yet available, the overall impression is that former Warsaw Pact states have contributed only a relatively small percentage to the marked increase in the foreign population. In fact, most of the new immigrants have come from the two traditional sending states of labour immigration in Austria, i.e. former Yugoslavia and Turkey. 40 per cent of the additional 115,500 foreign workers between 1988 and 1991 are from republics of the former Yugoslavia and 20 per cent from Turkey (BMAS). In 1992, the share of Turkish workers among all foreigners employed was 20.3 per cent (Table 9.1), which is only slightly less than the highest ever share of 23.4 per cent in 1989.

Immigrants from former Warsaw Pact states thus accounted for 14 per cent of total foreign employment in 1990, 15 per cent in 1991 and 16 per cent in 1992.

This is no doubt a substantial increase compared to the previously marginal position of Eastern European immigrants. But the point remains that the bulk of additional foreign labour migrated from the same countries as

Table 9.1   Shares of sending states in total foreign employment in 1992 (monthly average)

Yugoslavia, Croatia and Slovenia	49.7%
Turkey	20.3%
CSFR	3.9%
Poland	4.1%
Hungary	3,7%
Romania	3,4%
Bulgaria	0,6%
CIS	0,3%
Germany	5.0%
Other countries	9.0%

Source: BMAS.

before the 1989 revolutions. Even assuming a very large number of illegal immigrants from Eastern Europe, the vast majority of new immigrants have come from the traditional sending areas.

The main explanation for this scarcely perceived phenomenon is that while new push factors and emigration opportunities have emerged in Eastern Europe after 1989, internal pull factors in Austria have simultaneously gained in strength. In effect, since 1989 and the German unification, the Austrian economy has experienced an economic boom which only came to an end in 1992. Sectors such as construction and tourism, which traditionally relied on foreign labour, have been among the main beneficiaries of sustained growth. Although this strong increase in demand for foreign labour coincided with the opening up of Eastern European borders, employers continued to recruit foreign labour from traditional sending countries. Against this background, immigrants have been able to re-establish patterns of chain migration from the former recruitment countries. There is also some anecdotal evidence that guestworkers who had been laid off and had returned to their countries of origin between 1974 and 1984, have come back to their former employers.

Due to the dramatic failure of economic and political reform in Yugoslavia before its break-up, former Yugoslavian citizens largely contributed to the development of chain migration to Austria. It would thus appear that the overall pattern of post-1989 labour immigration has to be explained in terms of a combination of supply and demand shocks (Althaler *et al.* 1991) and of revitalised chain migration. These events have eroded established instruments for controlling foreign employment and have prompted a wave of new legislation.

LEGAL REGULATIONS AND THE INTEGRATION OF IMMIGRANTS

In spite of its long tradition as a country of immigration, Austria did not have a proper immigration law until 1992. This is the consequence of policy decisions taken in the 1960s, when employers were given permission to recruit guestworkers as a rotating workforce but not as permanent immigrants. Immigration was not primarily regulated at the national borders, but in the access of foreigners to the labour market. The neo-corporatist framework of social partnership played a decisive role in shaping this policy. Immigration was considered a matter of negotiation between employers and trade unions; but not as an immediate concern for parliamentary and governmental policy making (Bauböck and Wimmer 1988).

In 1975, the law on employment of foreigners (Ausländerbeschäftigungsgesetz) was adopted. Its basic provision was that foreigners could only be employed if their employer received the proper one-year, renewable permit (Beschäftigungsbewilligung). Employment permits, which are tied to a specified job, are issued by the labour exchange offices under very restrictive conditions which include a general evaluation of the situation of labour markets, the unavailability of unemployed Austrian citizens who could apply for the job, compliance with the usual working conditions and wages, and proof of suitable accommodation. Until 1990, eight years of continuing employment were the condition for obtaining a so-called exemption permit (Befreiungsschein) which entitled a foreigner to take up employment under the same conditions as Austrian citizens.

The reform of 1992 established new restrictions on the employment of foreigners. The first restriction still consists of the employment permit. After more than a year of continuing employment, the immigrant can claim a work permit (Arbeitserlaubnis) which is renewable after two years and entitles the holder to change jobs within a federal province. An exemption permit can be obtained by three categories of immigrants: those who are married to an Austrian citizen; second generation immigrants who have spent half of their life or half of their schooling in Austria and whose parents have lived in the country for five years; and foreigners who have been employed for five years within the last eight years. The exemption permit must be renewed every five years and can be revoked if employment is interrupted for too long. The percentage of immigrant workers whose exemption permit entitles them to free movement in the labour market has never surpassed 40 per cent; because of the larger number of new arrivals it has currently fallen to a mere third of all foreigners employed (BMAS).

General exemption from the law, without temporal restrictions, is only granted to refugees after they have obtained asylum, as well as to a few occupations such as journalists employed by foreign media, priests, or diplomatic personnel. In the most recent amendment of July 1992, the law was adapted to the conditions of free movement of labour in the future European Economic Area. Citizens of these states will no longer be subject to the law. As this was seen to create unfair inequalities for foreigners married to Austrian citizens, that group too will be exempted. Compared with other countries, even the reformed law strongly restricts not only access of new immigrants to legal employment, but also the mobility of already established foreigners and their family members.

Apart from controlling individual access to employment, the law also contains important provisions for regulating overall numbers. In 1990, a national quota for foreign employment at the level of 10 per cent of the total workforce was introduced. But in reaction to strong pressure from employers, the Ministry for Social Affairs decided to readjust the quota by eliminating double counts and by excluding from the quota those immigrants for whom employment permits had been issued but who had not taken up work. Furthermore, nationals of the European Economic Area will not be included in the quota after 1993.

One obvious way for immigrants and employers to circumvent quota regulations would be naturalisation. However, as in many other countries of immigration, naturalisations in Austria have been extremely low compared to both the size of the resident immigrant population and the number of foreigners who would qualify for Austrian citizenship. Thus after a record 3.7 per cent in 1986, the naturalisation rate in Austria has remained stable at 2.9 per cent since 1987 (these figures include acquisitions of Austrian citizenship abroad). This means, of course, an increase in absolute figures which amounts to +9 per cent from 1989 to 1990 and +24 per cent from 1990 to 1991. International comparisons show that Austria occupies a middle position in Europe, well below Sweden or Norway but far above Belgium, Switzerland and Germany (SOPEMI 1992: 36).

Comparing the various nationalities of origin also reveals some interesting differences. Immigrants from the former Warsaw Pact countries tend to naturalise in higher rates than other groups. This can be explained by patterns established in previous waves of refugee migration (it is well known that refugees are generally more inclined to naturalise than labour immigrants). In many countries the former are also given easier access to indigenous citizenship. Polish and Romanian citizens today account for two thirds of all naturalisations from Eastern European states. Romanian refugees from 1988 have now cumulated the required four years of residence and will probably apply in large numbers in the coming months. The naturalisation rate of immigrants from former Yugoslavia and from Turkey in 1991 is only 1.6 per cent.

The main requirement for obtaining Austrian citizenship is continuous residence for ten years. For certain groups, such as refugees, this may be shortened to four years. Decisions on applications are made by the provincial authorities who use their discretion in very different ways. While in most provinces the ten year requirement is strictly respected and tests of assimilation are applied, the provincial government of Vienna has followed a more liberal policy. The most important obstacle to naturalisation, however, is the strict exclusion of dual citizenship. Whereas other European countries have recently changed their policies to allow many immigrants to retain their previous citizenship, this idea would probably be strongly resisted by most Austrian provincial governments.

Another area in which the negative effects of the overall orientation of guestworker policies have become particularly acute is education and professional qualifications. There is now a general awareness of the lack of skilled workers in certain trades and industries. In public debates, one of the main goals of the new immigration law has been to select immigrants from Eastern Europe with the required skills. However, among those who presently take part in training schemes for skilled occupations (Lehrberufe), no more than 5.5 per cent are foreigners (December 1991, BWK), far less than their share in the according age group. Education statistics thus point to the fact that, contrary to the situation in other countries, the second and third generation of immigrants in Austria have not yet experienced any significant upwards mobility through education and training.

CURRENT POLICY ISSUES

Within current policy changes, the desire to regulate new immigration has completely pushed to the background unresolved problems of previous immigration. Simulations have shown that surplus immigration in 1990 and 1991 (i.e. immigration beyond the level of previous years) has contributed about 0.8 percentage points to the overall growth rate of the GDP, but has simultaneously diminished GDP per capita by 1.25 (Pichelmann 1991). Over the last few years, employment and unemployment have risen simultaneously. About three quarters of the 2.3 per cent rise in total employment between 1989 and 1990 is due to additional employment of foreigners (Althaler *et al.* 1991: 294ff.). The total rate of unemployment rose from 5.0 per cent in 1989 to 5.9 per cent in 1991. Older workers, both indigenous and foreign, have been particularly affected. In 1991, the unemployment rate within the age group 50–60 rose to 8.3 per cent (Biffl 1992: 5). There is, then, some empirical evidence that new immigration not only helped to expand the economy but was also used to replace older immigrants and indigenous workers in sectors which traditionally relied on immigrant labour. One should also mention the electoral successes of the neopopulist FPÖ (Freedom Party), which were based strongly on the party's anti-immigrant platforms. These economic, social and political background factors led to a marked shift in immigration policies in 1991 and 1992.

The first major reform concerned refugee policies. During the 1980s, the number of asylum seekers registered in Austria rose from its lowest levels in 1983 (5,898) to 21,882 in 1989, 22,769 in 1990 and 27,306 in 1991. The rate of positive decisions regarding asylum dropped simultaneously from 85 per cent in 1982 to 19 per cent in 1989 and to 6.8 per cent in 1990. It rose again to 12.6 per cent in 1991 and stabilised at 12.3 per cent during the first half of 1992. Since the new law came into effect, the number of asylum applications has dwindled to a mere 500 per month.

Important policy changes were introduced in 1990, including: the assignment of Austrian soldiers to control the borders along Hungary; the accelerated procedure for processing the applications of asylum seekers from Romania; attempts to secure a more even regional distribution of refugees in camps; subsidised accommodation throughout the federal provinces; and a temporary liberalisation (until 1991) in the access of asylum seekers to the labour market.

The new law on asylum came into force in June 1992. A new federal office was entrusted with the processing of applications, and asylum was extended to the families of successful applicants. Improved consultation during the application procedure, the use of interpreters, and assistance for integration were considered as positive elements of reform by organisations lobbying for refugees. However other policy changes, such as the fact that entry can be denied to asylum seekers who do not arrive directly from the country in which they have been persecuted, led to vigorous but unsuccessful campaigns against the new law. Due to the fact that all of Austria's neighbouring states have now become signatories to the Geneva Convention, this rule can be used to effectively deny entry and residence to any refugee taking a land route into Austria. So far, the vast majority of refugees have come via the Eastern and Southern land borders. Only a small number, most of them from Third World countries, arrived at Vienna International Airport. It is thus widely expected that these new rules will effectively lead to a reduction in asylum seekers from Eastern European countries.

Another aspect of the new law, severely criticised by organisations such as the United Nations High Commissioner for Refugees and Amnesty

International, is that asylum can be denied *a priori* if the applicant cannot produce adequate documents for personal identification or if his or her state of origin is regarded as a safe country.

While the number of applicants from Third World countries has risen during the last few years, the proportion of asylum seekers from Eastern European states steadily declined (88 per cent in 1988, 72 per cent in 1989, 67 per cent in 1990, 62 per cent in 1991). During the first half of 1992, however, the war in Yugoslavia reversed this trend. More than half of all new applicants for asylum came from republics of former Yugoslavia, 90 per cent of whom (5,385) from Serbia or Montenegro. The great majority of refugees from this area do not appear in asylum statistics, however. Although a generous interpretation of the Geneva Convention would have concluded that war refugees and displaced persons from this area left their countries because of a well-founded fear of persecution for reasons of nationality or religion, Austria's policy has excluded such refugees from asylum procedures. This can be explained, to a great extent, by the fact that admission of these refugees was intended as a purely temporary emergency measure.

Preparations for a refugee crisis were already under way when the Yugoslavian army begun fighting to stop the secession of Slovenia. A large number of refugees arrived a few months later when war erupted in Croatia. Most of these refugees have since gone back to Croatia. The situation of the 50,000 refugees from Bosnia who took up residence in Austria in 1992 is clearly different. The amount of destruction and the uncertain future of an independent Bosnian state will prevent these refugees from returning to their country of origin and will probably lead to many more people seeking asylum in Austria or in other western countries.

After unsuccessfully lobbying other European states to admit more refugees, Austria has introduced a visa requirement for immigrants with Serbian passports. The rigid enforcement of the first country and safe country rules in European asylum policies has mainly served to curb inflows into Western Europe and to shift the burden towards the newly democratised states of Eastern and Central Europe. This is also true for the Bosnian refugee crisis, which has affected Croatia, Slovenia and Hungary more acutely. However, because of its geographical location, its traditional immigration from Yugoslavia and its early support of the dissolution of Yugoslavia, Austria has taken a comparatively larger share of refugees from former Yugoslavia than have other Western European countries.

Generally, *de facto* refugees from Croatia and Bosnia are in a very insecure legal and social position. In February 1992, some 44,000 Bosnian war refugees received public assistance. Refugees are generally given a three-month residence permit, but are denied access to regular employment. Some of them, however, are given the opportunity to work part-time in their local communities, with charitable organisations, or in cleaning services. Finally, the Yugoslavian crisis also led to the inclusion of a special provision in the new immigration law regarding *de facto* refugees: During heightened international tension, armed conflicts or other circumstances which threaten the security of given populations, the Austrian government will be able to grant temporary residence to foreigners who are directly threatened and who cannot find protection elsewhere.

A new law on regular labour immigration and family reunion was passed in June 1992 and came into force in July 1993. Under this law, the total number of yearly permits is fixed in advance by governmental decree. It depends on developments in the labour and housing markets, in school and health services, on the number of foreigners living in Austria, on the number of asylum seekers during the previous year and on the expected number of family reunifications. This broad spectrum of rather vague criteria in fact ensures that the number of new permits is primarily influenced by the electoral motivations of political parties and by negotiations between employers and trade unions. Currently, a yearly contingent of 20,000 new permits has been proposed by government representatives. If the present inflows of war refugees and expected family reunifications are taken into account, this could lead to a halt in new legal admissions for labour migrants.

Another important provision of the new law is that provincial governments are able to decide, ultimately, on individual applications. In addition to the federal contingent, a separate quota for each province has been established, and provinces with a percentage of foreign population above the national average have been given permission to cut their quota even further. This devolution of immigration policies is explained by the need to coordinate housing policies (which are already the responsibility of provincial and local authorities) with new immigrant admissions.

Employer associations have successfully lobbied for a special provision for seasonal employment and short term contract labour. In the event of labour shortages, immigrants will be allowed up to six months employment without having to go through the individual application procedure. These are the only types of immigrant who will be able to apply for a regular permit from within Austria. However, they will not be given priority over applications submitted outside of Austria and in most cases they will have to leave the country after their contract has expired. They will not, thus, be in a position to receive unemployment benefit or to bring in their family.

Rather than replacing the existing law on the employment of foreigners, as had been originally planned, the new law has been adapted to the established mode of regulation. Regular immigrants still need employment permits, which will determine their chances to have their residence permits renewed. The duration of both types of permit have been coordinated. Residence permits are granted initially for six months only, but are renewable for another six months, and then twice for two years. After five years, permanent residence can be obtained.

During the public debates on the new legislation the government was also urged from very different sides of the political spectrum to consider regularisation of illegal immigrants. This request was consistently rejected. The law only permits legal residents to exchange their current permits for the new ones. At the same time, illegal employment of foreigners is now exposed to tougher employer sanctions and to deportation of undocumented workers. It is widely believed, however, that the restrictive provisions of the new immigration law will encourage increased illegal immigration and undocumented employment.

CONCLUSIONS

Austria has been slow in officially acknowledging its status as a country of permanent settlement for refugees and labour immigrants. The most recent wave of new immigration since 1989 has not been higher than previous waves after 1945, in 1956 and around 1973, but it has led to a marked change of perspective. Previous massive inflows were attributed to exceptional circumstances, and political instruments were available for redirecting immigrants towards other receiving countries or to their countries of origin. Post-1989 immigration, on the contrary, was determined by longer term changes in Eastern Europe, consisting of the opening up of external borders, long periods of economic stagnation and restructuring, and the potential for political upheavals, civil wars and violent ethnic conflicts. As a country bordering three states undergoing radical transformations, Austria expects to become a major destination for economic migrants and different categories of asylum seeker. At the same time, Austria has redefined its position towards Western European integration by becoming the first EFTA country to apply for EC membership since the inclusion of Spain, Portugal and Greece, and by actively negotiating the EEA treaty. Austrian ministers have sought to become involved in the Schengen and TREVI negotiations and have followed the policies of other EC countries in tightening up asylum procedures and shifting the burden towards Central and Eastern European countries, which are now considered as safe countries. The Yugoslavian refugee crisis, however, made government officials aware that Austria would be in a position to itself become a first destination and that it would need to share the burden with its richer Western neighbours.

In refugee migration, external push factors and state regulations regarding admission and residence determine the size of the flows. In labour migration, internal pull factors need to be taken into account as well. This has largely been neglected in public debates on the steep rise in legal and undocumented employment of foreigners in Austria. A sustained economic boom in sectors such as tourism and construction, which have relied strongly on immigrant labour, has coincided with new opportunities for emigration from Eastern European countries and with the aggravation of economic conditions in traditional sending countries such as Yugoslavia and Turkey. At the same time, the existing legal framework for regulating employment has to some extent been eroded by policies aimed at promoting more flexibility. Many employers have seen this erosion as an opportunity to exchange part of their workforce for new immigrants. A lack of control and sanctions, strong clientele relations between public administration and employers, and the weak presence of trade unions in enterprises with many immigrant workers have encouraged many firms to think that they can employ undocumented foreigners without being penalised. Although there is now more determination to fight this development, the emphasis is clearly on restrictions on new admissions rather than on employer sanctions and controls at the workplace. This will leave a substantial number of immigrants in an irregular situation unless either a massive wave of expulsions is carried through or regularisation is offered.

It is notoriously difficult to predict migratory flows. In the case of East–West migration, this has become an almost impossible task because political factors which could prompt massive waves of refugees are virtually unpredictable. Most experts now operate with scenarios rather than prognoses. In 1991, demographers and economists developed three 'realistic' scenarios for Austria, which assume, for the near future, a yearly net migration of between 15,000 and 50,000 people. One scenario assumes an additional inflow of 150,000 within a single year because of a political crisis in an Eastern European state. However, due to internal demographic developments over the long term, unemployment rates will only be negatively affected in the event of an inflow of 50,000 per year. According to this study, the main challenge will be in housing, education and generally in the necessary development of urban infrastructure (Fassmann *et al.* 1991).

Austrian membership of the European Economic Area and, at a later stage, of the European Community, will establish free mobility of labour. As a result, it is anticipated that Austria will experience further net emigration towards Western countries. Compared to neighbouring countries such as Germany and Switzerland, Austria is still a country with distinctively lower wages. The long tradition of labour migration of Austrian citizens across its Western borders will be accelerated with the new liberalisation of labour mobility. Most experts believe that additional emigration will be more marked among highly qualified nationals. At the same time, even after the lifting of the present immigration restrictions, Austria is unlikely to become an attractive target for migrants from the less prosperous EC Southern belt who have already established chains of migration in other Western European countries.

The logic of this development would support policies aimed at controlling new admissions while promoting equal treatment and citizenship for legally admitted foreigners. In the Western European political arena, the Austrian government has already attempted to lobby for better coordination of European policies in the field of labour and refugee migration. It has also presented its new legislation as a possible example to be followed by other European states. At the same time, however, Austrian politicians, trade unionists and employers have expressed their reluctance to abandon those elements of the existing regulatory framework which have entailed strong legal and social discrimination against established immigrant communities. While this policy can no longer be applied to EEA citizens, it may, however, be strengthened *vis-à-vis* 'third country aliens'. To a great extent, the reluctance to abandon some of the existing regulations can be attributed to the new political prominence of anti-immigrant sentiments, which are mainly promoted by the Freedom Party. While, in previous decades, immigration issues had generally been the domain of the social partners, they have now come to dominate domestic politics. Both Conservatives and Social Democrats in government have attempted to regain terrain from the neopopulist FPÖ by meeting some of its demands.

During the current Yugoslavian crisis there has been a growing understanding among the population that Austria had a special responsibility towards refugees from this area. This has temporarily pushed to the background anti-immigrant sentiments and it has also shown that, rather than being inversely determined by prejudice and hostility among the indigenous population, political commitment could change public attitudes and mobilise additional resources and capacities for new immigrant admissions.

Abbreviations

BMAS (Bundesministerium für Arbeit und Soziales) (Federal Department for Labour and Social Affairs).
BMI = Bundesministerium für Inneres (Federal Department of the Interior).
BWK = Bundeswirtschaftskammer (Federal Chamber of Commerce).
ÖSTZA = Österreichisches Statistisches Zentralamt (Austrian Central Office for Statistics).

References

Althaler, Karl, Wilfried Altzinger, Ernst Fehr, Thomas Grandner and Markus Marterbauer (1991). 'Arbeitsmarkt: Angebotsschock oder Nachfragesog?', *Wirtschaft und Gesellschaft*, 3/91: 285–307.
Bauböck, Rainer (1986). 'Demographische und soziale Struktur der jugoslawischen und türkischen Wohnbevölkerung in Österreich', in Hannes Wimmer (ed.), *Ausländische Arbeitskräfte in Österreich*, Frankfurt: Campus: 181–240.
Bauböck, Rainer and Hannes Wimmer (1988). 'Social Partnership and "Foreigners Policy": on Special Features of Austria's Guest-Worker System', *European Journal of Political Research*, 16: 659–81.
Biffl, Gudrun (1992). *Report on Labour Migration. Austria 1991/92*, Contribution for SOPEMI, OECD, Austrian Institute of Economic Research.
Fassmann, Heinz and Rainer Münz (1992). *Einwanderungsland Österreich? Gastarbeiter – Flüchtlinge – Immigranten*, Demographic Institute of the Austrian Academy of Sciences, Vienna.
Fassmann, Heinz, Peter Findl and Rainer Münz (1991). *Die Auswirkungen der internationalen Wanderungen auf Österreich. Szenarien zur regionalen Bevölkerungsentwicklung 1991–2031*, ÖROK, Wien.
Fischer, Gero (1986). 'Aspekte der Beschulungspolitik der Gastarbeiterkinder in Österreich', in Hannes Wimmer (ed.), *Ausländische Arbeitskräfte in Österreich*, Frankfurt: Campus: 307–30.
Pichelmann, Karl (1991). *Ein Simulationsexperiment zu den makroökonomischen Konsequenzen des Arbeitskräfteangebotsschocks 1990/91*, Institute for Advanced Studies, Vienna.
SOPEMI (1992). *Trends in International Migration*, OECD: Paris.
United Nations (1951). *The Refugee in the Post-War World. Preliminary Report of a Survey of the Refugee Problem*, Geneva.
Wimmer, Hannes (1986). 'Zur Ausländerbeschäftigungspolitik in Österreich', in Hannes Wimmer (ed.), *Ausländische Arbeitskräfte in Österreich*, Frankfurt: Campus: 5–32.

10 Italy

Carla Collicelli and Franco Salvatori

The radical political, economic and social changes which took place in Central and Eastern Europe after the collapse of communism opened up new immigration channels to Italy. Most immigration from Central and Eastern Europe is econmically driven, while the flow of asylum seekers who can no longer be recognised after the liberalisation process begun in this region is gradually decreasing.

In contrast to the alarmist migration forecasts after 1989, legal migration to Italy from Central and Eastern Europe is relatively moderate, particularly in comparison to levels of migration from this region to other Western countries, such as Austria and Germany. In fact a significant proportion of the flow involves Poles, Albanians, Romanians and citizens from the Republics of former Yugoslavia, due to geographic proximity and traditional historical and cultural ties.

On the other hand, Italy is experiencing substantial immigration of tourists and illegal immigrants, two categories which are difficult to define and measure given that tourist visits often become temporary or seasonal stays for work.

Demographic pressure and, to a certain extent unemployment, are less significant causes of emigration from Central and Eastern European countries, at least compared to the causes of traditional immigration from Maghreb, the Philippines, and from other African and Asian countries. In the case of Central and Eastern Europe, one of the fundamental causes of immigration is the difference in welfare between the countries of origin and Italy, coupled with expectations of higher earnings.

The phenomenon of repatriation of ethnic minorities from Central and Eastern Europe affects Italy only to a marginal extent. Since the shifting of borders at the end of the 1943–5 war, an Italian community has been established in the territory of the Yugoslavian federation, which community is now recognised by Italy through emergency provisions. The Italian minority which entered Italy after the 1st of September 1991 is offered the possibility of obtaining a renewable residence permit and of entering the labour market.

While entry visas for countries with a high propensity to emigrate to Italy, such as Maghreb, Senegal, Turkey and Gambia, have been reintroduced, relations with Eastern European countries are now being liberalised and visa requirements for some countries (e.g. Czechoslovakia and Poland) have been lifted.

One of the main reasons that Italy is becoming an attractive destination for immigrants is the possibility to work illegally or to extend a tourist visit with a request for asylum. The suppression of entry visas for Poles and Czechs, by facilitating potential illegal labour migration, could therefore have disruptive effects which are hard to foresee and control.

THE QUANTITATIVE ASPECTS

According to official statistics of the Ministry of the Interior, in July 1992 the main communities from Central and Eastern Europe in a regular situation consisted of Yugoslavs (37,878, in addition to 152 Croats and 59 Slovenes), Albanians (26,378), Poles (19,256) and Romanians (14,259). A small number of citizens from the former USSR (8,115), mainly from Lithuania, Latvia, the Ukraine, Belorussia and Uzbekistan, were also registered in Italy.

The total number of nationals from Central and Eastern Europe (104,415) thus continues to be low relative both to the total emigration from these countries and to the total immigration to Italy.

In fact, in the middle of 1992 immigration from the East accounted for only 12 per cent of the foreign presence in Italy, or 22 per cent of immigrants from developing countries.

As a country of recent immigration, after decades of Italian emigration to the United States, Latin America and Northern Europe, Italy is experiencing moderate immigration from Third World countries.

After two acts of amnesty for illegal migrants in 1986 and 1990 regularised over 300,000 foreigners, the recent restrictions introduced by the Martelli Act and by government decrees limiting the issue of residence permits, coupled with the difficulty of migrating legally to Italy for employment purposes, have increased the illegal presence of foreigners in Italy. It is in fact in this group (composed of about 200,000 to 300,000 people), that the majority of nationals from Central and Eastern Europe can be found.

Until July 1992, employment was the first motive invoked by the 726,623 non-EC registered citizens who requested a residence permit. 93,356 foreigners are resident in Italy for family reunion motives, while 36,291 are resident for educational purposes and about 17,000 for reasons linked to political asylum.

THE NORMATIVE ASPECTS

Through the Martelli Act (N. 39, 1990), which aimed to put a stop to uncontrolled immigration and clandestine residence in Italy by means of an act of amnesty, many illegal immigrants from Eastern European countries were able to legalise their situation.

The act of amnesty, which is considered to be the most liberal ever applied in Europe, allowed for the regularisation of approximately 230,000 people, among which numerous Yugoslavs and Poles. The act guaranteed a residence permit for two years and the subsequent issuing of a work permit or registration at the unemployment office. Free medical insurance was also guaranteed for one year.

At the beginning of 1992, less than half of the regularised foreigners fulfilled all the necessary conditions for the renewal of their residence permits, that is a regular job and/or an income of at least 400,000 lire per month. Their residence was nevertheless extended: four years for those with a regular job, two years for all others.

The 1990 Act also established an annual planning of new entries, which is designed to fulfill three major criteria:

-   the needs of the national economy;
-   the priority given to the employment of unemployed foreigners living in Italy;
-   international relations.

Up to the end of 1992, the annual planning of entries under the Martelli Act consisted of two decrees, one for 1991 and one for 1992, both of which established a 'zero planning' (no entries at all), with the following three exceptions:

-   requests for asylum;
-   family reunion;
-   domestic staff with a nominal job offer who have already obtained a residence permit.

In fact, all Central and Eastern European countries, including Russia, would be in favour of a system of planning of labour flows to Italy through annual quotas within each occupational group.

This would allow both Italy and the countries of origin to control the flows, and would facilitate the job placements on the Italian labour market and the flow of remittances to the countries of origin. Negotiations which were initiated in this respect, however, have not yet produced any agreement. For the time being, Italy is thus confining its actions to emergency situations, such as the Albanian exodus or the problem of refugees from the republics of former Yugoslavia.

In order to respond to the short-term needs of the Italian labour market and in order to contain the pressure from clandestine immigrants in search of temporary employment, the Italian government has also drafted an act on seasonal work. If approved, this act will lead to the legalisation of a large number of non-registered activities, a sector which increasingly employs nationals from Central and Eastern Europe. Entry and work permits would be given for periods of up to six months, on the basis of labour market demand (particularly in agriculture, construction, and tourism) and special bilateral agreements with certain countries of origin.

In accordance with general European agreements (i.e. Conferences of Vienna, Prague, Luxembourg and Berlin), Italy is also considering controlling entries in an organised manner with a view to reducing both the pressure on the Italian labour market and the negative effects of brain migration in Central and Eastern Europe. It should also be mentioned that in February 1992, Italy passed a law for 'cooperation with Central and Eastern European countries', which has the explicit aim of 'favouring transition towards forms of market economy' by way of, among other things, technical assistance, vocational training, and training of medium/ upper level executives.

THE SITUATION OF THE REFUGEES

For many years, East Europeans in Italy were political refugees. Since the end of the 1980s, however, Italy has moved from its traditional role as a transit country towards becoming a country of prolonged asylum, as placement in other countries has become more difficult. During the last 10 years, approximately 5,000 requests for asylum have been registered annually, with a peak of 27,000 in 1991 after the immigration of Albanians. However recognition of refugee status has remained very low, at a quota of 4–5 per cent. This said, applicants who are denied political asylum are rarely deported; they are tolerated for humanitarian reasons, not because of obligations resulting from adherence to the Geneva Convention, but in conformity with Section 10 of the Italian Constitution.

Above all, Italy has been a transit country for Poles and Soviet Jews. During the first decades of the post-war period, requests for asylum mainly stemmed from Yugoslavs (58 per cent), Hungarians (11 per cent) and Poles (7 per cent). Since 1984, there has been a major flow of Poles fleeing the adverse political conditions in Poland. Flows from Eastern European countries increased between the end of the 1980s and the beginning of the 1990s in response to political and economic changes and the liberalisation of exit visas.

In November 1987, faced with growing (and mainly economically-driven) migration from Poland, the Ministry of the Interior issued a directive introducing a 'green stamp' for immigrants from Poland (restricting the right to work and the duration of residence) and denying asylum to refugees arriving through Yugoslavia.

Yugoslavia has traditionally been a liberal transit country for Eastern European nationals migrating to the West, although a few years ago, it introduced a system of controls and restrictions to screen alleged political refugees. The illegal flow of refugees from the East, crossing Yugoslavia with the hope of entering Austria or Italy, nevertheless continued to increase until the emergency situation in 1992. Whereas, in 1989, 95 per cent of the migrants who were denied entry at the Italian and Austrian borders were from Africa and Asia, in 1990, 98 per cent of the same category of migrants consisted of Romanians, Soviets, Poles and nationals of other Eastern European countries.

Today the situation has changed, following Italy's signing of the Schenghen agreement in November 1990 and the Dublin Refugee Convention in June 1990. Recognition of the refugee status of applicants from Central and Eastern started to decrease as most of these countries became 'safe' and democratic.

THE INDIVIDUAL NATIONAL GROUPS

The Poles

The first group of Polish immigrants in Italy (approximately 200,000 people, of whom 8,000 stayed in Italy while the others subsequently emigrated to Argentina, Australia and Canada) was composed of soldiers from the Polish army at the end of the war. These were followed, in the 1950s and 1960s, by political dissidents and subsequently by groups of workers and engineers recruited (mainly in the Piedmont and Sardinia regions) on the basis of intergovernmental agreements.

The major inflow of official and clandestine Polish immigrants took place in 1986–1988 as a result of the liberalisation of emigration from

Poland and the restrictive immigration measures implemented in certain European countries during the same period. Official Polish sources indicate that 2,010 Poles migrated to Italy in 1986, 2,700 in 1987, and 1,375 in 1988. In 1989 and 1990, departures fell steeply to 351 and 179 respectively. Although residence permits followed a similar trend, their number was more significant: 4,342 in 1986 and 9,500 in 1987. The difference is due to clandestine entries and to the extension of tourist visas into residence permits.

Of the seven Central and Eastern European countries, only Czechoslovakia and Poland regularly publish official emigration statistics. Poland also has data on Poles who have illegally extended their stay abroad and registers data according to age, sex, level of education, occupation, residence and destination. With regard to legal emigration, women reach the same quota as men; most of the Polish immigrants in Italy come from towns.

The Yugoslavs

Despite the fact that former Yugoslavia (now the Slovenian Republic) has common borders with Italy, flows have always been moderate and often seasonal (e.g. employment in construction and tourism). This is also due to the fact that no intergovernmental agreements on labour migration have ever been concluded. Migration was mainly directed towards North-Eastern Italy (particularly in the Veneto region, where there is a strong community in the textile sector, and a steady border movement in Friuli Venezia-Giulia) and the coastal regions of the Lower Adriatic (Apulia). The population from former Yugoslavia increased progressively from 29,790 in 1990, (half of which were recent immigrants or former clandestines who were regularised), to 35,171 in 1991 and 37,878 in July 1992.

The war in former Yugoslavia does not appear to have increased immigration to Italy, at least until the end of 1992. There are currently about 10,000 refugees from former Yugoslavia (mainly Bosnians) in Italy, 2169 of whom are receiving direct assistance from public institutions. The numbers are extremely variable, given that new arrivals often coincide with the departure of those who wish to regain possession of the houses in Croatia and Bosnia from which they had been expelled during the war.

Entry and reception of refugees are regulated by the law of 24.9.92, which authorises the issuing of a temporary, renewable visa valid for sixty days. The law also authorises the entry and reception of young citizens from the former Yugoslavian republics who have reached the age of conscription or are called up by the army, or who are deserters or conscientious objectors. In addition, Italy has contributed 1.5 billion dollars to UNHCR's aid programme for refugees still in Yugoslavia.

The number of refugees in Italy seems modest compared to the situation in other countries, not only in Hungary and Turkey, but also in Germany, Austria, Sweden and Switzerland. The attempt to reach a European agreement aimed at raising and distributing evenly the quotas of refugees from former Yugoslavia has failed.

The Hungarians

Migration from Hungary is relatively limited and involves many qualified and highly qualified personnel, including a considerable proportion of engineers. There are numerous mixed marriages, sometimes 'false' ones.

At the end of 1990, 4,147 Hungarians were officially resident in Italy (of which only 500 had migrated after the 1989 revolutions). After a further increase of more than 10 per cent in 1991, a decrease was reported in the course of the first quarter of 1992, bringing the total Hungarian population to 4,460.

The Romanians

Many mixed marriages have also been recorded among the Romanians (10,000 in 1991 alone). A notable proportion of Romanian women, who are nurses or nursery school teachers, have also been registered. Romanian immigrants are mainly young people from large families. In general, adults are at a high professional level, often trained in chemistry, physics or electronics.

The number of Romanians in Italy more than doubled after the dissolution of the Soviet empire and the opening up of the borders. Immigration is mainly economically-driven, although nearly 1,000 requests for asylum were made in 1990 (220 of which were accepted, 570 still being under consideration).

According to data supplied by the Romanian authorities, 3,193 people asked to migrate to Italy between January 1990 and September 1992. Italy is the eighth most important country of destination for Romanian emigrants (Germany, Hungary and the United States are the major countries of immigration). It is estimated that a total of 165,796 Romanians have settled abroad.

More than 20 per cent of the requests for immigration to Italy come from holders of secondary school certificates and graduates. There is a slight majority of women and a strong presence of minors (approximately 25 per cent in 1990 and 35 per cent in 1991) and of people older than 60.

The Bulgarians

In 1992, there were over 5,000 Bulgarian citizens present in Italy, although the Bulgarian authorities consider that more than half of the 10,000 people who entered Italy with a tourist visa have stayed on illegally in search of work. Many declare themselves to be political refugees, despite the fact that the possibility of official recognition of their status is now considerably reduced. The clandestine residents mainly come from the countryside and have little education or vocational training. They usually find temporary employment in construction and in the lower positions of the tertiary sector.

The Czechs

The increase in new entries from Eastern Europe is also relatively significant in relation to the Czech population in Italy, which, starting from a low quota, grew to 4,240 in July 1992.

Czech immigrants are often well qualified, with a secondary school certificate or a university degree, and they tend to be quite young. They include a number of au-pair girls. The number of clandestine Czechs in Rome is estimated at 2,000.

Citizens of the Community of Independent States

The new immigration flows from the republics of the former Soviet Union are still modest and it is difficult to measure the relative importance of flows from the individual republics (citizens are still registered under the broad 'USSR' heading).

8,115 people were registered under the heading USSR in July 1992, a figure considerably lower than in 1991, whereas from 1990 to 1991 an increase of 5 per cent had been registered.

On the other hand, the distribution of exit visas from the former Soviet republics has not yet been completely liberalised. The effects of the Russian Law of May 1991, which authorised unrestricted emigration as from January 1993, are anxiously awaited.

The Russian government has also requested that an intergovernmental agreement on seasonal work be concluded with Italy.

The Gypsies

Some reflections should also be made with respect to gypsies, who do not form a true group of immigrants. Groups who have recently emigrated from the

Southern Yugoslavia, together with other nomads who have been coming to Italy for several centuries, are all classified as 'gypsies'. Gypsies, in fact, belong to ethnic groups which are increasingly diversified according to economic and socio-cultural characteristics and nationality (many are Italian citizens).

Within the group of immigrants from Eastern Europe, gypsies consist of the Lovara and Kalderasa, who originate from the Danubian-Carpathian area and who arrived in Italy at the turn of the century. There are also the Rom Khorakne and Kanjarja from Central-Southern Yugoslavia (Serbia, Bosnia, Herzegovina, Montenegro, Macedonia and Kossovo). Some of the latter group are Muslim and others are Orthodox. Their immigration started during the 60s, and increased during the 70s, also as a result of the Yugoslavian crisis. The Rudari originate from Romania and still speak Romanian among themselves. They started to migrate to Italy in the 1960s.

The principal activities of the gypsies are begging, working in fairs and as street vendors or tinkers, and selling flowers. The Gypsy population is very young (60 per cent are under 20), with a high illiteracy rate (44.3 per cent). The gypsies mainly live in mobile camps (caravans and huts) on the edge of large and small towns, and form a group which is very hard to integrate in Italian society.

The Case of the Albanians

The emigration of Albanians to Italy took on the same dimensions as the boat people tragedy, when tens of thousands of Albanians, compelled to leave their country because of immense poverty and an authoritarian and repressive political situation, flooded the Italian coasts. The flow was also prompted by the images of consumer well-being, shown continually on Italian TV in Albanian homes and on Albanian streets.

The two main flows of Albanians to Italy occurred on the 8th of March and on the 7th of August 1991. The proximity of the Albanian and the Italian coasts, coupled with the ties created under the Italian protectorate, created the conditions for this desperate exodus. It has also been assumed that the government of Tirana tolerated, or even favoured, the exodus with a view to reducing pressure exerted by the unemployed and the political opposition.

In March 1991, approximately 25,000 Albanians disembarked on the Italian coast in a mass exodus from Albania. The majority arrived in Brindisi on the 8th of March, with the agreement of the Italian government (given the emergency situation) and contrary to Italian law. Of this group, slightly over 3,000 returned to their native land after a couple of weeks (not having seriously intended to immigrate to Italy), while the remaining Albanians were accepted, with reservation, as temporary immigrants.

In April 1991, in contravention of the law in force, the Ministry of Labour authorised the issue of a temporary residence permit aimed at enabling the Albanians to register at the employment office 'until the procedures for immigrating to other countries is completed or until the desire to return to Albania is expressed'. Refugee status was only recognised in exceptional cases. A joint state-regional plan for the reception of the Albanians was designed with the aim of evaluating the reception capacity of each region and commune according to various criteria (e.g. the population density, the socio-economic situation, the availability of aid structures and organisations, and the presence of other immigrant communities).

A survey carried out among 600 Albanians staying in a camp site at Frassanito in the province of Otranto (Apulia) showed that 60 per cent were young people under 26 (nearly all unmarried males), 25 per cent had been to primary school, 70 per cent were in possession of secondary school certificates, and 5 per cent were university students or graduates. 85 per cent were factory workers, more than half of whom were qualified.

In September 1991, of the 21,292 Albanians distributed among the various Italian regions, 645 had been granted political asylum, 1,143 had returned to Albania, 322 had been deported, 1,500 could not be traced, and approximately 600 were receiving care as minors. 6,300 were registered at the employment office and 480 had found employment. By the end of 1991, 16,580 Albanians were registered at the employment office and 11,000 had been hired.

With respect to the second exodus of 7 August 1991, 17,000 Albanians were immediately sent back in accordance with an agreement between the Italian and Albanian authorities. By September 1991, only 183 of these refugees were still in Italy, all of whom were awaiting repatriation.

Following the emergency which arose from the two exoduses, a cooperation plan between Italy and Albania for the preventive control of ports and the sea was concluded. In addition, a humanitarian aid programme was also developed and economic cooperation agreements aimed at reorganising and modernising Albania are currently being negotiated. Discussions are also underway with a view to concluding an agreement for organised labour migration of Albanians, itself aimed at promoting remittances in foreign currency.

CHOOSING FUTURE STRATEGIES

As a phenomenon which is still in its early stages and which is badly documented, the task of defining the level, nature and effects of future migration to Italy is clearly a perilous one.

Population imbalances, different levels of wealth, political or religious repression, geographic proximity, access policies, networks of friends and family chains are all factors which combine in determining the direction and intensity of migration across the world, including in Europe and in Italy. However, with the improvement of means of communication and diffusion of images and information, 'proximity' has now become 'planetary'. During the last 20 years, the links and interdependence between geographic areas have become so extensive and ramified that geographic proximity and colonial links between countries of departure and countries of destination are no longer of primary importance in determining the choice of countries of immigration.

The main causes of migration from Eastern Europe to Italy are certainly more economically than politically-driven. But this fundamental choice holds sociological as well as psychological paradigms. In general, immigrants come to Italy in order to participate in a well-off consumer society. It is not the pressure of over-population and the consequent lack of jobs which lead to emigration, but the discrepancies between the levels of pay and standards of living. The flows are therefore intense at the moment, but there is a clear preference for a temporary stay and temporary employment. This can be attributed to predictions of recovery in the national economies of the countries of origin as a result of political change and economic reconversion.

Does this mean that migration is becoming more of a commuting process ('circular migration') than proper immigration with permanent settling? The development of transport and communications could certainly support this argument. The insignificant differences between Eastern and Western population growth, the lack of any traditional network of relations between the two regions (unlike those which exist between the North and the South due to colonial history, and exempting specific East–West relations between, for example, Poland and France and Germany), and the prospect of economic recovery and democratisation in Central and Eastern Europe (which will generate a new spirit of national belonging), would all tend to contradict alarmist theories on future immigration to Italy from Eastern and Central Europe.

Steady, permanent immigration from the three countries in which the transition process is progressing more rapidly (i.e. Hungary, Czechoslovakia and Poland) can thus be excluded. The migratory thrust from these three countries will be mainly of a temporary nature. Poland, however, could to a certain extent be an exception in that the migratory chains established in the 1980s and the initiatives of certain Italian companies, aimed at attracting medium and highly skilled labour, could act as a pull factor.

With respect to the three other countries undergoing a more traumatic transition (the former Soviet Union, Bulgaria and the Baltic States), the populations most likely to emigrate have characteristics which make a mass flow towards Italy unrealistic. The Baltic States could witness migration of part of their population to the Scandinavian countries; Bulgarians of Turkish and Macedonian origin, and gypsies resident in Bulgaria, will tend to migrate to Turkey and Hungary, two countries with which they have close ties. The same could hold true for Romanians of Magyar origin living in Romanian Transylvania. However, that several thousand people from Romania will still prefer to emigrate to Italy, due both to linguistic similarities and to the presence in Romania of an Italian community of craftsmen and bricklayers which might decide to return to Italy, should not to be excluded .

Forecasts with respect to Yugoslavia and Albania are rather more worrying. Although the two countries show different characteristics (Albanian emigrants are poorer and more needy, whereas those from Yugoslavia leave their country for war and political reasons, and are more in favour of a rapid return), the two flows will run the risk of creating significant pressure at the Italian borders over the course of the next few years.

According to experts, the gradual opening up of the borders of the former Soviet Republics is likely to produce growing migratory flows, even though predictions of a catastrophic mass exodus seem unrealistic. The flows will be diverse and will not necessarily head towards the West. It can be anticipated, for instance, that a portion of the Soviet emigrants with medium and high level qualifications who will leave their countries of origin due to economic crisis, the so-called 'European emigration' (i.e. emigrants from Russia, Belorussia, Ukraine and Uzbekistan), will choose to migrate to Italy. On the contrary, it is unlikely that the so-called 'Asian emigration', which consists of unqualified workers leaving the Southern and Eastern republics because of demographic pressure, will significantly affect a country like Italy. But no one can yet predict the direction of 'ethnic migration' of Russians from the 'colonialised' former Soviet republics (25 million Russians established primarily in Kazakistan, the Ukraine, Latvia and Estonia), although the flow will be directed initially towards the Russian Federation.

The level of education and the cultural and social affinity of European citizens coming from the former communist countries lead us to think that this segment of foreign immigration to Italy will receive more favourable treatment and will achieve a higher level of integration, both economic and in Italian society. It is the view of some experts that immigration from Eastern and Central Europe will also be privileged in order to oppose, in the long-term, further waves of immigration from Africa and Asia, which objectively give rise to stronger elements of socio-cultural contrast and stronger resistance to integration.

Italy will continue to provide favourable conditions for temporary as well as for permanent immigration, both on an institutional level (because of inefficient control of illegal immigrants and tolerance of their presence) and with respect to the characteristics of the productive system and the decentralised, flexible labour market. Many observers explain East European migration to Italy as a flow which is determined by qualitative, rather than quantitative, imbalances on the labour market. The Italian economy is extremely deregulated and enjoys large segments of secondary and/or submerged markets, which allows for contractual flexibility during the current phase of economic stagnation. In particular, the temporary nature of the work, and the possibility of commuting, contribute to the willigness of Eastern European migrants to accept unstable and badly paid jobs.

Eastern European labour is all the more attractive to Italian employers in that young Italians, due to their expectations in terms of quality of employment, and due to the financial support they receive from their families, are increasingly reluctant to accept jobs in marginal sectors such as the lower tertiary sector, unskilled work in heavy industry, in farms or in fishing.

Despite the above, and bearing in mind the current shortage of qualified manpower, it can be anticipated that in the medium and long term, Eastern European labour will be increasingly required to fill high and medium level professional positions, leaving the unskilled and unwanted tasks to the African and Asian workforce. It is also likely that, in the near future, Italy will attempt to resolve its current contradictions, where the virtual closure of external borders coexists with the tolerance of high numbers of clandestine immigrants. Despite the slower economic growth rate, the Italian labour market is still showing a steady demand for labour. On the other hand, Italy cannot disappoint the expectations of Eastern European citizens looking at the 'free and well-off' West, just as it cannot avoid devising bilateral labour agreements, which are currently being negotiated with the new Eastern and Central European states, as components of the more general agreements on economic cooperation.

Indeed, one of the possible scenarios, the most realistic for Italy too, is that of a gradual shifting from a 'crisis migration' (collapse of dictatorial regimes, economic crises) to a 'normal migration' (mainly of a temporary nature), following the elimination of all obstacles to free migration and the organisation of stable currents of temporary migration based on intergovernmental agreements.

11 United Kingdom
Patricia Goldey

When one compares the UK situation with that of other North European countries, there are very distinctive patterns of migration, and of policies and legal responses by government towards migratory movements that make the British experience of migration somewhat different from that of France, Switzerland or Germany, the major countries of European immigration in this generation. In the 1970s, 10 per cent of the labour force in France was foreign; in Switzerland 30 per cent. In Britain, by comparison, the proportion of foreign workers has been relatively small. Between 1965 and 1980 immigrants accounted for as much as half the population expansion in Germany, while in Britain they accounted for only a fifth, at a time when the birth rates of the two indigenous populations were declining. The impact of labour migrants on the British economy has been statistically small in comparison with France, Germany or Switzerland.

The composition of the migrant population in Britain is also different from that of its north European neighbours. Most labour migrants to Britain in the past thirty years have not come from Europe as such but from three main areas of origin: Ireland, the Caribbean and Asia. While there are significant numbers of Portuguese, Italians, Greeks, Turks and Cypriots in the capital and smaller nuclei of these populations in the major industrial towns (Manchester, Liverpool, Birmingham Glasgow, Newcastle, Bristol), they constitute collectively the lesser part of the migrant or immigrant population.

Compared with other West European states, the United Kingdom has not experienced as yet any substantial immigration from Eastern Europe; however it does face along with other EC countries increasing immigrant pressures from developing countries outside the Community and pressures from former Yugoslav asylum-seekers.

The main rationale and features of UK's migration policy differs from that of other major West European states. In the perspective of post-Maastricht negotiations on coordination of national immigration policies, this chapter examines the recent policy and legal shifts in the UK, and discusses the areas of conflict or disagreement between national law and international accords established through European legislation.

MIGRATION TO THE UK FROM 1960 TO 1992: THE HISTORICAL
CONTEXT OF POLICY

Discussions on migration, and governmental responses to migration have
tended in Britain, because of the dominant pattern of the migration flow,
to become entangled with discussions on race; migration 'problems' have
tended to be seen in the context of racial issues. References in news-
papers and government papers to 'second generation immigrants', itself a
contradiction in terms, underline this equation made at all levels in British society between migrant status and racial origin. The overlap between
categories of migrant status and racial origin affects most studies, and the
statistical data base; in 1966 the New Commonwealth immigration population was about 900,000: by 1974, with the inclusion of UK born
descendants it had risen to 1 million and by 1982, to 2.2 million. Of the
'black' population presently counted, over 40 per cent were born in the
UK. The Office of Population Censuses and Surveys gives the total population of people of Asian and West Indian origin as 1,651,000 (1982): that
is to say just over 3 per cent of the population. Half of the white British
population lives in towns or villages that have less than half of one per
cent of residents from ethnic minorities. One-third of all people of Asian
origin, and one-half of those of West Indian origin live in the Greater
London area.

This then is one major problem in any discussion of migration issues in
Britain; the problem of the entanglement of racial issues with migrant
issues. Most academic migrant studies in the UK focus on those survey
populations where the head of household is of Caribbean or Asian origin;
most government studies have also focused on these populations.

Migration law since the 1960s has meant the development of a system of
control designed to reduce the number of settlers; the New Commonwealth
citizens were of special concern; that is to say, citizens of the formerly
dependent territories of Africa, Asia and the Caribbean as opposed to the
Dominions. There were three main policy areas to be considered during the
1960s in relation to migration: commonwealth policy; official estimates of
labour demand; the social consequences of migration.

(a) Commonwealth Policy: with the growing independence of previously
colonial territories, and the growing recognition of Europe as the
focus, the future, there was a conflicting pull, a confusion, in the public mind; now too, but especially then, market loyalties and relationships were divided between Commonwealth outlets and imports and
those in Europe.

(b) Labour demand: this was a second area of public confusion. Given the general awareness that the UK was entering a period of technological change and industrial reorganisation, there was uncertainty about industrial labour needs. Migrants were seen as a pool of spare capacity, able to work in the service sector and only presenting a small burden on public expenditure.

(c) Social consequences: there was little attention given to how many labour migrants would settle in Britain; immigration, employment, health, education were concerns of different government departments and there was no co-ordinated view on the treatment of, or facilities for, migrants.

Between the Commonwealth Immigration Act of 1962 and the Nationality Act of 1981 primary immigration from the Commonwealth had stopped. The British Nationality Act of 1981 attempted to define citizenship afresh, while correlating it with immigration control. It offered a field day to lawyers, and a jungle for individuals to try to fight through. Before the courts of law, the migration rules as Lord Denning said are 'not rules of law. They are rules of practice laid down for the guidance of immigration officers and tribunals' (Lord Denning quoted in Bevan, 1986: p. 14).

Since 1983 there have been three further changes in immigration law, all of them controversial.

(a) Wives have been reduced to the level of husbands for entry considerations, since a primary purpose test has been introduced for all spouses.

(b) A visa requirement has been introduced for visitors from selected Commonwealth countries; Bangladesh, India, Ghana, Nigeria, Pakistan, Sri Lanka.

(c) The Courts and Immigration Appeals Tribunal was established, and gained increasing importance, (720 cases in 1982, 1,067 in 1984 and 1,297 in 1985 (MacDonald, 1987)).

Not all migrants enter the country legally: there are four recognised ways of illegal entry:

(a) use of false documents before the entry clearance officer;
(b) use of false documents at the port of entry;
(c) covert entry;
(d) overstaying.

Policy is strict on detection of illegal immigrants and on their removal; the basis of removal, even many years after illegal entry, was laid down by the 1971 Act, which now is enforced through raids, stop and search encounters and the regular contact of immigrants with government departments like the Police, DSS, and Inland Revenue. The 1971 Act strengthened the power to deport. Aliens who enter the UK clandestinely, without going through immigration control, have committed a criminal offence and can be deported, but until 1968, Commonwealth citizens who escaped detection for 24 hours had not committed an offence and could not be deported. After 1968, clandestine entry was one crime punished by deportation of both aliens and Commonwealth citizens. Before 1971, illegal entrants to the UK could, after five years ordinary residence, expect exemption from deportation.

The 1971 Act involved the establishment of special intelligence units set up to detect illegal immigrants and overstayers. It applied deportation 'conducive to the public good' to both aliens and to Commonwealth citizens. By 1976 leave to stay obtained by deception was ineffective; the person could be treated as an illegal entrant, and so detained or deported.

One recent estimate suggests there could be as many as 250,000 illegal immigrants in the UK, including those who have either overstayed their permits to remain, or who have gained entry under false pretences.

UK AND THE EC

Over the past decade, changes in the law and regulations covering immigration have produced tighter controls and increased the capacity for official intervention in individual cases. The EC law with the legal provisions for freedom of movement, right of entry, and lifted border controls, appears to stand in stark opposition to the trend in British immigration policy and law over the past twenty years.

'Ease' of entry for EC nationals is seen by some in the UK to be in sharp contrast to the tight controls placed on entry for other nationals; added to the existing differentiation between so-called Old Commonwealth, and New Commonwealth country nationals, this has been seen by some as leading to further racial discrimination, where 'white' foreigners are preferred as migrant workers.

Right of entry for Commonwealth citizens is now very controlled and compares adversely with the rights of citizens from EC countries. Under EC law a worker can be admitted to the UK for an initial six-month period.

He/she should be employed before the family can join, and installed in housing 'considered as normal for national workers in the region where he is employed'. He/she can then apply for a residence permit which is a proof of entitlement. The permit can only be withdrawn for reasons of public policy or if the holder has left employment voluntarily.

An EC national working in the UK has the right to equal treatment with nationals in conditions and terms of employment (art.7/1), in social and tax advantages (7/2), vocational training, trade union membership and benefits (8/1) and housing (9). The rules of nationality and patriality define who has the right of residence and is free from immigration control. British nationality is no longer determined in the traditional manner of birth in UK territory: the 1981 Act requires a new-born child to have one parent who was either born in the UK, or who has 'settled' status under the immigration laws (British Nationality Act 1981 s.11). EC law allows for extensive free movement of workers, the self-employed, and those establishing business; it is quite separate from the provisions of the Immigration Act or the Immigration Rules and where the two come into conflict, the EC Law prevails.

There are striking differences between the treatment of EC migrants and non-EC migrants. For EC workers, dependents also have the right of entry; there is no sex discrimination; and in addition to dependent children, grandparents may also enter (article 10 (2) of 1612/88).

Until March 1980 the immigration rules for aliens and Commonwealth citizens were separate documents; after that they were embodied in one main document (HC169, February 1983) amended in 1985 (HC503, August 1985). Visa requirements were introduced between May 1985 and January 1987.

It is a cause of some disquiet to some groups in the UK that the 'ease' of entry for EC nationals contrasts so sharply with the restrictions placed against non-EC immigrants.

In 1983, the total number of passengers given permission to enter the UK was about 11.5 million, rising in 1984 to 12.5 million; of these over 5 million were EC nationals. Those accepted for settlement decline steadily throughout the 1980s, as reflected in official statistics. (1980, 69800; 1981, 59,100; 1982, 53,900; 1983, 53,500; 1984, 50,950). Of the 50,950 accepted for settlement in 1984, 26,720 were Commonwealth citizens, 24,230 were foreign nationals (Iran, Pakistan, USA and others). Residence permits issued to EC nationals have stayed at between 6,000 and 8,000 per year since 1975: in 1984, 6,940 residence permits were issued. On average, about 50 per cent of permits go to workers.

Despite the fear of 'swamping', so dominant in the rhetoric of both major political parties in the UK since the 1970s, in recent years it is the case that

(a)   the majority of work permits now go to aliens rather than Commonwealth citizens,
(b)   the USA, Canada and Europe (west and east) supply the seasonal workers required (in agriculture or domestic work),
(c)   if workers are required, the origin of these workers will be the countries of the EC.

In theory, it is possible for businesses to import workers depending on specific need. Work permits are obtainable through the Department of Employment; if demand arises in a particular area, in theory the demand can be met in a carefully calculated way. The prospective employer has first to convince the Department of Employment of the necessity of employing foreign immigrant labour. There are requisite conditions to be met:

(a)   the work itself must require that foreign labour,
(b)   the employer should first advertise locally and nationally for at least three weeks before applying for a permit and guarantee that no resident will be displaced or excluded by the employment of the foreigner,
(c)   wages must not be lower than those paid to indigenous workers,
(d)   the age of the worker should be between 23 and 54, and a professional skill or qualification should be required.

The work permit scheme is a tight method of control for the immigration of non-EC workers: even in the UK National Health Service, where presently about 18,000 foreign doctors are employed, and where traditionally there has been a heavy reliance on imported labour, tighter controls have been introduced since 1985 (Bevan, 1986: p. 287).

The protection of employment opportunities for UK nationals remains one rationale of immigration control, especially in a period of recession and high unemployment. In 1990 the European Community produced a paper on migration policy which identified certain areas in which the Community might exercise a common role:

–   the integration of groups into their host area;
–   the harmonisation of rules on family unification;
–   illegal immigration;

- deportation of illegal migrants;
- the organisation of short-term contracts for workers;
- the use of Aid and Development funds to offset pressures to migrate.

The common agenda was discussed with EFTA countries who will get free movement rights and with East European states who were partly seen as a buffer but also as a potential threat.

EC legislation extended national rights to non-citizens but only to those who are nationals of the EC countries; it guaranteed a policy of free movement of workers, goods, services and capital across national frontiers. Fears of being 'swamped' by movements from poorer to richer countries within the community were quelled by restraining the free movement of workers from a five to a seven year period in the case of GrECe, and from five to an eight year period in the case of Portugal and Spain. In fact so far as statistics show until now there has been little movement of EC nationals across frontiers; those who are taking advantage of their new rights are professionals and middle managers, and not so much unskilled workers. Of the estimated 15 million people in the EC who are not nationals of the state in which they live, two-thirds are not EC nationals (8–10 million depending on the count of illegal immigrants). There has been then, until now, a relatively limited national movement of EC nationals. However, while the EC gives rights to individuals over and above the rights they have as nationals, the right to nationality or citizenship is given by the member state. Countries within the EC vary in how nationality is given, and therefore in how inclusive or exclusive is the policy towards immigrants and their national or social integration in the state.

Countries within the EC have varied in their response to the concept of free movement of people, and the aim of a frontier-free Europe. Removal of controls and checks at national frontiers implies the development of alternative systems of control and surveillance, as the concept of legality or right of entry has not shifted, only the ways by which it is monitored. Controls over drug trafficking, illegal entry of individuals have still to be maintained albeit away from the frontier. The UK government, along with Ireland and Denmark, has maintained that the UK is justified in maintaining border controls to check on non-EC nationals: while France, and Germany have through the 1980s removed their controls. At various levels within the EC administration, discussions on the controversial issue of free movement have taken place since the mid-1980s; with the *ad hoc* group of Immigration Ministers convened first in 1986, and the Coordinators group set up in 1988. While not all border barriers have been lifted, pressures that they should not be lifted have been growing from those various interest groups who fear that the harmonisation of procedures and policies within the countries of the EC will make it more difficult for non-EC nationals to get into any of the countries of the community.

Pressures to defend national and community interests have increased since 1990; in part in response to the fear of potential migration from the eastern European countries; in part a response to the war in former Yugoslavia; in part in response to a growing fear of loss of national power and legitimacy.

Since 1990 member states have permitted the Commission to take the lead, to make proposals through expert groups and the like, on immigration. Events have however overtaken policy. The 750,000 guest workers from former Yugoslavia have been joined by relatives in Germany; the twenty million Russians thought to be wanting to leave Russia may now get passports to do so. Germans are returning to Germany from Russia, a 'rare migration where grandparents are leading their children and grandchildren home' (Ignatieff, 1992), a right permitted to them because of German nationality law and its 'right of return', but no longer permitted to many British nationals, and no longer to Brazilians whose special relationship with Portugal had to be surrendered by 1993.

All this in the midst of an economic recession, interpreted also by some as a moral and social crisis. At a time of possible growing immigration, economic priorities have demanded cutbacks in UK programmes aimed at 'integration'. Cutbacks in the funding allocated for certain programmes carried out under local or national governments in 1992 were feared to have a disproportionately negative impact on the ethnic minority population resident in Britain, mainly in inner-city areas.

Although controversial and always a cause of debate, the policy of integration on equal terms and social service provision aimed at achieving that policy, was fundamentally accepted by most political parties. Money allocated through the programmes, although never sufficient, was quite substantial. The implication of the cutbacks is also presumably that no such 'integrative' services will be made available by government to any new immigrant groups, a point to be developed later.

ASYLUM SEEKERS AND REFUGEES

In 1990 the Dublin convention on asylum which attempted to harmonize asylum procedures between member states of the Community was signed by all, but not ratified by all. Pressures opposed to a community-wide policy on asylum seekers have grown, mainly from those groups who believe it would be more difficult for non-EC nationals to enter the Community where the different member countries to have a common policy. The perceived implications of freeing the borders include: a dependence on identity cards to help with checks away from the border, a possibility fiercely opposed by Denmark, Britain and Ireland; greater control or responsibility put on the airlines and airport authorities; easier transferability of personal data so as to control illegal entry. Some government members also see a wider problem: that so much of the negotiation process has taken place outside the parliamentary arena that little or no space is allowed for renegotiation of agreements.

The specific UK problem, as yet unclear and unresolved, focuses on the signing of the Treaty of Maastricht; now it appears that signing the treaty as negotiated a year ago might create a parliamentary crisis, given the present divisions among and within political parties: not signing the treaty would bring UK relations with Europe to a final collapse. Although in a minority, the thirty or so potential Conservative Party rebels are genuinely appalled by the idea of a federal Europe, and might be prepared to trade the survival of the present government for an independent, future Britain. The Foreign Office appears to believe that if Britain decides not to opt out of the Social Chapter, the whole treaty will have to be re-ratified by the other 11 countries. In practice Britain's opting into the treaty should pose few problems, given the flexibility of rules and regulations in the community. In practice too the Social Chapter involves mainly a set of guidelines which would probably have to be passed into British law in any case.

The present discourse over Maastricht in Britain represents yet another example of British ambivalence over European unity on the legal side. The UK government has maintained, along with Ireland and Denmark that the UK is justified in maintaining its border controls to check on non-EC nationals, and the Home Office has denied that immigration policy would be subsumed under a European policy. Maastricht does however begin to formalise a coordination between Ministers of Justice on asylum seekers and refugees.

In 1992 the EC Interior Ministers appeared to destroy, or set aside, internationally recognised definitions of what is a refugee, resulting in accusations from within Europe and outside of imposing a 'Fortress Europe' regime. Active on this issue amongst EC Ministers was the British Home Secretary, Kenneth Clarke, who tried to force the responsibility of protection of asylum seekers back onto their countries of origin; and persuade EC Ministers to force asylum seekers to find protection from within their own countries. Mr Claude Moraes, Director of the Joint Council for the Welfare of Immigrants, described Mr Clarke's proposals as 'new and frightening'.

EC Ministers agreed on measures aimed to identify 'bogus' asylum seekers, and to harmonise laws and policies; the German Chancellor's call for common EC asylum laws was based explicitly on a plea to combat the growth of violence against refugees, through a common refugee policy. Calls to 'share the burden' of asylum seekers, were on the whole resisted; for example the Italians, finding little or no support from the EC with the influx of Albanians in 1992, sent them back forcibly.

Eastern Europe raises the spectre of 'millions' of potential migrants waiting and ready to leave their countries as soon as they get a passport; Yugoslavia raises the spectre of refugees, a very significant increase in asylum seekers from within Europe to add to the thousands of Somalis, Sudanese, Sri-Lankans already seeking refuge in the West.

While issues of asylum and immigration can be kept conceptually and legalistically distinct, they are now entwined in policy statements: asylum seekers can be reclassified as immigrants, 'economic migrants', in a more verbal than real distinction from 'real' refugees.

The flexibility of practice in comparison to the apparent rigidity of regulation is particularly seen in the application of rules to refugees. Most of the UK press space given to those entering the UK during 1992 concerns refugees, their poor treatment at the hands of the authorities and the bending of policy and back-tracking on the part of those authorities. In August 1992, the UK deported 36 refugees from the former Yugoslavia; following criticism in the light of this incident, and British policy on refugees from Bosnia, asylum rules were somewhat relaxed. In September 1992 while the government agreed to make greater efforts to allow entry to Bosnians, the Foreign Minister rejected the German appeal for the UK to take a greater share of Bosnian refugees. In October 1992, a hundred Bosnians were stranded at Gatwick airport having been refused entry. By December the UK had agreed to double its intake of Bosnian refugees.

Towards the end of 1992 pressure from local authorities pleading approaching bankruptcy because of pressures to care for refugees resulted in the Home Secretary offering the prospect of financial help to those local authorities faced with housing refugees, while imposing visa requirements on most travellers from former Yugoslavia, and opening a visa office in Croatia to deal with refugees from Bosnia.

The steady stream of refugees has provoked strong government response, but a fluctuating policy. While Amnesty International and like non-governmental organisations accused the government of turning its back on special pleas for help from the UNHCR, asylum seekers were, despite government reluctance, being admitted to the UK (2,717 in January

1993 from the former Yugoslavia), but with long delays expected in the processing of asylum applications.

Volunteer groups are still arranging private assistance: planeloads of women and children were supported by a Worthing-based charity arranging rescue flights to London, some groups of Yugoslavs arrived by sea at Harwich and a Liverpool-based group supported the entry of several bus-loads of Bosnians having pressured the government to admit them. Such groups are critical of Britain's policy, especially given the size of the burden in comparison to other European countries: the fewer than 3,000 applications for asylum stand in comparison to the 44,000 accepted by Sweden, and the 200,000 by Germany. Britain was also criticised for ignoring requests from Amnesty International and other agencies not to return refugees to other Europeans countries in the interests of 'international burden-sharing'. Since August 1992, the behaviour of the government has been questioned by the volunteer agencies about the expulsion of Yugoslavs to other countries from which they had come. Amnesty International's British Director, David Bull, was reported in the press as having expressed his 'surprise and concern' to the Home Secretary, Kenneth Clarke, and as having declared that the government had shown 'little if any flexibility' in the application of the asylum regulations. Mr Bull was also reported as asking Mr Clarke to ensure that Britain complied with a UNHCR request to refrain from 'third country removals' of Yugoslav asylum seekers during the present Yugoslav crisis in the spirit of 'international burden-sharing'. Pressure groups and other voluntary associations have been able to make special cause and work around policy restrictions. This is also exemplified by the case of the Kurds; there are about 18,000 Kurdish refugees in the UK, mainly in the London area but also in Colchester, Manchester Cardiff and Glasgow – the last three towns being historical dispersion points for refugees. The Kurdish Housing Association, working mainly in the three London boroughs of Lambeth, Hackney and Harringey was established in 1989 to assist refugees find homes.

The Asylum Bill of 22 October 1992 changed the access to appeal of immigrants and asylum seekers: refugees refused asylum were granted an automatic right of appeal with an oral hearing before an adjudicate. However, prospective visitors who are refused a visa, and prospective immigrants had their right to appeal withdrawn, in the latter case of immigrants affecting only those whose grounds for appeal are considered 'manifestly unfounded'.

For those who have access to appeal there is a long wait as the backlog of about 26,000 cases means a delay of about two years before appeals will be heard.

Asylum applications have grown; from an annual figure in 1968 of 4,000 to an estimated 57,000 in 1991. The Home Office Asylum Office estimated an official figure of 44,000 for 1991.

In comparison to the situation facing Germany, the British asylum situation is a modest problem: in 1992 reports from Germany indicated approximately 500,000 asylum seekers entering in the year, with a further 500,000 making up the backlog of applications awaiting processing. Of these many are Romanians, and many of the Romanians, perhaps as many as 80 per cent, are gypsies.

Deportation, a temporary solution to the problem of undesired immigration is a tool used to varying extents by different European governments. In 1992 there were about 300,000 deportations in 1992 of Romanian Gypsies from Germany.

The atmosphere in the EC, outside the UK, seemed to be towards the end of 1992, a willingness to reduce the queues of asylum seekers allowed admission into Europe while officials decide whether they are or are not 'genuine' refugees.

During the British presidency in July 1992, a draft paper was drawn up proposing a common approach for identifying those asylum seekers who could be classified as 'clearly unfounded' or 'obviously deserving'. The *ad hoc* Ministerial Group said 'Those who genuinely feel compelled to leave their own country should seek protection in the first country to which they come.' In effect, and not only, this suggests that asylum seekers should look for help within their own continents. However, it also implies that 'fast-track' applications would be considered to leave the door open to 'genuine' cases.

While the 1961 Geneva convention guarantees asylum to people with a well-founded fear of persecution, discussions on definitions of what constitutes a refugee continued at ministerial level among EC nations during 1992. The general argument seemed to be that running from war, hunger, starvation or extreme poverty were not covered by the 1961 convention. The asylum package for discussion in December at the Edinburgh summit was generally seen as a measure to deter waves of asylum seekers from the Third World, which however, even if it reached conclusions, would not have legislative force, though they could be adopted by national governments.

Arguments from proximity also put paid to a German initiative to establish quotas for other EC countries to burden-share, which was rejected after other EC countries claimed, based on a UNHCR statement that people fleeing a civil war should be accommodated as close as possible to their original homes in order to allow a speedy return to their homes, pushing refugees back to the region from which they originate. This would mean for example that Sri-Lankan disputes should be resolved within the Indian sub-continent, and that Zairean refugees should reach asylum in the surrounding countries.

In 1991, with Kenneth Baker as Home Secretary, there were 50,000 asylum applications in the UK but with an increase in immigration staff and 'more rigorous' examination of claims numbers in 1992 fell to around 30,000. (Baker in 'Europe can't give refuge to the world', *Daily Express* 7.9.1992). In the 1980s there was a steady but small flow of 2,000–3,000 refugees per year into the UK: this has been rising, with the 1991 figure of 50,000 representing a tenfold increase on the 5,000 applications figure of 1988. This should however stand beside the 400,000 refugees that Germany received in 1992, a sharp increase from the 250,000 in 1991.

New fast track vetting procedures allow applicants to make an oral representation, when before they had no right of a hearing before an adjudicator. However, the old time limit remains: 48 hours for some, 15 days for others, to collect evidence and marshall a case.

UK government retains control on its periphery by imposing fines on airlines for unauthorised travellers and the strict control it keeps on visas. Even temporary visitors find it harder to come to Britain, as tourists, businessmen, relatives who want to pay a brief visit have had their right to appeal to a visa rejection withdrawn in the immigration section of the 1992 Bill. Almost 2,000 of the 10,000 who appealed last year had their claims upheld.

THE WIDER ISSUES AND WIDER COMMUNITY

(a) From Receiving to Repelling

After the start of the energy crisis in 1973 the main receiving countries of northern and central Europe, France, Germany, Holland, Switzerland, Austria and Belgium, introduced changes in their immigration policies; firstly, employment of new foreign workers was reduced to the lowest level possible; secondly, return of migrants to their country of origin was encouraged; thirdly, measures were initiated to try to integrate those foreign workers and their families most necessary to or already most integrated within the host country (OECD, 1978). Changes in migration policy were thus interlinked with the cyclical movements in the national economies of the countries of immigration, and with broader, more international issues of technical and technological development, demographic changes, core-periphery inequalities and systemic disharmony.

Economic crises in Europe led to increased national unemployment levels, and increased dismissals of foreign workers. This resulted by 1980 in the acceleration of the reunification of families, which in 1980 represented 70 per cent of total Western European Immigration (UN, 1982). November 1983 saw the passing of the law in Germany 'Stimulating foreigners to return to their countries of origin', with a financial incentive for workers who chose to return 'home'. Already by the 1980s in northern Europe feelings were expressed, and policies implemented, on the basis that there were 'too many foreigners' in certain countries of immigration. In 1981 there were 10.7 million foreigners in the five receiving countries of France, West Germany, Holland, Sweden and Switzerland (OECD, 1983).

This attitude was certainly changed from the welcome afforded to immigrants in the 1960s. In 1964 when the millionth 'foreign worker' arrived in West Germany from Portugal, he was greeted with gifts and music. Immigration from the European 'periphery' continued into the 1970s, after a twenty year period during which the Northern European countries were clearly dependent, in their economic boom period, on imported labour, although not always so well advertised, nor indeed so welcome as in the German case above. Since 1973 or shortly thereafter policies of welcome turned to policies of repulsion. One problem, not unique to Britain, is the reconciliation of twenty years of restraint or repulsion of migrants with the concept of the open frontier, in a situation where the limitations of the apparent 'open-door' policy are not well understood outside the legal setting. British immigration authorities have become accustomed to a policy of exclusion and restriction. This sits uneasily with the more liberal policy espoused by the Treaty of Rome, and the EC, of extending the scope of free movement and reducing the restrictive powers of member states. However in practice restrictive regulations in the UK have in the past year been relaxed to allow the entry of specific groups (claiming refugee status) into the UK, due to the ability in Britain of pressure and special interest groups to move constituency representatives and play the political game at the local level with humanitarian motives.

The presence in the UK of long-established, concentrated East European (Polish, Hungarian, Czech) communities from the 1930s, 1940s and 1950s has made it possible for thousands to join relatives and for those seeking entry to find patrons or support.

There continues to be seasonal migration of students and other young people from Eastern Europe to work mainly in agricultural tasks such as fruit-picking, work traditionally done in previous generations by poor urban British families in lieu of a holiday under the Seasonal Agricultural Workers' Scheme. Some students are brought in for training schemes under the Employment Department's Training and Work Experience Scheme. Some employment agencies have grown up specifically to help non-British workers, usually with specific skills or of managerial level, to find work in Britain, and also help companies circumvent the restrictions. However, employment statistics show that the entry of workers from Eastern European countries is insignificant as yet in comparison to that of other nationalities.

(b) Labour Market Trends

It is difficult to produce any economic motive or 'pull' factor that might at the moment attract European migrant labour to the UK in any significant numbers. Wages and family benefits are higher in other West European countries; the previous attractions of the UK such as the National Health Service and educational system appear to be in crisis or decline, depending on one's viewpoint. British tax laws now give a marginal incentive to richer social groups to live or invest in the UK. However, for the migrant non-refugee coming from Eastern or Southern Europe, it is difficult to identify the market opportunities in a period of recession and, some would say, industrial decline. The low skills of the British labour force, 44 per cent of whom appear to have no academic or professional qualification, may however provide gaps in the labour market for particular categories of skilled workers, for example in civil construction, which can only be met by skilled imported labour.

The present rate of indigenous and immigrant unemployment, highest among the manual and semi- or non-skilled groups must surely be a deterrent for would-be migrants with low skills. The unemployment figures of January 1993 topped the three million line; a figure that has symbolic significance in Britain. The figure means that three million were collecting unemployment benefit, not including those categories previously excluded from entitlement to benefit through a series of policy shifts during the current and previous Conservative governments. Representing 10.5 per cent of the British workforce, the three million figure, despite the doctoring of statistics, recalls the unemployment levels of the mid 1980s, and signifies to the population at large that the economic recession continues.

However, seasonal migrants still come, from the South and the East. Statistics for seasonal workers are handled outside the employment conventions. Even in times of high unemployment, specialists and highly skilled workers in professions in deficit might be welcomed as immigrants, especially given the noted lack of skills among the working population.

(c) National Rights, Human Rights

In the earlier migration phase pre-1973, some national attention was given to problems faced by migrants in Western Europe, the status of migrants' rights, and the question of political integration and rights, especially in the context of 'basic human needs' or 'equity'. While the 'basic human needs' approach to the analysis of human rights is still of fundamental importance, it has rather been swamped by considerations of nationality taking prior place to humanitarian concerns.

The import of migrant workers in northern Europe to do poorly paid work has often activated the latent xenophobic and hostile tendencies in the indigenous populations, strengthened at times by the multi-ethnic composition of the migrant population. Absorption or integration has at times meant accepting a weak legal and political status, becoming 'ethnic minorities', subject to special integrative measures, or standing outside the mainstream provision provided for other UK citizens. The ambiguous nature of laws and regulations within the EC allows for arbitrary interpretations and an ambiguous treatment of 'rights'. Civil rights, political and social rights of the individual shift as he/she shifts across frontiers: individuals move from being citizens, to foreigners with residence and work permits, over time, if they choose, to being citizens again as they are 'included' in their host country of work and residence. Restrictions on social and economic rights in the Western European context has been gradually lifted in recent years. Despite the British preference to maintain national control over immigration policy the EC countries have agreed to operate a common visa system, the first step to a common migration policy.

While fears of a massive East European influx of migrants seems unrealistic in the UK, it is certainly an issue for the EC. Given previous experiences of migration it might be assumed that 'open' societies of the West are able to absorb free circulation, but, in practice, the German experience of the past two years makes that hard to sustain. Another paradox is that while EC States now apparently refuse to see themselves as countries of immigration, they still are, but with very little support capacity.

However, regional integration and the consolidation of trading blocks may mean that West and East Europe develop some balance – counter balance between trade and labour prospects: affluent migrants are always welcome during a recession, and then also more likely to move; while countries like UK suffer high unemployment now, the demographic trend generally in Western Europe indicates that more workers will be needed to make up worker shortages in those countries with demographic imbalances.

References

Banton, M. (1985). *Promoting Racial Harmony*, Cambridge: CUP.

Bevan, V. (1986). *The Development of British Immigration Law*, Beckenham: Croom Helm.

Brown, C. (1984). *Black and White Britain: the Third PSI Survey*, London: Heinemann.

Home Affairs Committee (UK). *Number and Legal Status of Future British Overseas Citizens without other Citizenship*, HC158, 1980–81.

Home Affairs Committee (UK). *Immigration from the Indian Sub-continent*, HC90-1, 1981–2.

Home Affairs Committee (UK). *Revised Immigration Rules*, HC526, 1981–2.

Home Affairs Committee (UK). *The Work of the Immigration and Nationality Department*, 1984.

House of Commons Select Committee on Race Relations and Immigration (UK). *Reports 1968–1978*.

Jackson, J. (1986). *Migration*, London: Longmans.

MacDonald, I.A. (1987). *Immigration Law and Practice in the United Kingdom*, London: Butterworths.

Nationality and Employment Statistics. 1990–92.

OECD (1978). *The Mighty Chain*, Paris: OECD.

OECD (1979). *Migration, Growth and Development*, Paris: OECD.

OECD (1983). *Continuous Supporting System on Migration (SOPEMI)*, Paris: OECD.

United Nations (1982). *International Migration Policies and Programmes: a World Survey*, New York: UN.

12 Switzerland and the EFTA Countries

Thomas Straubhaar

It was only at the end of the 19th century that Switzerland became a country of immigration. Immigration remained practically free until the early 1960s, when the stock of foreign residents in Switzerland approached one million people, or more than one eighth of the total population. In 1970, a global ceiling system was introduced with a view to stabilising the share of the foreign population. It turned migration policy in Switzerland into an increasingly restricted and regulated *bargaining process* between administration, employers and interest groups. In December 1992, Switzerland's forthcoming membership of the European Economic Area was rejected by public referendum.

This chapter aims to review Switzerland's migration policy in the light, in particular, of the current and forthcoming labour mobility within the EC and the EEA areas; it also addresses the possible effects of future migration within the European Economic Area in the face of increasing migratory pressures in Central and Eastern Europe; it anticipates, finally, the major consequences for migration of Switzerland's rejection of European integration.

SWISS MIGRATION POLICY AND TRENDS

Switzerland enjoys a relatively capital-abundant economy with a correspondingly high labour productivity and a structural shortage of domestic labour. The share of foreigners living in Switzerland rose markedly after 1945. In the early sixties, the stock of foreign nationals approached one million people (16.7 per cent of the total population in 1965), and fears of *foreignerisation*[1] led to considerable political tension. Since the end of the 1960s, six referendums, aimed at a revision of the Swiss constitution,[2] were held at the initiative of xenophobic groups. Although they were all rejected by an increasing majority of Swiss voters, the political pressure caused by these initiatives exerted a decisive influence on the development of Switzerland's migration policy.

Despite the introduction of the first *ceiling control system* in 1963, which was followed by the adoption, in 1970, of the *global centrally administered ceiling system*,[3] the number of foreigners continued to increase steadily until 1973, when over 1.2 million foreign nationals lived in Switzerland. After the oil price shock, Switzerland was hit by a comparatively severe economic crisis. Foreign employment decreased from 894,000 in 1973 to 643,000 in 1977. From 1979 onwards, the immigrant population started to grow at a moderate pace, totalling, in August 1991, 989,457 workers (27.7 per cent of total employment) and 1,284,928 residents.[4]

In 1991, over 72 per cent of foreigners in Switzerland were EC nationals, while EFTA nationals accounted for 4.3 per cent of the foreign population. However, the share of workers from Turkey and Yugoslavia also increased significantly, from 13.8 per cent in 1980 to 18.7 per cent in 1991.

At this time, the majority of foreigners in Switzerland were employed in lesser skilled positions (whatever their actual qualifications) in the metal industry (19 per cent), construction (16 per cent), hotels and restaurants (11 per cent), public health (6 per cent) and textile and cloth manufacturing (3 per cent).

MAJOR EFFECTS OF MIGRATION TO SWITZERLAND

Originally, the underlying intention of Switzerland's migration policy was to stabilise the proportion of foreigners within the total population; to satisfy labour market needs; to improve the business cycle policy; and to implement an effective regional development policy.

The introduction of the global ceiling system did not appear to affect the proportion of foreign population living in Switzerland, which continued to increase until the oil crisis of 1973, and again after 1977. In migration theory, the so-called push/pull approach helps to analyse the causality and the levels of labour mobility. It explains migration as an interplay between (i) push factors influencing labour supply, (ii) pull factors determining labour demand, and (iii) the intervention of institutional or informal obstacles. In the case of Switzerland, despite the high degree of central political intervention, migration has remained a purely economic demand-determined process. Administrative restrictions, however, have hampered the efficient allocation of foreign labour.

In a recent study, Dhima (1991) analysed the employment patterns of foreign workers who had been employed in Switzerland from 1981 to 1989. The study showed that 66 per cent of the immigrants sampled had entered the country as seasonal workers. Because, through the political bargaining process, work permits were more easily granted for employment in the Swiss mountain areas, the majority of seasonal workers were originally employed in poorly qualified jobs in the agriculture, construction, hotels and restaurants, and public health sectors. However, after they had obtained a one-year residence permit, they gradually left the mountains and moved into more demanding jobs in industry, banking, insurance, the chemical industry, and trade.

In assessing the average productivity of branches in which workers were employed before obtaining a one-year permit, as well as the productivity of branches to which they subsequently moved, a difference of more than $3,600 per worker/year was evidenced. This means that the relatively inefficient allocation of foreign labour permitted to immigrate in 1981 resulted in an annual economic loss of more than $70 million.

At the social level, immigration to Switzerland had the following major effects. First, since immigration has been composed, primarily, of poorly qualified labour recruited for unskilled jobs, foreign employment resulted in a stratification of the Swiss labour market. 'Dirty' jobs were accepted by foreigners, which meant that poorly qualified Swiss workers could improve their labour market position. On the other hand, however, in times of economic depression, unskilled segments of the Swiss labour force had to compete with foreign workers. Social attitudes towards foreigners therefore depended, to a great extent, upon Switzerland's economic performance.

Second, due to the fact that immigrants were considered to be short-term guest workers, the public welfare system was not adapted in the slightest to the needs of the increasing share of foreigners who intended to stay (and to a large extent succeeded in staying) in Switzerland with their families.

THE NEW CHALLENGES

During the past few years, Switzerland has been confronted with a number of new challenges, which have gradually led to a fundamental reorientation of the national migration policy. Three major factors currently influence the development of Switzerland's migration policy: (i) the ageing of the Swiss population; (ii) European integration and political developments in Central and Eastern Europe; (iii) refugee policy.

(a) Growth and Ageing of the Swiss Society

Like most other highly developed European countries, Switzerland is experiencing a decline in the fertility patterns of its native population. In the absence of new immigration (i.e. assuming a net migration balance equal to zero), the Swiss population is expected to decrease by 17 per cent during the next half a century (i.e. from 6.8 million in 1993 to 5.62 million in 2040). This would mean a decrease in the total labour force from 62 per cent of the total population in 1993 to 54 per cent in 2040 (Straubhaar/Luthi, 1990).

In theory, there are two ways to influence population growth. Population policies may aim to change the fertility behaviour of natives; or they may try to influence population growth through new immigration. The former type of policy proved to be an ethically delicate issue in Switzerland, and one which gathered little consensus. The latter policy is also questionable. Empirical evidence shows that, in general, immigrants rapidly adapt their fertility behaviour to that of the natives of the receiving countries.

The changing age structure of the population resident in Switzerland over the next 50 years was recently calculated using three different scenarios:

(a) The 'restrictive scenario', which assumed the absence of any new immigration (or an annual *net* migration equal to zero).

(b) The 'liberalisation scenario', which assumed a sudden abolition of immigration restrictions, the consequences of which would first result in a immigration surplus of 50,000 per year, and would then, after ten years, reach an equilibrium of + 20,000 immigrants each year.

(c) The 'expansive scenario', which assumed a net migration surplus of + 50,000 immigrants every year.

In all three scenarios, there is a moderate increase in the total population until the year 2000. After 2000, the restrictive scenario predicts a decline to 5.6 million inabitants in 2040, while the expansive scenario foresees an increase to 8.7 million residents by the same year. The liberalisation scenario anticipates an increase in the Swiss population of approximately 500,000 people until 2010, followed by negative growth rates, and a surplus of + 200,000 inhabitants in 2040 (as compared with 1993).

Although immigration cannot fully invert Switzerland's decreasing population trends, the demographic input of new immigration is nevertheless influencing the current debate on migration issues and the negative side-effects of a highly restrictive immigration policy.

(b) European Integration and the Political Changes in Central and Eastern Europe

The Swiss economy has for long been dependent on other European countries. In 1989, 78 per cent of its imports originated from the planned

European Economic Area (EEA), and 63 per cent of its exports were directed towards the EEA. In relation to the European Community (EC), in 1989 Switzerland was the second exporter (after the USA) and the third importer (after the USA and Japan) (Hauser, 1991). With regard to foreign direct investment (FDI), 25 per cent of all inward flows, and 56 per cent of all outward flows, were evolving within the EEA (Leskela, 1991).

At the political level, the Swiss have traditionally perceived their country as an island in stormy European waters. For a long time, neutrality and political sovereignty constituted the main concepts of Switzerland's foreign policy. These concepts were also the most important determinants of Switzerland's rejection of the EEA referendum.

Against this background, and due to the fact that the development of EC integration has made it increasingly difficult and costly for Switzerland to remain isolated, and that neutrality has gradually lost its original justification after the collapse of the communist bloc, Switzerland's political identity and perceptions are starting to be questioned in intensive public discussions. It became clear that Switzerland would need to find its niche within a renewed Europe, and that this process would bring about increased political integration with other European countries, which would in turn require basic changes in Switzerland's migration policy.

Originally, the challenge of European integration and the creation of the common European Economic Area caused overt fear of mass immigration and of *foreignerisation*. In its first official statement on the EC 92 project, the Swiss government clearly identified the need to liberalise immigration policy as one of five major obstacles[5] to Switzerland's EC membership (Bundesblatt, 1988, 121). However, a closer evaluation of the effects of free labour mobility within the EC and the Nordic Common Labour Market[6] soon revealed that free migration between highly developed countries rarely caused mass migration and could, on the contrary, improve the functioning of domestic labour markets.

Recent estimates of the migratory consequences of the abolition of immigration restrictions for EC citizens predicted an increase of approximately 100,000 additional immigrants for the years 1990 to 2000. At the same time, however, they anticipated a 'crowding out' effect for migrants from Third World countries, which would amount, for the same period, to slightly more than 100,000 people (Straubhaar, 1991; Dhima, 1991). If these estimates prove to be accurate, net migration to Switzerland would decrease slightly compared with the migration balance registered under the current policy system. The political debate on the determinants and the level of future migration has made it clear, however, that intra-European free mobility of labour could not constitute a realistic alternative to migration from developing countries. What is more, the political changes in Central and Eastern Europe and in the former USSR have given rise to increased concern about the generation of a new migratory potential in these regions, which potential might no longer be met through immigration restrictions only. Thus in an official report (BIGA/BFA, 1991) on the priorities of Swiss migration policy in the nineties, the Swiss government acknowledged that due to its conventional approach, Swiss migration policy was not adapted to growing migration pressures worldwide. The report also recognised that while the problem of migration had traditionally been approached in the light of South–North population movements, political change in Central and Eastern Europe was now generating the potential for substantial East–West migration. According to the same report, 'handling this problem will be one of the greatest challenges in the years to come, and will require instruments other than conventional immigration and asylum policies. Not even the conventional development cooperation instruments will be adapted to the new challenges. For example, the need to create jobs or other opportunities for migrants willing to return to their countries of origin will require resources which will clearly exceed the capacity of Switzerland or the immigration countries as a whole. However, efforts in that direction will need to be intensified in the years to come' (BIGA/BFA, 1991, p. 58).

(c) Refugee Policy

While the number of asylum seekers did not exceed 1,803 people in 1970 and 3,020 in 1980, the demand for asylum rose drastically throughout the 1980s. In 1991, 41,629 people applied for asylum in Switzerland. While, in previous decades, refugees were traditionally from Central and Eastern Europe, asylum seekers in the eighties were predominantly of non-European origin. In 1990, the main groups were from Sri Lanka, Turkey, India, Pakistan and Angola. After the beginning of the civil war, Yugoslavians became, in 1991, the most important national group of asylum seekers.

Within current Swiss politics, Eastern European states are regarded as 'safe countries'. Consequently, the number of asylum seekers from Eastern Europe and Russia remained negligible. In 1991, 120 people from the former USSR, mainly Russian Jews, applied for asylum in Switzerland. Immigrants from Central and Eastern Europe are not presently accepted under labour market criteria.

The challenge associated with the current Swiss refugee policy is twofold. Firstly, Swiss authorities are increasingly confronted with the difficulty of distinguishing between genuine (i.e. politically persecuted) and economic refugees. The idea has thus been expressed of integrating refugees into a more comprehensive migration policy.[7] Secondly, it became clear that, in order to prevent rising migratory pressures in the countries of origin, more attention should be given to the specific causes of emigration. It was therefore decided to gradually develop a national migration policy which would include measures aimed at reducing migratory pressures in the sending countries.

THE FUTURE OF MIGRATION TO SWITZERLAND

In its report of May 1991 on a new refugee and immigration policy, the Swiss government introduced what has been referred to as a *three circle model* (Bundesblatt, 1991, p. 245; OECD, 1991e). This new approach brought about a fundamental reorientation in Switzerland's migration policy. According to this report, the existing bargaining system would be replaced, by and large, by the free mobility of European labour and by the reliance on market forces to attract, as appropriate, new foreign labour. The seasonal work permits would also be abolished and replaced by 'normal' residence permits.

In practice, citizens of EC and EFTA countries would belong to the *first circle* of foreign labour, and enjoy complete freedom to take up jobs in Switzerland. Workers required by the labour market and belonging not to EC or EFTA states but to traditional recruitment areas (above all Turkey, at a later stage East European countries. Former Yugoslavia was excluded from the traditional labour recruitment areas in 1991) would comprise the *second circle*. They would enjoy simplified administrative procedures for obtaining an exceptional right to work in Switzerland. However, immigration from second circle countries would become more restrictive. Workers from all other countries would belong to the *third circle*. They would not be allowed to enter Switzerland for work or residence. Temporary exceptions, however, could be made for scientific, research and teaching, and development assistance purposes.

The granting of asylum will remain strictly confined to political grounds. In order to reduce migratory pressures from former 'second world' and third world countries, economic and development aid policies will be increasingly promoted.

The Swiss government's proposal of May 1991 found considerable political support. It was commonly viewed as a scheme which would be able to attract more qualified and 'adapted' labour from European countries, while 'crowding out' less 'profitable' seasonal workers currently employed in Switzerland.

After Switzerland's potential membership of the EEA was rejected by public referendum in December 1992, the Swiss government attempted to introduce more dynamic aspects into the functioning of the Swiss labour market. It soon appeared, however, that economic interest groups would again be able to determine the directions of Switzerland's future migration policy. The government interpreted the rejection of the EEA treaty as a sign that Swiss citizens were against the free movement of labour (not of people) within the EEA. As a result, the immigration market will continue to be highly regulated, and the regional and industry quotas wil be maintained. The Swiss government also plans to abolish the right of the 'Saisonnierstatut' (i.e. seasonal workers who do not have the right to move either geographically nor in terms of occupation over a period of four years) to obtain a one-year residence permit after four years of employment.

On the other hand, Swiss leaders are well aware of the fact that in order to confront the problem of mass migration, asylum seekers and illegal migration, Switzerland will need to resort to international cooperation. With regard to East–West migration, the official BIGA/BFA report (1991:81–83) indicated that 'Switzerland should not try to solve this problem without cooperation, particularly if there is a need to deal with irregular migration'. This need for international cooperation and coordination will certainly intensify the relations between Switzerland and the EC and other EFTA countries. This will happen even if Switzerland continues to reject membership of the EEA.

EFTA AND THE EUROPEAN ECONOMIC AREA (EEA)

As a free trade association, EFTA has no common position on international migration. Within the EEA, all workers belonging to a member state will be entitled to migrate, and it is anticipated that free labour mobility will allow for a more efficient allocation of the labour force (a factor which ʾtually motivated the creation of the European Economic Area). On the er hand, all EEA member states (the EC and EFTA countries) will ʾin free to devise their own migration policy *vis-à-vis* non-member including Central and East European countries.

formation of the EEA completely neglects migration flows from ʾber states. As a result, two adverse effects can be anticipated:

as the EEA member states are free to devise their own policy non-EEA migrants, the efficient allocation of production

factors within the EEA will be considerably reduced, given that the equalisation of the marginal productivity of labour will be prevented.
2. As long as free movement of labour is restricted to EEA citizens, the EEA economies will not be in a position to contribute to the improvement of welfare in non-member states. In the long term, such restrictions could negatively affect the EEA economies, since the improvement of welfare in Eastern European countries would considerably reduce the incentive to migrate to the EEA member states.

The way migration is currently approached by EEA member states could thus contribute to increasing immigration pressures from the outside world. Barriers to trade from the countries outside the Common Market will clearly stimulate international labour migration, while EEA member states will increasingly appear as a 'Fortress Europe'. The efficient allocation of labour would thus require that the EEA member states adopt a common policy *vis-à-vis* non-EEA citizens, particularly those from Central and Eastern Europe. As long as foreign labour is regulated by national legislation, factor prices within the integrated area will be difficult to equalise. It is only by allowing free mobility of non-EEA citizens, therefore, that the European Economic Area will effectively achieve its fundamental principles of establishing an economic space free of any barriers to the movement of factors of production.

CONCLUSIONS

1. Although subject to a migration policy which was more and more centrally-administered, after 1945 immigration to Switzerland remained a predominantly demand-determined process. The vast majority of immigrants moved from European countries for labour market motives. A large number attempted to stay in Switzerland permanently. The economic benefits of the reallocation of labour under the existing foreign labour system were overriden by the structural inefficiencies of the political/economic bargaining procedures inherent in the distribution of new work permits in Switzerland.

   In brief, Swiss migration policy has consisted, primarily, of restricting immigration and of distributing permits. By and large, the distributional aspects outstripped the allocational efficiency. While Switzerland continued to suffer from a structural shortage of highly qualified labour, new permits have been, and to a certain extent still are, granted for relatively lesser qualified jobs. All in all, the economic benefits of the Swiss-administered labour market policy thus remained negligible.

2. Based on this experience, it appears that liberal market mechanisms of reallocating foreign labour are more effective than centrally administered bargaining systems. In the absence of marked differences of wealth causing mass migration, allocational gains of increased labour mobility offset distributional losses. From this point of view, Switzerland's intention to abolish its guest worker system and to participate in a common European labour market seemed consistent.

3. If additional labour immigration from non-EEA countries is to be allowed, quotas will need to be imposed. In Switzerland, consideration is currently being given to allowing such immigration from Turkey, from some Eastern European countries and, at a later stage, from Croatia or Slovenia.

4. Due to the turnover principle underlying the Swiss guest worker system and the lack of any public policy to support the social integration of foreigners, immigration to Switzerland has generated considerable economic and social costs. Affirmative action to integrate immigrants into Swiss society would have avoided the social costs associated with the intensive rotation of foreign labour inherent in the guest worker system.

5. Switzerland's attempts to develop a regional policy by means of a targeted distribution of foreign labour have not been successful. The objectives underlying such a policy would have been better pursued through direct fiscal policy measures.

6. Free labour migration is not a realistic alternative to the economic development of Third World or Eastern European countries or to the closing of developmental gaps and wealth differentials with developed countries. If at all, large-scale migration can only be prevented by means of a consistent common international migration policy involving all major industrialised countries. Recent global challenges demonstrate the vital importance for all the leading economies to work towards a *General Agreement on Migration Policy* (i.e. the GAMP, drawing upon the agreement reached under the GATT system).

The GAMP should aim to reduce the potential for migration in the countries of origin. Measures to be considered could consist of coordinating efforts to reduce income gaps (e.g. through additional trade liberalisation, capital investment incentives, development cooperation); to promote new employment opportunities in less developed economies; to reduce the relative deprivation in the countries of emigration; and to discourage false expectations regarding employment opportunities and living conditions in potential countries of immigration. On the other hand, sustainable supranational action aimed at promoting basic human, political and democratic rights in certain countries of emigration would contribute to reducing political refugee migration.[8]

Notes

1. The term *foreignerisation* attempts to translate the almost untranslatable german term *Ueberfremdung*, which designates an increasing presence of foreigners perceived by natives as a danger to their own identity and cultural independance.

2. In Switzerland, every Swiss citizen has the right to propose a change in the national constitution. If such a proposal (called an *initiative*) is supported by the signature of at least 100,000 Swiss, it has to be discussed in parliament and must finally be accepted or rejected in a public vote (called a *referendum*).

3. The ceiling control system of 1963 focused on single enterprises and aimed to limit the share of foreign employment within each company. In practice, the system produced, above all, an incentive for migrant workers to move to companies with a low share of foreign labour. The global ceiling system of 1970, which is still effective today, aims to stabilise the share of foreign population by fixing the number of new permits issued every year. This number is calculated by computing the desired volume of the foreign population on the basis of (i) the stock of foreigners already resident, and (ii) the number of foreigners who left the country during the year under review. Quotas are fixed every year for each one of Switzerland's 24 districts, in addition to a national quota for special occupations.

4. In 1990, 57.7 per cent of the foreign population was composed of permanent residents, 18.8 per cent of one-year permit holders, 12.5 per cent of frontier workers, 8.5 per cent of guest-workers, and 2.5 per cent of asylum-seekers.

5. The other four obstacles were: (i) neutrality; (ii) political sovereignty, particularly in foreign affairs; (iii) Swiss federalism; and (iv) direct democratic rights such as the referendums and the initiatives.

6. For a detailed evaluation of the free movement of labour within the EC see, for instance, Straubhaar, 1991; in relation to the Nordic Common Labour Market, see Fischer/Straubhaar, 1991.

7. In its latest legislation (Bundesblatt 1991, p. 254), the Federal Council of Ministers chose to reject this idea. Numerous interest groups had expressed fundamental opposition to this project from fear of seeing economic interests mixed up with politically-driven immigration regulations.

8. For a more detailed discussion of this proposal, see Straubhaar, 1991.

References

AS. *Amtliche Sammlung der Eidgenössischen Gesetze*, periodical, ann., Bern.

BIGA. *Possible Swiss Strategy for a Refugee and Asylum Policy in the 1990s*, Bundesamt für Industrie, Gewerbe und Arbeit (BIGA), Bern 1989.

BIGA/BFA. *Bericht uber Konzeption und Prioritaten der schweizerischen Auslanderpolitik der neunziger jahre*, Bern 1991.

Blattner, Niklaus, Schwarz, Heinrich and Sheldon, George. 'Die Ausländerbeschäftigung als Determinante von Wirtschaftswachstum und Produktivität in einem Industrieland: Das Beispiel der Schweiz', in Giersch, Herbert (ed.); *Probleme und Perspektiven der weltwirtschaftlichen Entwicklung*, Jahrestagung des Vereins für Socialpolitik, Duncker & Humblot, Berlin 1985.

Bundesamt für Statistik. *Statistisches Jahrbuch der Schweiz 1990*, NZZ Verlag, Zürich 1990.

Bundesblatt. *Bericht über die Stellung der Schweiz im europäischen Integrationsprozess*, vom 24. August 1988. Bundesblatt IV/1988, pp. 121 *et seq.*, Bern 1988.

Bundesblatt. *Informationsbericht des Budesrates über die Stellung der Schweiz im europäischen Integrationsbericht*, vom 26, November 1990, Bundesblatt IV/ 1990, pp. 291 *et seq.*, Bern 1990.

Bundesblatt. *Bericht des Bundesrates zur Ausländer und Flüchtlingspolitik*, vom 15, May 1991, Bundesblatt III/1991, pp. 291 *et seq.*, Bern 1991.

Dhima, Giorgio. *Politische Oekonomie der schweizerischen Ausländerregelung, eine empirische Untersuchung über die schweizerische Migrationspolitik und Vorschläge für Ihre künftige Gestaltung*, Verlag Rüegger, Chur/Zürich 1991.

Fassmann, Heinz and Münz, Rainer. 'Migration und Bevölkerungspolitik. Oesterreich im internationalen Vergleich', in Felderer, Bernhard (ed.), *Bevölkerung und Wirtschaft, Jahrestagung des Vereins fHr Socialpolitik 1989*, Duncker & Humblot, Berlin, 1990.

Feichtinger, Gustav and Steinmann, Gunter. 'Immgrants to Germany', *Population Studies*, 1991.

Fischer, Peter Arnold and Straubhaar, Thomas. 'Integration und Migration in Nordeuropa: Freizügigkeit im Gemeinsamen Nordischen Arbeitsmarkt (Free Movement of Labour within the Nordic Common Labour Market; with an English Summary)', Intermediate Report of the Project 'Freizügigkeit im Gemeinsamen Nordischen Arbeitsmarkt', Institute of Economics, University of Berne, Bern, 1991.

Gnehm, Adrian. *Ausländische Arbeitskräfte – Ihre Bedeutung für Konjunktur und Wachstum dargestellt am Beispiel der Schweiz*, Paul Haupt Verlag, Bern and Stuttgart 1966.

Hagmann, Hermann Michel. 'La Suisse/Switzerland. Country Analyses', in Rallu, Jean Louis and Blum, Alain (ed.), *European Population, vol. I, Country Analyses*, John Libbey, Montrouge/London/Rome 1991.

Hammar, Tomas. *Democracy and the Nation State. Aliens, Denizens and Citizens in a World of International Migration*, Aldershot, Avebury, 1990.

Haug, Walter: *... und es kamen Menschen, Ausländerpolitik und Fremdarbeit in der Schweiz 1914 bis 1980*, Z-Verlag, Basel, 1980.

Hauser, Heinz. *EWR-Vertrag, EG-Beitritt, Alleingang: Wirtschaftliche Konsequenzen für die Schweiz (unter Mitarbeit von Sven Bradke)*, Gutachten zu Handen des Bundesrates, Bundesamt für Konjunkturfragen, Bern, 1991.

Hoffmann-Nowotny, Hans Joachim and Killias, Martin. 'Switzerland', in Krane, R.E. (ed.), *International Labour Migration in Europe*. Praeger, New York, 1979.

Huber, Klaus. *Die ausländischen Arbeitskräfte in der Schweiz*, Vogt-Schild, Solothurn, 1963.

Kunz, Karl Ludwig. 'Ausländerkriminalität in der Schweiz – Umfang, Struktur und Erklärungsversuch', in *Schwiz. Zeitschrift für Strafrecht*, vol. 106, pp. 373–92, 1989.

Lee, E.S. 'A Theory of Migration', in *Demography*, vol. III, 1966.

Leskelä, Jukka. 'EFTA countries' foreign direct investment', in European Free Trade Association, *EFTA Trade 1990*, EFTA, Geneva, 1990.

Lewis, A.W. 'Development with Unlimited Supplies of Labour', in *The Manchester School of Economic and Social Studies*, vol. 22, pp. 129–91, Manchester, 1954.

Majava, Altti. 'Towards an Equitable Sharing of the Benefits of International Migration', in *Yearbook of Population Research in Finland*, vol. XXIX, pp. 93–8, Helsinki, 1991.

Mauron, Thierry. *Rapport du Correspondant Suisse. Report for the Continous Reporting System of Migration of OECD (SOPEMI)*, Bern/Paris, 1991.

Nabholz, Ruth and Artho, Markus. 'Auswanderung aus der Schweiz als Folge einer Freizügigkeit im EG-Raum', thesis at the University of Berne, Switzerland, 1992 (mimeo).

OECD (1991a). *Labour Force Statistics, 1968–88*, ann., Paris, 1991.

OECD (1991b). *OECD Economic Surveys 1990/91 – Switzerland'*, OECD, Paris, 1991.

OECD (1991c). *National Accounts, Main Aggregates*, vol. 1, OECD, Paris, 1991.

OECD (1991d). *Quarterly Labour Force Statistics*, No. 2/91. OECD, Paris, 1991.

OECD (1991e). 'The Swiss Delegation's Contribution', Conference Paper, International Conference on Migration, Rome, March 13–15, OECD, Paris, 1991.

OECD (1991f). 'Historical Statistics 1960–89'. *OECD Economic Outlook*, OECD, Paris 1991.

Schwarz, Heinrich. *Volkswirtschaftliche Wirkungen der Ausländerbeschäftigung in der Schweiz*, Verlag Rüegger, Chur/Zürich, 1988.

Siebert, Horst and Koop, M.J.. 'Institutional Competition. A Concept for Europe?', in *Aussenwirtschaft*, vol. 45/1991.

Straubhaar, Thomas. *On the Economics of International Labour Migration*, Verlag Paul Haupt, Bern and Stuttgart 1988.

Straubhaar, Thomas and Lüthi, Ambros. 'EG-Freizügigkeit und schweizerische Ausländerpolitik', in *Schweizerische Zeitschrift für Volkswirtschaft und Statistik*, Heft 3, 1990.

Straubhaar, Thomas (1991a). *Schweizerische Ausländerpolitik im Strukturwandel. Strukturberichterstattung, Bundesamt für Konjunkturforschung*, Bern, 1991.

Straubhaar, Thomas (1991b). 'Migration Pressure', in Böhning, W.R., Schaeffer, P.V. and Straubhaar Th. (ed.), *Migration Pressure: What Is It? What Can One Do About It?*, Working Paper, International Migration for Employment, ILO, Geneva 1991.

Todaro, M.P. and Harris, J.R. 'Migration, Unemployment and Development', *American Economic Review*, vol. 60/3, 1970

Tuchtfeldt, Egon. 'Die schweizerische Arbeitsmarktentwicklung – Ein Sonderfall?', in Issing, Othmar (ed.), *Aktuelle Probleme der Arbeitslosigkeit*, Duncker & Humboldt, Berlin, 1978.

Part IV
Prospects

13 The Future of East–West Migration

Bimal Ghosh

INTRODUCTION

In the second half of 1989, alongside dramatic political and economic changes in Eastern Europe, 1.3 million people surged across the borders to the West.[1] East–West migration has since emerged as a major challenge facing Europe. The crescendo of euphoria created by the collapse of the communist régime and the easing of emigration restrictions in East European states has now died down. Instead, East–West population movements are contributing to the feeling of a looming migration crisis in Western Europe. The concern is shared, though in varying degrees, by several East-Central European countries, especially those faced with large immigration flows from within the eastern region and outside. The proliferation of meetings and the extensive debate held over the past few years on East–West migration are a measure of the widespread anxiety that now surrounds these movements.

The alarmist scenarios of mass exodus from the East, as depicted by many in the wake of the 1989 movements, have not materialised. But, the migratory movements have clearly persisted; and pressures for emigration from new and emerging sources are building up. As the fledgling democracies in East Europe strive towards reforms, signs of political tensions have surfaced in several of them. Economic restructuring implicit in the transition to the market economy has led to widespread social hardships in virtually all East European countries. Despite the signs of a modest upturn in the industrial production of the Central European countries in 1993, the whole eastern region, including in particular the Commonwealth of Independent States (CIS), continues to face high levels of unemployment, falling living standards and inadequate social safety nets.

Clearly, these factors add to the emigration potential. But the most powerful source of increasing migratory pressures lies in ethno-political tensions and violent conflicts, such as those already occurring in strife-torn former Yugoslavia. They hold the potential for massive and unpredictable movements of people, both inside and outside Eastern Europe.

217

It is this volatility of the political, economic and ethnic situation in Eastern Europe that makes East–West migration one of the most complex and unpredictable population movements of modern times. The current movements, coupled with the build-up of a massive migration potential, has exacerbated the feeling of losing control over immigration in West European states. The fact that these movements are taking place at a time when total immigration flows from developing countries in the South have reached record levels since the mid-1970s, has heightened the perception of an impending migration crisis.

West Europe's own integration adds another dimension to the migration challenge. Economic coordination and increasing inter-dependence entail, both as a means and an end, harmonisation of policies, including those governing migration. But immigration policies have been traditionally viewed as a prerogative of national sovereignty; they are perceived to be closely linked to national identity. As the European Community (EC) countries move towards closer economic and, more haltingly, political union, they also undergo a stressful process of adapting their national moorings and identities. At this juncture, large inflows of immigrants from outside the Community, with diverse religious and less familiar cultural backgrounds, only serve to enhance their anxiety.

There is a perceptible danger that as the pressure for emigration from neighbouring states increases and the fear of an uncontrolled immigration takes hold, policy makers in West Europe might be induced or impelled to follow a crisis management strategy. Such an approach is most likely to lead to, and rely on, short-term, restrictive measures, discounting or ignoring the need for a more active and forward-looking policy. Europe's new migration challenge no doubt needs to be addressed urgently. The policy makers might otherwise be overtaken by events, as foreshadowed by rapidly increasing anti-immigration acts and xenophobic violence in several European states. But there is no reason why this should be allowed to impede the development of a dynamic and long-range policy, contributing to, and at the same time deriving support from, the process of East–West cooperation.

The present chapter deals with some of the major aspects of this challenge.[2] It analyses the combined impact of East–West and South–North immigration on the policies of West Europe and the prospects of a common European migration policy. These provide the background and much of the rationale for the final sections which succinctly relate to some of the common findings of the previous chapters and highlight the main elements of a policy package to deal effectively with East–West migration in the 1990s and beyond.

MIGRATION POLICIES AND EUROPEAN POLITICAL TRENDS:
A COMPLEX INTERFACE

Complex political and economic changes in both West and East Europe
since the late 1980s have profoundly influenced Europe's migration situation. The move by twelve West European nations towards closer economic integration and the consequent realignment of inter-state relations
within the European Community have had major implications for migration. In Eastern Europe,[3] the collapse of the communist régime and the disintegration of nation-states contrasted with the process of integration in
West Europe. But their effect on Europe's migration situation has been
equally, if not even more, far-reaching. Policy response to the new migration challenge has proved difficult to shape. Many of the hard issues
involved remain interlinked with the political and institutional evolution of
the EC and, indeed, of Europe as a whole, in the months and years to come.
Long range migration policies are thus still in the making.

Within the EC, current efforts at shaping migration policies are marked
by an interplay of conflicting forces. The influence of Europe's political
liberalism and bitter memories of inter-state conflicts, including two large-
scale wars, favour an open system of cooperation and international
exchange. It propels them to construct through joint efforts a border-free
Community, to be buttressed by the economic advantages of a large,
unified market. At the same time, the inward-looking, statist tradition pulls
the member nations in the opposite direction, inducing them to close their
doors, firmly protect their frontiers and placate anti-immigrant sentiments
among the public. Strong adherence to the concept of sovereignty makes
them reluctant to surrender the prerogatives of the nation-state or even in
pooling them together within a regional framework for the pursuit of a
common interest. These inner conflicts, as the following discussion will
show, account for much of the EC's current tribulations in formulating a
coherent migration policy within the Community and in relation to the
world outside.

THE DILEMMA AND PREDICAMENTS OF THE EC COUNTRIES

The European Community, established under the 1957 Treaty of Rome, is
envisaged as an area for free movement of goods, persons, services and
capital under the Single European Act (1985) which came into force in
1987. As the project for a border-free Community was taking shape, the
pressure for immigration to West Europe had already been rising. Alongside

a continual stream of family reunification and the increasing admission, as in the case of the Federal Republic of Germany, of immigrants who could claim citizenship of the receiving country on ethnic grounds, there was a sharp rise in the number of asylum seekers which jumped from 16,000 a year in the first half of the 1970s to 200,000 during 1985–89. Adding to these flows, there were large numbers of irregular migrants, mostly from across the Mediterranean, who entered the southern European states – Italy, Spain and Greece, all former labour-exporting countries. Within the EC, there were signs of a growing concern about the ability of the member states to control immigration at the external borders.

The late 1989 migratory waves from East Europe sharpened this concern of the EC member states; they also gave rise to new predicaments. It was not just the suddenness of the eastern movements or their scale which posed problems in policy formulation. The nature of these movements, especially the political context in which they were occurring, brought into play many of the conflicting forces which, as already noted, have long been embedded in West Europe's political system and thought.

For more than 40 years the West had pressed for freer emigration from the East European states as a mark of political liberalisation; it had upheld freedom of movement as a cherished goal, subsequently enshrined in the Helsinki Accords. Just as the East Europeans had been making use of the newly found freedom to travel abroad, it could not close its door without diminishing its moral standing and political credibility. Equally important, West European states have been conscious that liberal entry arrangements are a vital part of their declared policy of support to the fledgling democracies and fragile economies of East Europe. At the same time, however, they were afraid that a liberal entry policy might open the floodgate of East European migration, which they would be unable to cope with.

The dilemma of the West European states would have been less overwhelming had they been able to avoid or reduce the flows from the developing countries of the South. But both practical realities and political considerations largely ruled out this possibility. As already mentioned, much of the South–North flows, to which West European states had become exposed, were taking place in defiance of their regular immigration procedure. Politically, few West European states would find it expedient to adopt a preferential immigration régime for East Europeans which could openly discriminate, or may be perceived to discriminate, against the emigration countries of the South. Nor were they keen that new immigrants from East Europe should displace other immigrants who had already been living and working in their territories (OECD/SOPEMI, 1990). Although, unlike the United States, West Europe does not have a powerful immigrant lobby, discriminatory immigration control measures could have serious negative repercussions for the integration of legally resident immigration populations, a declared objective of all West European states.

While most West European countries faced this complex dilemma, nowhere were the predicaments more pronounced than among the EC nations which had committed themselves to dismantle their internal borders by 1 January 1993. The attainment of this objective warranted an agreed migration policy. Free movements within the Single Market implied that the situation in one member country could directly or indirectly impact on that in other countries, not only through the admission of new immigrants but also through changes in labour market conditions and in the social situation resulting from high levels of immigration or unsuccessful integration of immigrant groups. The social and political consequences of migration in one country could spill over into other countries in many different ways, including a strengthening of intra-European networks of extreme right-wing political groups and joint action by the immigrant groups across EC countries (Colinson 1993). The need for a common migration policy or at least a harmonisation of migration policies and procedures was thus increasingly recognised by the EC member states.

There are certain common elements in the policies and principles adopted by individual EC countries that could seemingly help the process of policy harmonization at the Community level. These include the commitment of all EC countries to uphold a set of basic human rights as enshrined in the European Convention on Human Rights and other international and European human rights instruments. Based on the fundamental principle of family unity, for example, all EC countries allow a limited degree of family reunification. Similarly, they all profess a commitment to the protection of refugees in keeping with the provisions of the 1951 UN Convention on the Status of Refugees (and the 1967 Protocol), and to an effective integration of the legally resident immigrant groups. Apart from combatting irregular immigration and abuse of asylum procedures, all EC countries have also shown a common interest in restricting immigration, as reflected in their policies to curb labour immigration and to reduce emigration pressures in existing or potential sending countries.

However, despite the self-evident need to evolve a Community-wide approach to migration, especially as regards the entry of new immigrants and the integration of existing ones, and their common adherence to certain goals and principles, EC countries have found it difficult to harmonize their policies within a coherent framework – not to speak of developing a common policy on migration, whether from the East or the South. Shared principles have led to comparable difficulties; member countries have also found themselves in different situations – differences stemming from countries' past immigration patterns and links, from their divergent political and social traditions and from variations in current and projected immigration pressures. As the *ad hoc* Group on Immigration, set up in October 1986 within the EC Council Secretariat, observed in a recent report, 'Immigration policies are a complicated issue, not all areas of which lend themselves to immediate harmonisation' (*ad hoc* Group on Immigration, 1991).

POLICY-MAKING IN A RESTRICTIVE CLIMATE

As these differences impeded the development of a Community-wide policy on migration, the thrust of the harmonisation process has gravitated towards restrictive measures regarding access to the Community area, border control, visa regulations and expulsions. Several additional factors have converged to reinforce the restrictive trends in policy formulation. First, while the divergence of interest and approach among the EC member states inhibited a prompt agreement on the substantive aspects of an active migration policy, the fear of large waves of immigration from the East and the South created a sense of urgency for devising measures to restrict the flows and protect the common external border. Second, the Community's lack of direct competence in external migration matters under the Single European Act of 1985 has underlined the primacy of national sovereignty and prerogatives, encouraging the statist (as opposed to liberal) trends to dominate the politics of migration in most EC countries in recent years. Thirdly, in the absence of a prior definition of basic principles of a European migration policy, including agreement on a set of liberal and humanitarian concepts, harmonisation of external border control measures has veered towards the lowest common denominators. This is reflected, for example, in the introduction of new immigration controls and visa requirements by the southern European countries comparable to those operating elsewhere in Western Europe. To quote once again the *ad hoc* Group on Immigration, '... if the harmonisation process were initiated without defining basic principles, harmonisation may be carried out at the lowest level. Assuming that immigration into Member states must remain limited, it is above all the restrictive opinions which could dominate.'

In recent years, it is indeed the restrictive opinions that have strongly influenced the policies of EC member states. As discussed later in this chapter, there have been some initiatives on the part of a number of EC states to relax this approach on a limited scale or on an *ad hoc* basis ir case of East–West migration. [Bi-lateral arrangements for temporary employment and training of nationals of East (mainly East-Central) European countries and the granting of facilities for visa-free travel as tourists are indicative of such initiatives]. But, over all, the restrictive approach has prevailed.

Although in the past few years the restrictive measures seem to have gained additional ground among the EC states, as elsewhere in West Europe, the trend is not entirely new. Even as the EC nations were preparing for liberalisation of internal (intra-EC) movements, they saw the clear need for a common policy to protect the external borders. For example, the Schengen Agreement,[4] which was initially signed by France, the Federal Republic of Germany and the Benelux group of countries in June 1985 as a forerunner of the harmonisation of arrangements within the EC as a whole, 'provides [more] evidence of movement toward internal liberalization, but with externally protectionist overtones' (Hollifield, 1992). In fact, in seeking to abolish controls within the territories of the signatory states, the agreement provides for coordinated controls on immigration from outside through harmonisation of visa and asylum policies and the coordinated policing of external borders.[5] The Agreement has come under criticism from human and civil rights groups which 'consider it overly restrictionist and at odds with the liberal asylum and human rights policies of member state governments' (Hollifield, 1992).

The Schengen Agreement was followed by two conventions as major instruments to ensure free movement of people within the EC: one on the crossing of external borders (the Borders Convention); and the other concerning determination of the State responsibility for examining asylum applications (the so-called Dublin Convention). Both Conventions are of direct relevance to the future of East–West migration.

The Borders Convention (the signing of which has been held up due to a conflict between the United Kingdom and Spain over the status of Gibraltar) deals with several issues. These include, in particular: (a) the mutual recognition of national visas between the member states and (b) the abolition of visa requirements for non-EC nationals legally resident in one member state – when visiting another member state for a period not exceeding three months. The Dublin Convention, adopted in June 1990 but not yet ratified by all EC member states, is designed to (a) prevent the submission of multiple or successive applications by an asylum seeker in more than one state; and (b) avoid the problem caused by no state accepting the responsibility for particular asylum seekers. The Statement accompanying the signing of the Convention emphasizes that the aim was not to amend the rules for examining applications for asylum and refugee status which would continue to be covered by the national law of each state.

Although the two instruments deal with different subjects, they share certain common features in terms of policy approach. Like the Schengen Agreement, they reflect the fact that issues of immigration, border control and asylum seeking are still subjects of national competence of individual EC member states. They also reveal that the harmonisation efforts are focussed more on methods and procedures of inter-state cooperation than on the principles or substance of migration policies. The latter continue to be covered by the national régime of each state. As one analyst has put it 'Movements of people, asylum seekers and issues of immigration and border controls are areas where nationalism tends to survive, not ultimately for technical reasons, but for a 'political culture' and the fear of introducing surreptitiously the concept of federation or confederation' (Callovi, 1992).

In the EC, as in the rest of West Europe, statist policies have often gone hand-in-hand with restrictive measures. In the case of the Dublin Convention, for example, the restrictive approach seems to have considerably influenced, if not dominated, the humanitarian considerations underlying EC nations' commitment to protection of refugees. The question is further discussed later in this chapter in the context of burden-sharing.

THE MAASTRICHT TREATY AND ITS IMPLICATIONS FOR MIGRATION

The Treaty on European Union, signed in Maastricht in December 1991, was a compromise between the statist and the Community approach to migration issues. It marked a modest advance over the statist trends by establishing (under Article 100C) the Community's legal competence in determining the third countries whose nationals will need visas when crossing to external borders and, before 1 January 1996, a uniform format for visas. But, with the exception of the visa question (and measures to cope with an emergency situation created by sudden inflows of nationals from a third country), issues of migration remain outside Community competence. The Treaty lists (Title VI, Article K) several areas of 'common interest' which include: asylum policy, rules governing the crossing of external borders; immigration policy (conditions of entry and movement of third country nationals, residence, family reunion and access to employment of third country nationals and unauthorized migration).

These matters of inter-governmental cooperation might however be amenable to Community-level action if the EC Council so decides. Asylum policy is mentioned in a declaration attached to the Treaty as a possible priority item for such transfer to the Community list by the end of 1993. Foreign and security policy which has important implications for East–West movements, caused by ethno-political conflicts and suppression of minority rights, remain outside the Community's direct competence. The Maastricht Treaty has, however, opened up the possibilities of a joint approach in these areas and foresees, under Article V, paragraph 2, a new Conference in 1996 to carry forward its work.

Since the negative Danish vote in June 1992 on the Maastricht Treaty, the Community's internal divergence and asymmetry have become increasingly visible. The inability of the member states to develop a common and effective strategy in the face of the deepening crisis in former Yugoslavia has revealed the inadequacy of the Community's political cohesiveness, just as the turbulence in the European exchange rate mechanism has strengthened doubts in some quarters about the prospects of the projected European monetary union. EC leaders' continuing preoccupation with these and other related issues have inevitably stifled the prospects of a bold, new initiative in favour of an active, Community-wide migration policy. If anything, action has lately been swinging towards restrictive measures through inter-governmental mechanisms in which statist policies have prevailed.

Indicative of this trend was the decision of the EC summit, which met at Edinburgh in December 1992, to delay the lifting of controls on free movement of people within the Community until late 1993 and possibly beyond. Underlying the various legal and technical arguments used against the abolition of controls by the three EC nations – Denmark, Ireland and, especially, the United Kingdom – there was a general concern: protection of the national territory by preventing the entry of unwanted non-EC nationals, whether from the East or the South. Internal political considerations in several other EC member states, including France and Germany, accounted for their willing acquiescence to the postponement of the project for border free Community. At the same time, the endorsement by the EC summit of a resolution, already adopted by the EC ministers responsible for migration, (London, November 1992), revealed the persistent efforts of EC nations to minimize their exposure to refugee inflows through restrictive measures. Action envisaged under the resolution is applicable to flows both from the East and the South. But, given the Balkan crisis, it could have, as further discussed in a separate section, immediate and particularly important implications for East Europe.

EMERGING EAST–WEST POLICY ALIGNMENTS: VISA AND BORDER CONTROL

Tighter immigration control at the EC's external borders has given rise to a growing concern about concentration of migrants, especially asylum seekers and irregular migrants, in states bordering on the Community. This has served as an additional inducement for the EFTA countries to move towards harmonising their visa and border control policies for nationals from non-OECD countries. As a result, the immigration pressure on countries in East-Central Europe, notably Hungary, the Czech Republic and Slovakia and, to a lesser extent, Poland, from within East Europe and countries of the South has been visibly rising.

Central European countries, in turn, are now preparing themselves to tighten their own visa policies and border control measures. To a large extent, this also results from the closer political and economic ties that have been developing between these countries and those in West Europe. Hungary, Poland and the Czech and Slovak republics have already concluded bilateral agreements which permit their nationals to travel without visa to a number of West European countries. As the latter would like to make sure that third country nationals do not use the peripheral Central European countries as a bridgehead for illegal entry into their own territories, they would expect and encourage the Central European countries to assume a coordinated responsibility for examining visas and enforcing border control measures. The Communiqué of the Ministerial Conference on East–West migration (Vienna, 1991), which was attended by several East European countries, envisages such coordination of policies and practices concerning visas and frontier formalities and a common responsibility for entry and travel regulations.

For Central and East European countries such a joint approach would imply bringing in new immigration laws and active cooperation among themselves and with West European countries.

It remains to be seen whether and to what extent such cooperation between Central and East European countries would develop at policy and operational levels. There are however indications that, the growing economic cooperation within the Visegard Group of four Central European countries – Hungary, Poland and the Czech and Slovak republics – would lead them to develop a common or harmonised approach to migration issues (just as they can be expected to align their immigration control policies to those of West Europe). Better economic prospects and proximity to West Europe make these countries more attractive as final destinations or transit points for migrants originating, in particular, from Romania, the

CIS, the former Yugoslavia and many developing countries; they could thus have a common interest to tighten and harmonise their border control measures.

In the coming years, as the Central and East European countries move closer, both economically and politically, to the EC, coordination of border control and migration policies too, is likely to gather further momentum. Recent developments in the EC have already enhanced the prospects of such cooperation. Since the Danish negative vote (June 1992) on the Maastricht Treaty, the opinion in several EC states has been swinging in favour of fostering closer ties in the eastern region as a step towards enlarging the Community. At the Edinburgh EC Summit in December 1992, it was decided to initiate preparations for the accession of the eastern countries to the EC. In taking over the EC presidency in January 1993, the Danish government confirmed that this subject would be high on the Community's agenda; the point has been reiterated by several EC leaders following the Second Danish vote (May 1993) on the Maastricht Treaty.

The Central European states, followed by Bulgaria and Romania – states already linked to the Community through association agreements – are likely to move faster on the road to accession than those farther on the east. Of special significance in this context is the revival of interest in a proposal which had been tentatively put toward in 1991 by Mr. Frans Andriesen, former EC External Affairs Commissioner. Under the proposal, some of the non-EC member states could be allowed to participate in certain specific EC activities, and not in others. Since the Maastricht Treaty makes external migration essentially a subject of inter-governmental cooperation at least until the end of 1993, without the involvement of the European Council or Parliament, cooperation between the EC and Central European countries can be arranged through inter-governmental mechanisms.

Clearly, much will depend on how the institutional relationship between the EC, EFTA and Central Eastern European countries evolve in the coming months and years. It may be recalled that the political agreement reached in Luxembourg on 22 October 1991 between the EC and seven EFTA countries (including Switzerland) provides for the establishment of European Economic Area (EEA) where free movement of people (with some temporary exceptions and under certain conditions) would prevail by 1993 after ratification of all nineteen members of EEA. At the time of writing, the EC and EFTA members (minus Switzerland) were set to finalise arrangements for bringing into force the EEA during 1993. Parallel to this, the EC would continue negotiations with Austria, Finland and Sweden on their applications for full membership of the Community. A successful conclusion of these negotiations could conceivably create a new dynamic for widening the Community to the east, but it is difficult to prejudge its exact impact on the institutional relationship between the EC and Central/East European countries or on East–West migration policies.

There is little doubt, however, that the closer the Eastern, and especially the Central European countries move towards the EC, either directly or through the EFTA, the greater could be the pressure for aligning their border control and migration policies with those of the Community. Meanwhile, as discussed below, efforts to persuade the sending countries in the eastern region to take part in a joint East–West approach to the problem of containing refugee flows and irregular migration have been stepped up.

ASYLUM-SEEKING AND REFUGEE MOVEMENTS: PROSPECTS OF EAST–WEST SUB-REGIONAL INITIATIVES

The EC countries may have successfully converged to keep the flows from former Yugoslavia away from their respective borders, but their statist policies have not been conducive to intra-EC solidarity in terms of burden-sharing. The Dublin Convention itself tends to weaken the principle of burden-sharing among member states, as it makes the first country of arrival responsible for processing asylum applications. Indeed, burden sharing has emerged as an issue of wide disagreement between EC member states in dealing with war refugees and asylum seekers. The recent ministerial-level conference on East–West migration (Budapest, February 1993) revealed the discord, or at least the limits of cooperation, within the EC, as within West Europe, on this matter. The major recipients of war refugees from former Yugoslavia – Germany, Switzerland, Austria and Sweden – were unable to persuade other EC or West European states to share the burden. Several of the latter states resisted the move as they were more concerned with the recent increase of influxes from other regions. The argument of proximity – that war refugees should be accommodated as closely as possible to their original homes to allow a speedy return – was also used to justify their stand.

These trends cast doubts on the immediate possibility of evolving a common EC policy on asylum, including its basic content. There are indications, as presaged by the agreements signed between Austria, the Czech Republic, Poland, Slovakia and Slovenia in March 1993, that if the ethnopolitical situation in the eastern region worsens further, this could spur new sub-regional arrangements based on bilateral or plurilateral agreements among the states in East and West Europe which may be mostly directly exposed to refugee flows.

Most of the asylum seekers in West European countries are now coming from East Europe and Turkey. Between 1986 and 1991, for example, the inflow from within Europe increased by 487 per cent, compared with an overall increase of 264 per cent. The war in Yugoslavia has further exacerbated this influx. Since mid-1991, the conflict has produced about 2.6 million refugees and displaced persons, of which nearly 600,000 are outside the ex-Yugoslav territory. Any further deterioration of the ethnopolitical situation in Bosnia could, as further discussed below, have a spillover not only in Kosovo and Macedonia, but far beyond in the eastern region, including the Baltic states and the CIS.

The policy of EC countries has been to minimize their exposure to refugee inflows from the eastern region and, as far as possible, to divert them to 'safe' third countries outside the Community area. Under the Dublin Convention the participating states are already authorized to send back an asylum applicant to the first EC country he or she had landed in. Under the new resolution on asylum seeking, endorsed by the Edinburgh Summit, the EC states can send an asylum seeker back to a 'host third country' outside the Community, as long as it is considered safe and is not the country from which he or she had originally fled.

In the context of the Balkan crisis, the host third countries are most likely to be those closest to the conflicts such as Croatia, Slovenia, Hungary, Poland and the Czech Republic. As Germany tightens its liberal asylum system through a change in its constitution, the pressure on the eastern countries could be particularly heavy. But none of these states has the necessary infrastructure, resources or experience to deal with large numbers of refugees; and at least some of them such as Croatia, Hungary and Slovenia are already carrying a heavy burden of refugees. Up to November 1992, Slovenia had accepted 75,000 refugees – about 4 per cent of total population; and Croatia was hosting 750,000 refugees and displaced persons resulting from the Yugoslav conflict – 16 per cent of a total population of 4.7 million. This is equivalent to 10 million intakes for Germany and about 8 million for France or Britain. And, if the eastern countries, too, follow the EC's lead and opt for the same rules of consignment of refugees to safe first country, there could be considerable jig-saw human movements based on a conceivably endless exchange of different groups of asylum seekers between them. It is possible, however, to envision an alternative scenario. The pressure of these refugees, combined with their own internal ethno-political tensions, may lead to a breakdown of law and order in one or more of the fragile eastern states. If this happens, it could unleash new, uncontrolled flows of refugees westward – precisely what the EC is trying to avoid.

Significantly, at the recent (February 1993) Budapest Conference, Germany sought to allay the fears of Poland and the Czech Republic that they would become part of a 'refugee zone' in Europe. Germany has signed agreements with Romania and Bulgaria committing the latter countries to repatriate rejected asylum seekers in return for financial aid (International Herald Tribune, 13 November 1992). A similar agreement signed with Poland in May 1993 provides for German aid of DM 120 million ($76.4) in 1993 and 1994 to finance refugee shelters in Poland and improve surveillance of its own borders with equipment purchased from Germany with the aid money. The agreement was expected to serve as a model for an analogous arrangement between Germany and the Czech Republic later in the year (IHT, 8–9 May 1993). These agreements have come under criticism in Germany and elsewhere for appearing to legitimise demands of rightist groups for mass deportation of asylum seekers. Even so, the situation, as mentioned above, can open a new window of cooperation between the countries of West Europe (e.g. Austria, Germany and Switzerland) and those of East Europe (e.g. Hungary, the Czech Republic and Poland), based on burden-sharing arrangements.

The situation concerning joint East–West action to combat irregular migration is more straightforward. The Ministerial conference on illegal migration held in Berlin (October, 1991) recommended the adoption by West and East European countries of a series of practical measures, including tighter and harmonised control procedures at certain key points; arrangements for the return to the country of departure or origin of persons who have illegally entered another country; conclusion of bilateral or multilateral readmission agreements and harmonisation of visa policies in a spirit of mutual cooperation. In keeping with these decisions, the Budapest Conference agreed to further toughen measures against illegal East–West migration. The pressure for coordinated East–West action to combat illegal inflows will certainly rise in the future, alongside the likely increase in the potential for such migration. But these short-term restrictive and punitive measures, however useful, cannot be a substitute for a long-range policy aimed at tackling the root causes.

INADEQUACY OF A RESTRICTIVE APPROACH

Experience indicates that restrictive policy measures, even if seemingly useful in the short-run, have a limited enduring effect on migratory flows. When there are powerful push factors in the sending countries or pull factors in the receiving countries, and especially when they combine to reinforce each other, restrictive immigration policies are hardly successful in arresting the flows; they are simply diverted to irregular channels of entry. Despite the ban on recruitment of foreign labour since 1973–4, West Europe witnessed continued flows of immigrants, many of whom came through irregular channels, especially after the mid-1980s. Equally significant was the presence in the United States of between 2.5 and 3.5 million irregular migrants mainly from the neighbouring countries even after large-scale legalisation involving some 3 million aliens had been carried out under the Immigration Reform and Control Act of 1986. These are not isolated examples.

The migratory pressures in East Europe are at present reinforced by the disparities in the levels of income and prosperity between the two parts of Europe, the geographical contiguity and easy access to West Europe resulting from low transportation costs, the networks and ethnic links already created by past movements and the persistent demand (despite high levels of overall unemployment) for foreign labour in certain occupations and branches of industry in West Europe. Given the circumstances, it is unrealistic to think that West Europe can stop the East–West migration flows simply by implementing restrictive immigration policies and tightening the control mechanism. Nor can liberal democracies take draconian measures such as mass expulsions to discourage future immigrants. If the intention is to slow down the flows or stem disruptive mass immigration, public policies can be more effectively used in two, largely inter-related ways. The first relates to policy measures which provide the framework for making the movements more orderly, predictable and productive, and the second consists in addressing the root causes that propel massive migratory movements. Policy interventions are generally more useful when they are deployed to help the push and pull factors reach the level of a dynamic equilibrium, and not when their existence is ignored.

IMMIGRATION VIEWED AS AN OPPORTUNITY

But even if it were possible for West Europe to shut itself in and seek isolation from the East and the rest of the world, will it serve West Europe's own longer term interest? Immigration can be perceived as a threat, but it can also be seen as an avenue which West Europe can use to meet its own needs and policy objectives in several inter-related areas (Ghosh, 1993).

Demographic growth is one such area. Despite a slight increase in the fertility rates in the late 1980s, the natural increase (excess of births over deaths) in West Europe's population growth is just above the reproduction level – it was less than 0.24 per cent in 1989. By the year 2015 it would reach the zero-level or will be declining. In the 1980s international migration became the dominant component of the moderate, total increase in West Europe's population. During the first half of that decade, with low immigration levels and birth rates, several West European countries witnessed negative demographic growth rates in different years – Austria (1982–3), Belgium (1983), Denmark (1981–4), Federal Republic of Germany (1982–5), and the United Kingdom (1982–5) (Council of Europe, 1991).

On the reasonable assumption that West European nations will be unwilling to see a steady decline in their populations, the question needs to be asked as to how the current trend could be reversed. Increase in the birth rates of the national population is one option; but will West Europeans be willing to accept families of a larger size than they have become used to? Almost throughout Western Europe, families with three or more children have become rare. At the same time, the proportion of women without children has been rising, largely due to a fall in the rates of marriage. Except in a few countries, the negative effect of the declining marriage rates on birth rates has not been compensated by an increase in the number of births outside the wedlock. Indications are that West Europeans are not likely to re-embrace the concept of larger families and the profound changes that this would imply in their way of living. Nor will it be easy to reverse the current socio-cultural trends, often reinforced by economic factors, that are shaping women's attitude to marriage and child bearing in West Europe.

Can immigration be an answer to the problem? The snag here is that with time as the immigrant families are socially and culturally better integrated with the local populations, they, too, prefer to have less children. Even so, since young adults, between the ages of 25 and 45, are more prone to move, immigration can at least delay the process of population decline which many West European countries might otherwise be facing already by the turn of the century.

Linked to the above is the issue of West Europe's future labour market needs. As West Europe's population is heading towards stagnation or decline, it is also aging. A smaller proportion of population in the age group of 0–14 years in West Europe (around 19 per cent of total population, compared with world average of 33.5 per cent), alongside a relatively large group of people, aged 65 years or more, implies that the growth of its labour force is nearly at an end. By the turn of the century West Europe would be unable to meet the manpower requirements of its economic growth. France, for example, will suffer from a shortage of manpower as from the year 2000. The National Scientific Research Institute estimates that annually the country will need 165,000 additional workers from outside between the years 2000 and 2009 and up to 365,000 between 2020 and 2029 to meet its manpower requirements. Similarly, it is foreseen that West Europe's labour force would lag behind the projected expansion of employment in the coming decades. One study shows that with West Europe's labour force contracting by 5,5 per cent over next three decades from 145 million in 1990 to 137 million by 2020, several countries in West Europe will soon face shortage of trained workers which would have a negative impact on output. According to the study, France, the Netherlands, Portugal, Spain and the United Kingdom may not face the same immediate problems but increasing labour difficulties are likely to emerge from the beginning of the next decade (Business Strategies, 1990).[6]

West Europeans cannot be expected to accept willingly a fall in their living standards. If so, how will the manpower requirements of economic growth be met?[7]

As West Europe's aging process continues, other social and economic problems will arise. The population group of 65 years plus now represents more than 15 per cent of the total population in several West European countries such as Austria, Denmark, Norway, Sweden and the United Kingdom compared to the global average of about 6 per cent. In many of them the ratio of non-working to the working age population is 50 per cent or above. The fiscal and social burdens are shifting towards an increasingly smaller group of working age population. In future, there will be fewer and fewer people of working age to support each elderly person or child. The process is already placing a heavy strain on the social security system in West Europe; it could lead to an erosion of the traditional solidarity between the older and younger generations. Inflow of young immigrants could be of fiscal advantage to West European countries; it can help avert a crisis in the social security arrangements just as it can contribute to demographic revitalisation.

Two other considerations may be taken into account in assessing the potential benefits that West Europe could derive from immigration, especially from the East–West movements. In West Europe low labour mobility, together with rigidity in wages and high unemployment benefits, contributes to persistently high levels of unemployment in times of economic slowdown. This contrasts with the United States where a recent study shows that, if employment in a particular state falls by 1000 in any year, then, on average, 300 workers remain unemployed, 50 drop out from the labour market and as many as 650 leave the State (Blanchard and Katz, 1992). Eventually, out-migration erases the effect on unemployment and participation rates. But migration does not play the same kind of equilibrating role within or between European countries. In 1987, 2.8 per cent of the US population changed their state of residence compared to

1.1 per cent of Germans who changed their region of residence, 1.3 per cent in France and 1.1 per cent in the United Kingdom (OECD, 1992; *Financial Times*, 19 January 1993).

Even after free circulation of people within the Community is more formally recognised, this situation is not likely to change soon. The EC's employment creation programme may promote new job opportunities, but their geographical distribution may not be evenly spread. Low labour mobility of EC workers would contribute to inter- (and intra-) state divergence in employment rates and tend to depress the overall employment level. The inflow of immigrants may improve labour mobility and help even out employment differentials between EC countries and thus contribute to economic integration and convergence.

Immigration can sometimes distort the skill composition of the local labour force, with an adverse effect on the local wage structure. In the case of East–West migration, however, this danger is much less apparent. Although the levels of skills in Eastern Europe are generally lower than those in West Europe, the mix of available skills is not very dissimilar. It should therefore be possible to ensure that the skills brought in by eastern immigrants are those that East Europe can spare and West Europe can easily use. At least, in accepting East European immigrants, it should not be difficult to avoid any serious distortion in the skill distribution of the local workforce or in the local wage structure in the form, for example, of a widening of the wage differential among West European workers (Richard Layard *et al.*, 1992). The real challenge of course lies in ensuring that the inflows of skills from Eastern Europe are fully co-related to those industrial sectors and occupations where West Europe is facing, or projected to face, a critical manpower shortage.

ELEMENTS OF A FORWARD-LOOKING POLICY: REGULATED OPENNESS

What, then, should be West Europe's policy approach to East–West migration? An approach which seeks to make West Europe a 'fortress' is, as we have seen, not viable in the face of the contemporary migration realities; nor does it serve the longer-term interests of Europe, East or West. A new, forward-looking policy must be realistic enough to be sustainable over time; must serve, to the maximum extent possible, the common interest of the two parts of Europe; and be consistent with Europe's liberal tradition. In essence, it should be a policy of regulated openness.

Such a policy could be built on three essential pillars: (i) allowing a limited flow of orderly and regular immigration; (ii) promoting, through bilateral and multilateral arrangements, movements linked to cultural exchange, training, and fixed-term employment, and labour mobility as part of cross-border trade in services, without involving permanent immigration and (iii) reducing the pressures for massive and disorderly emigration by dealing with the root causes in the potential sending countries.

SHOULD EUROPE ADOPT A FLEXIBLE QUOTA SYSTEM? THE PROS AND CONS

Could a flexible quota system be used in order to allow a limited flow of regular immigration? From several points of view, the quota arrangement may not seem to be an ideal one. The political right would suspect it as a surreptitious device to turn West Europe into an area of foreign immigration for ever, negating all future options. The left could find it too restrictive. But, with all its shortcomings, real or perceived, the flexible quota system could help West European countries meet their own manpower and demographic needs; provide a safety-valve for high emigration pressure in East Europe; and create a favourable political climate for closer cooperation between West Europe and the potential sending countries. An attractive feature of the system is that the annual or multi-year quota of intakes could be adjusted (it may even be allowed to drop temporarily to zero-level) to changes in the labour markets of West European countries and their overall capacity to absorb immigrants. In a report prepared for the International Organization for Migration in 1990, and later submitted to the Ministerial level conference on East–West migration in Vienna (January 1991), I raised the possibility of European receiving states opting for such a flexible quota system as part of a new migration policy (Council of Europe, 1991). Similar proposals have recently been made to the competent bodies of the Council of Europe. Despite (or because of) today's restrictive climate, several West European countries, including Austria, Italy and Spain, have already opted for or are moving towards a flexible quota system. In France, Germany and Switzerland, the approach, though still controversial, has aroused considerable public interest.

EXPANDING OPPORTUNITIES FOR FIXED-TERM EMPLOYMENT AND TRAINING: RISKS AND REWARDS

Meanwhile some progress has already been made by West European states in putting in place arrangements for short- and fixed- term inward movements of people from East Europe. Several West European countries – for example, Germany, Belgium, France and Switzerland – have signed agreements with countries of East Europe, notably the Czech and Slovak republics, Hungary and Poland – covering a wide variety of arrangements to provide short-term employment to immigrants and help them with vocational and language training. These include: project-tied work or projects undertaken by foreign firms using their own workers (as, for instance, in Germany); seasonal jobs (agriculture in France) or frontier jobs (in Germany, Austria and Finland) and temporary employment (in Germany, Belgium, France and Switzerland, among others) (OECD, SOPEMI: 1992).

Despite their obvious merits, the implementation of these schemes entails some potential pitfalls. For example, in some West European receiving countries, e.g. Germany, concern has been expressed that training and temporary employment schemes may be a useful device to use cheap immigrant labour, substituting a proper labour immigration policy (Hofler, 1992). There are also fears of wage depressing effects in certain situations such as the concentration of East European workers in seasonal industries or in the border areas. Some of these schemes could also open the way for irregular immigration through, for example, illegal lending of workers and unauthorized prolongation of stay. But most of these difficulties could be overcome or at least minimised through effective monitoring, inspection and supervision. A more serious problem arises in the case of a mismatch between the training offered and the skills likely to be in demand in the sending country. Essential to the success of all such schemes is close cooperation between West and East European states, which would also help in fostering a truly joint approach to the wider policy aspects of East–West migration.

ADDRESSING THE ROOT CAUSES: NEW MODALITIES OF ECONOMIC COOPERATION

But a policy of orderly or regulated immigration is not likely to be sustainable unless the mounting pressures for emigration in East European countries can at the same time be brought under control. Trade, aid and foreign direct investment can be used within a coherent policy framework to create jobs and generate incomes and new economic opportunities and thus reduce the migratory pressures. There is little doubt that even accelerated development will not be able to remove in the near future the wide income disparities – the average wage rate in West Europe is ten times the rate in

East Europe – that now separate the two parts of Europe. But new economic cooperation from West Europe and the world outside, coupled with sound domestic strategies, could promote in East European countries the kind of development which would generate employment, upgrade jobs, and provide at least a minimum level of economic relief and security to those who might otherwise be compelled to flee out of extreme poverty and economic despair.

For many poverty-driven migrants getting a regular job itself is equal to having gained a wage increase. When this happens, the search for employment – or, rather, the search for basic economic security – becomes a more powerful factor in international migration than wages (Ghosh, 1992: 2). In fact, migration, in general, responds more to variations in employment than in wages, although poverty-driven migrants are even more sensitive to job prospects. In Britain, for example, a 10 per cent lower wage in a region increases its annual net emigration by 0.6 per cent of its labour force, (Layard *et al.*, 1991). But a fall of 10 per cent in its employment rate increases annual net emigration by 0.8 per cent of the labour force. A similar situation is discernible in Spain (Bentolila and Dolado, 1991; Layard *et al.*, 1991).

If, alongside employment creation, economic cooperation can ignite new hopes among the East Europeans about the future of the home country economy, it can have a significant impact on attitudes towards outmigration. West Europe's own experience – Italy in 1967–8, Greece in 1971–85 and Spain and Portugal in the mid 1980s – shows that a general optimism and a positive perception about the future of the domestic economy may slow down emigration or can even encourage return migration (Ghosh, 1991, 1 & 2). Surveys carried out in Poland in the late 1980s tend to confirm that a pessimistic perception of the home country economy favoured emigration (Okolski, 1991).

STRATEGIC USE OF AID

Development aid can be used as an important component of international cooperation to reduce the pressure for mass emigration from Eastern countries. Aid, including technical cooperation, has traditionally been used, with varying degrees of success, for general development purposes, but without any particular attention to their effects on migration. With the exception of programmes of return migration and rehabilitation of refugees, the links between development aid and migration management has thus remained weak. If the full potential of aid for reducing pressure for mass migration from the East is to be exploited, a different approach will be needed, involving close cooperation between West European and other aid donors and the East European recipient states.

A strategic use of aid for this purpose should be envisaged at three different levels. At the general level, it should be used to help design and implement stable macro-economic policies as well as those concerned with trade liberalisation, foreign direct investment, demographic change and human resources development. Policies in all these areas have an important impact on employment, income and growth, and thus on migration. The interlinkages could be used to keep emigration within manageable limits, consistent with other development objectives of East European countries.

Aid money can be extremely valuable to East European countries in tiding over their external and internal financial difficulties during the reform process. For example, it can be prudently used to cope with the foreign exchange difficulties and loss of revenue by the trade liberalising countries during the transition period when imports are likely to grow faster than exports. Equally important, aid funds could be of critical help in providing social safety nets, and adjustment assistance increasing facilities for retraining workers, and thus in reducing the social and human costs of the reform process which add to migratory pressure.

At a more specific or micro level, aid can target on particular migrant producing areas or groups of potential migrants in East European countries. Aid can also be used at an 'intermediate' level, focussing on certain broad sectors such as the services and the small enterprises sector, which are of special relevance to East Europe's migration management. The development of service industries, especially professional and business services, for example, hold important potential for employment of skilled workers and for contributing to the growth and efficiency of other economic sectors. This, however, calls for, particularly in the case of computer and telecommunication based services, huge initial outlays for human capital formation, research and the development of transport and telematic infrastructure. Few East European countries can mobilise such resources without external assistance.

It is not implied that aid is not being used in East Europe for at least some of the proposals mentioned above; what is emphasized here is that, in very few cases, have the migration effects been an important consideration in determining the use of aid or the priorities of aid-supported projects. The five common priorities under the EC's assistance programme (PHARE) – initially launched for Poland and Hungary, and now extended to East Europe, including the Baltic states, but not the CIS, do not include migration as a specific priority area. More recently, in the face of the rising immigration from the East, several West European governments have launched a number of small scale bilateral aid projects – which are specifically geared to reducing migratory pressure. In general, however, these projects are too narrowly focussed. While targeting of aid on specific groups of migrants or areas of high emigration is important, unless the projects are at the same time closely integrated with the overall development strategies and priorities, their development impact is likely to be limited, as has generally been the case in the past with the micro-level, *ad hoc* aid projects linked to return migration.

The general deficiency in the planning and management of external aid to East Europe has circumscribed its potential role in improving the performance of eastern economies and thus in promoting optimism among the potential migrants. A recent study (Institute for East–West studies, 1992) has unveiled several of these weaknesses. The gap between pledges and disbursement, for example, is a major problem. The Group of 24 OECD nations have pledged $27 billion to Central Europe but only 2 per cent of the amount earmarked for former Czechoslovakia was disbursed in 1990; the proportion was 17 per cent for Hungary and 27 per cent for Poland. Part of the solution to the problem lies in adopting innovative measures, including catalytic use of technical cooperation, to enhance the aid absorption capacity of these countries, alongside a more pragmatic and modulated approach to the complex and sensitive issue of aid conditionality.

Except for EC's technical assistance programme and the UN funded activities, credits were usually offered on commercial terms; and in the bulk of the cases the grant element was less than 25 per cent. Official development assistance commitment (with at least a 25 per cent grant element) continues to be modest, as compared with, for example, export credits (ODI: 1992). Another key issue in aid effectiveness is coordination: lack of coherence between project objectives and duplication of activities could be wasteful and confusing. The early recognition at the political level of the need for effective coordination of Western aid activities in East Europe was wise and useful, but it has not solved all the practical problems implicit in aid coordination. The multiplicity of international and regional agencies, the divergence of interests and priorities among the donor countries, and not infrequently, their individual desire for visibility and aid-based leverage in the recipient country will continue to complicate the task of coordination (Ghosh: 1990: European Affairs).

TRADE AND MIGRATION: THE POLICY CONTRADICTIONS

But trade can help more than aid. Agriculture, steel and coal, and textiles and clothing are among the most competitive industries in countries like

Poland, Hungary and the Czech and Sloval republics; they account for around one-third of both employment and national income in these countries. Because they are labour-intensive they can also be more effective in reducing unemployment-induced emigration from these countries. The paradox in the present situation is that though anxious to curb immigration flows, West European countries, like other industrial nations, are pursuing a policy which produces the opposite effect. They struggle to protect their own markets for the products of those industries which have the highest potential for creating jobs in less affluent, labour-surplus countries. What is even more paradoxical is that many of these industries can survive in West Europe partly, if not largely, because they employ cheap immigrant labour.

A clear indication of this trend is discernible in the association agreements which were signed between the EC and the countries of the Visegard Group in East-Central Europe – Poland, Hungary, the Czech Republic and Slovakia (then Czechoslovakia) in 1991. The agreements provide for liberalisation of imports from the latter countries by 1999 and ensure improved access of several of their products in the intervening period. Similar association agreements have since been signed also with Romania and Bulgaria. But the distinction made in these agreements between steel and coal, textiles and agriculture, on the one hand, and the general industrial products, on the other, remains significant. It reflects the 'sensitivity' of the former group which will continue to face import restrictions in the EC. But, this is the group which includes most of those items in the current and potential export trade of the East European countries which hold the highest potential for easing unemployment-induced emigration. Significantly, the EC recently imposed 'punitive' tariffs against exports of steel from the Czech/ Slovak republics, which, in the wake of the removal of EC quotas, had risen by 12.6 per cent in the first four months of 1992 against the same period in the previous year. In 1991, the EC had run a trade deficit of $1.22 billion with East Europe. In 1992 it recorded a surplus of $3.1 billion with Hungary, Poland, Bulgaria, the Czech Republic and Slovakia.

The relationship between trade and migration is complex: depending on the circumstances trade can be a substitute for, or a complement to, labour migration. In general, however, the more the easterners would be able to sell products using their fertile land and plentiful labour, the less compelled they would feel to sell their services directly to the West. East Europe's trade expansion should have a positive effect on both employment and wages. The wage effects at least in the near future will fall far short of erasing the present wage disparities of 1:10 between East and West Europe, but the effect on East Europe's unemployment could be significant because of the labour-intensive composition of their exports. A recent estimate reveals that if, as a result of trade liberalisation, an eastern country were able to export 20 per cent of its GNP to the EC (compared to an average of 3.2 per cent in 1988) the effect, under a set of reasonable assumptions, including a rise in eastern wages, will be equivalent to the out-migration of 8 per cent of the workforce. And if the wages do not rise in proportion, trade can make a more substantial difference to unemployment in East Europe (Richard Layard *et al.*, 1992). This, in turn, can be expected to slow down eastern emigration, especially since, as we have seen, migration is generally more sensitive to changes in employment than to variation in wages.

Although in the coming years East Europe will be doing most of its trade with the EC countries, its gains from trade liberalisation will be greater if it would include the EFTA countries. After more than two years of difficult negotiations, the signing of a free trade agreement between EFTA and Hungary, followed by a similar agreement with Bulgaria, both of which are due to come into force on 1 July 1993, (*Financial Times*, 2 February and 28 February 1993), is an encouraging development; and so are the agreements signed earlier by EFTA with the Czech Republic and Slovakia, Poland and Romania.

As part of East–West trade liberalisation, arrangements for greater cross-border labour mobility related to trade in services holds considerable promise in easing skill migration or brain drain from Eastern Europe. There is, as already mentioned, considerable scope for developing, with external aid, East European service industries, including business and professional services, such as engineering, accounting, and data processing. There could be an increased cross-border trade with West Europe in the skill and knowledge-intensive services through the use of computer and telecommunication technology. But this would in many cases also call for temporary, cross-border movement of skilled and professional people, related directly to the delivery of services, as envisaged, for example, in the draft General Agreement on Trade in Services (GATS) under the Uruguay Round of trade negotiation. The encouragement of East–West mobility of such skilled manpower, as part of a fair and equitable international exchange, could be beneficial to both parts of Europe. West Europe would gain from its access to eastern skills, especially in sectors and occupations suffering from skill shortages at a reasonable cost and without having to face the problems of permanent or long-term immigration. For East Europe, such mobility would mean additional employment for its skilled workers, along-side an opportunity for them to widen their knowledge and experience. As the skills would be used abroad on a 'restorative' basis, the problem of brain drain, usually associated with long-term or permanent emigration, will be avoided or minimised.

Trade expansion will also enhance the prospect of an increased flow of foreign direct investment to East Europe. Continuing trade restrictions, on the other hand, would slow down foreign investment in these countries, since access to western markets from an eastern country base is an important incentive for such investment. Debt as a percentage of exports was particularly high for Poland (26 per cent) before the negotiated debt reduction (of up to 50 per cent) in April 1991; it continues to be relatively high for Bulgaria (21 per cent) and Hungary (15 per cent).[8] This strengthens the unfavourable perception of credit worthiness of East European countries and raise the cost of their commercial borrowing. Foreign direct investment could be critically important in all these countries as it can bring both capital and technology, but very little of it currently flows to these countries. The number of joint ventures and wholly owned foreign firms registered in the region doubled between the beginning of 1991 and January 1992, but foreign equity commitments amounted to only $9 billion, and the amounts actually invested were much smaller.

RETHORICS AND REALITIES OF NEW POLICY INITIATIVES

As West Europe faces increasing immigration pressure, and as restrictive measures are tightened up, some attention is being given to the possibility of using aid, trade and foreign direct investment within a more coherent economic co-operation policy to reduce the pressure at source. The Ministerial-level conference, organized by the Austrian Government and the Council of Europe (Vienna, January 1991), in the context of East–West migration, underlined the importance of development assistance, trade links and economic cooperation in preventing disorderly migration. These views were echoed in September of the same year by the Fourth Conference of European Minister Responsible for Migration at Luxembourg as it advocated bilateral and multilateral economic cooperation, including programmes of investment, training projects and other forms of assistance for economic development of the countries of origin as a means of stabilising migratory flows.

But the calls for such cooperation will remain public rhetorics unless they are firmly embedded in congruent domestic policies of both West and East European countries. If East European countries intend to reduce emigration pressure they need to adopt suitable domestic strategies for employment creation consistent with economic growth, alongside stable micro-economic policies conducive to increased flows of trade and foreign investment and more effective use of aid. West European countries, for their part, must be prepared to accept changes in their trade, aid and structural adjustment policies, supplemented by a more dynamic approach to East Europe's external debt problem.

The success of such a policy will also call for institutional changes at the national, bilateral and multilateral levels to ensure full policy coordination affecting aid, trade, foreign investment and facilitate a continuing dialogue between East and West European countries. Despite the progress made during the past 2–3 years in several of these areas in both parts of Europe, an acceleration of the process is clearly indicated.

NEW ECONOMIC COOPERATION NOT A SUBSTITUTE FOR ORDERLY IMMIGRATION

Could such an economic cooperation policy run parallel to, and be consistent with, a limited flow of orderly migration from East Europe? Doubts have been expressed by some that under such a dual policy, the young and more promising people will opt for emigration rather than wait for improvement of wages and incomes through national development (Tapinos, 1991). Elsewhere, I have argued that even if, as is likely, some workers do migrate, this should not defeat the basic objective of the cooperation policy. Admittedly, such a policy will add to the administrative burden of migration control at both ends of the flow because of a likely excess demand for entry. Arresting clandestine and irregular migration must have a high priority because of the social, economic and ethical problems it entails. But, even if the borders were completely closed, the problem of immigration control will remain, except that the migration authorities will be exclusively concerned with combatting irregular and clandestine movements.

The idea behind West Europe's new migration policy, in any case, is not to stop all East–West movements. Rather, the policy objective is to make these movements orderly, manageable and productive and avoid those which are clearly detrimental to the economic interest and welfare of either the sending or the receiving country or both. Disorderly mass migration, driven by poverty, economic insecurity and despair, could be disruptive at both ends of the flow, just as depletion of vital human resources, in the form of brain drain, could seriously impede economic recovery of the eastern countries. East–West economic cooperation could help attain this policy objective, but cannot leave out, or be a substitute for, migration.

MIGRATION INTERTWINES WITH A NEXUS OF ISSUES

Minority and ethnic issues are admittedly outside the realm of migration policy. They are the direct concerns of the states' foreign affairs, security and human rights policies. But the recent traumatic ethno-political conflicts in former Yugoslavia and the simmering ethnic and minority tensions in East Europe are clear signals that West Europe's new migration policy cannot be indifferent to these issues.

Ever since the end of the Second World War the approach of the international community, including the West European states, to the question of the collective rights of minorities, as distinct from the rights of individual members, has been tardy and inadequate. The international community's excessive concern over sovereign rights and the constraints imposed by the Cold War largely explain this situation. In the past many states with dormant minority problems within their own borders, were averse to placing the issue high on the global agenda lest it opened 'Pandora's box'. But the violent upheavals, mass displacements and human sufferings in the Balkans have now demonstrated the inadequacy of the erstwhile approach and the danger it entails.

Under the impact of the fast-moving events in ex-Yugoslavia and the simmering conflicts over minority rights elsewhere in the eastern region, West European states are now becoming more conscious of the need for a bolder and more coherent approach to the issue. The experts meeting, held in Geneva in June 1991 at the behest of the Conference on Security and Cooperation in Europe (CSCE), was unable or unwilling to come up with a definition of the collective rights of minorities. Even so, it did break new ground by recognizing the rights of minorities as an issue of international concern, and not just a domestic matter. Shortly afterwards, as the Yugoslav situation was heading towards a crisis, the EC Foreign Ministers agreed on an important principle – that the territories seeking independent status must fully guarantee the rights of ethnic minorities living inside these territories. These were steps towards a clearer recognition of the international dimension of the minorities issue and also of the collective rights of minorities inside nation-states, although the rights themselves still remained to be more precisely defined.

The whole of Eastern Europe, even the relatively homogeneous Poland and Hungary, are ethnically diversified societies, with ethnic minorities often cutting across national boundaries. Unless adequate protection to minority communities can be ensured throughout the region, restoring their feeling of security and sense of national participation, the minorities may feel compelled to move from the states to which they belong causing volatile mass migration; or they may try to move the inter-state borders leading to tensions and, possibly, violent conflicts. West European states, which are particularly exposed to the danger, can play a more forceful role through the CSCE process, the regional organizations and the United Nations to ensure that these rights are clearly defined, fully institutionalized and actively upheld. It seems unfortunate that the 1993 United Nations Human Rights Conference could not be sufficiently geared to this issue. Collective action to deal with one of the most potent causes of unpredictable outflows of migrants and refugees at the very source can make West Europe's new migration policy of regulated openness more realistic and sustainable.

WHERE DOES EUROPE GO FROM HERE?

Previous chapters of this book have depicted in some detail the landscape of East–West migration – the levels and nature of the movements, policies and perceptions – from the perspective of sending and receiving countries. The overall picture that emerges is a variegated one, marked by, as noted in the introductions to Parts II and III, both common characteristics and divergent features of the countries within each group. The analysis reveals how simplistic and misleading it would be to think of West and East Europe as perfectly homogeneous areas, respectively, of immigration and emigration, in the context of East–West movements. The similarity and divergence of conditions, interests and approaches are discernible not only within the two groups of countries but also, albeit to a lesser extent, across them. Countries of East-Central Europe, which, while continuing to be emigration areas, share a common concern with various West European countries about the influx of increasing numbers of war refugees from ex-Yugoslavia and irregular migrants from elsewhere are a case in point, but not the only one.

If the diversity of the migration situation is, as already discussed, making it difficult for the EC countries to harmonise their policies, it also applies to other countries of Europe, both East and West. At the same time, the commonality of problems and interests and similar perception of migration issues pulls individual countries together for joint action from within and outside existing inter-country economic groupings, such as the EC and EFTA. New alliances are forged and policies and measures are realigned on specific migration matters through bilateral agreements and plurilateral or sub-regional arrangements. Indicative of this trend are the bilateral agreements signed by Germany with various Central and East European countries, the accord reached between Austria and the Central European countries and Slovenia, and Poland's projected agreements with

Hungary and Ukraine on illegal immigration. These arrangements could be the building blocks for a common European migration policy but they could also reduce the pressure for developing a single, Europe-wide policy.

Policies of migration, including the making of migration policies, cannot be isolated as several chapters in this book have shown, from national attitudes, policies and politics. The British ambivalence over European political union is not just a historical accident; nor is its resistance to the immigration policy being submerged under a wider Community policy a political aberration. But national attitudes and policies are not necessarily immutable. They, too, can change under changed circumstances, as exemplified by the current, though still controversial, move in Germany to repeal its constitutional provision granting the right of asylum to all refugees. By the same token, if in East Europe migration policies are still in a flux, it reflects the extreme economic uncertainty and ethno-political volatility that prevail in many of the countries.

A key issue in East–West migration is how national politics might affect the EC's future policies. The positive Danish vote on the Maastricht Treaty in May 1993, and its expected ratification by the United Kingdom, could remove the uncertainty about the future of the Treaty, but not necessarily about the future political and institutional configuration of the EC. The indications, especially after the second Danish vote, are however that the 'statist' trends among the EC members, alongside a renewed emphasis on the 'subsidiarity' of the Community, will remain strong at least in the coming years. If so, attention will continue to be focussed more on reactive and restrictive migration measures than on a pro-active and forward-looking policy. At the same time the new political trends in EC countries would favour the 'widening' of the Community towards the East, as already reflected in the EC Commission's latest (May 1993) proposal on trade and economic concessions to the eastern countries.[9] This would create a more propitious climate for further cooperation between the EC and East European countries on migration matters.

Clearly, the present stressful process of change, which affects, though for different reasons and in different ways, both East and West Europe, adds to the constraints in designing a common, long-range European migration policy. And yet, as this chapter has indicated, both the EC and individual West European countries have taken a number of steps – the move towards a quota system of intakes, the acceptance of limited numbers of labour migrants under various time-bound employment and training schemes, and the promised assistance in creating political and economic conditions conducive to reducing the emigration pressures in the countries of origin – which could provide the basis for a common and coherent frame of approach to East–West migration. It would, *inter alia*, also make it easier to ensure that in future any specific or *ad hoc* measures of a reactive and urgent nature fit into the agreed, long-term policy approach and are not in conflict with it.

As East–West migration moves rapidly up the European agenda, policy makers need to bear in mind not only the common, long-term interest of the two parts of Europe but also of the role that Europe seeks to play on the global scene in the years to come. An isolationist migration policy is hardly congruent with Europe's potential role as a more powerful actor in world affairs. A response to the current concern over uncontrolled inflows must be part of this wider policy perspective.

Notes

1. The figure includes the movements, mainly of the Soviet Jews, to Israel and the United States. Also included in the figure are 320,000 Bulgarian Turks, nearly half of whom subsequently returned to Bulgaria.
2. Although the integration of immigrants from East Europe, including their status in the receiving countries of West Europe, is an important aspect of East–West migration policy, it is not included within the scope of this paper. Nor does it examine the future prospects of movements from West to East Europe and their impact on East–West migration policy.
3. The term refers to the eastern region of Europe, including the Commonwealth of Independent States, unless specifically indicated otherwise.
4. The Convention on the Application of the Shengen Agreement was signed in June 1990 and the group was enlarged by the adhesion of Italy in 1990 and by Spain and Portugal in 1991. Greece became a full member of the group in 1992.
5. A display of the highly statist view is found in the response of the United Kingdom Government which saw the Agreement, despite its protectionist approach, as an infringement of national sovereignty.
6. These projections, based on data published by EUROSTAT (The EC Statistical Office), do not take into account the full incidence of recent eastern inflows to West Europe, especially the Federal Republic of Germany. Another study made in 1989 (Prognos, 1989), shows a labour force shortfall of 4.9 million in the EC by 2000, even after account has been taken of migration from non-EC to EC countries and a higher female participation rate.
7. Some experts (e.g. Coleman) take the view that West Europe does not need to increase immigration as it has very substantial reserves of employable manpower. The optimism in such analyses about the upgrading training of existing workforce and the mobilisation of "hidden labour force" through a much higher rate of female participation can be questioned.
8. 1990 figures.
9. The proposals envisage improved, across-the-board market access for East European products; faster dismantling of EC tariffs; increased EC-led

lending to finance infrastructure and an EC commitment to eventual
membership of East European countries. At the time of writing, the proposal
was yet to be considered by the EC summit (Copenhagen, June 1993).

References

Bentolila, S. and Dolado, J. 'Mismatch and Internal Migration in Spain, 1962–86',
in Padoa-Schioppa (ed.), *Mismatch and Labour Mobility*, Cambridge University
Press, 1991.
Blanchard, O. and Katz, L. *Regional Evolution*, Washington, Brookings Institution,
1992.
Business Strategies Ltd. *People at Work – European Demographics in the 21st
Century*, London, 1990.
Callovi, G. 'Regulation of Immigration in 1993: Pieces of the European Community
Jig-Saw Puzzle', *International Migration Review*, vol. 26, Summer 1992.
Coleman, D. 'Does Europe Need Immigrants? Population and Workforce
Projections', *International Migration Review*, vol. 26, Summer 1992.
Coleman, D. 'The World on the Move? International Migration in 1992', Geneva,
UNECA, Council of Europe and UNFPA, 1992, Paper submitted at the
European Population Conference (Geneva, March 1993).
Colinson, S. *Migration in Perspective: Policy and Patterns in Western Europe*,
London, Royal Institute of International Affairs (1993).
Council of Europe. *Recent Demographic Developments in Europe*, Strasbourg,
Council of Europe, 1991.
Ghosh, B. 'Money Can't Buy Reform in East Europe', *European Affairs*, no. 3,
Autumn 1990.
Ghosh, B. 'Migratory Movements from Central and East European Countries: Some
Selected Aspects, Geneva and Strasbourg. International Organization for
Migration and the Council of Europe, 1991', Paper submitted at the Conference
of Ministers on the Movement of People from Central and Eastern Europe
(Vienna, January 1991).
Ghosh, B. 'East–West Migration: The European Perspective', Geneva, IOM, 1991,
Paper submitted at the IOM/Greek Government Regional Seminar on Prospects
of Migration in Europe Beyond 1992 (Athens, October 1991).
Ghosh, B. 'Migration-Development Linkages: Some Specific Issues and Practical
Policy Measures', Geneva, IOM, 1992, Paper submitted at the Tenth IOM
Seminar on Migration (Geneva, September 1992).
Ghosh, B. 'Migration, Trade and International Economic Cooperation: Do the Inter-
Linkages Work?', Geneva, IOM, 1992, Paper submitted at the Tenth IOM
Seminar on Migration (Geneva, September 1992).
Ghosh, B. 'L'immigration est un danger : l'immigration est une chance', *Le Temps
Stratégique*, no. 50, février 1993.
Ghosh, B. 'Movements of People: A Global Challenge', in *UNESCO Yearbook
on Peace and Conflict Studies, Special Issue on Non-Military Aspects of
International Security*, Paris, UNESCO (1994).
Hofler, L. *Migration Programmes of the Federal Republic of Germany Aimed at the
Training and Short-Term Employment of Workers Originating from Developing
Countries or Countries of Central and Eastern Europe*, Geneva, IOM, 1992.

Hollifield, J.F. 'Migration and International Relations: Cooperation and Control in the European Community', *International Migration Review*, vol. 26, Summer 1992.

Institute for East–West Studies. *Beyond Assistance*, New York, 1992.

ODI. *Aiding Eastern Europe and the Former Soviet Republics*, Briefing Paper, London, ODI, November 1992.

OECD, SOPEMI. *Trends in International Migration, Continuous Reporting System on Migration*, Paris: OECD, 1990, 1991, 1992.

OECD. *Employment Outlook*, Paris, OECD, 1992.

Okolski, M. *Migratory Movements from Countries of Central and Eastern Europe*, Council of Europe, Strasbourg, 1991.

Prognos, A.G. *The Labour Market in the EC Internal Market up to the Year 2000*, Basel, 1989.

Tapinos, G. 'Can International Cooperation be an Alternative to the Emigration of Workers?', Paper presented at the International Conference on Migration, OECD, Rome, March 1989.

Index